The First Book of

PC Tools® Deluxe

Second Edition

Gordon McComb

A Division of Macmillan Computer Publishing

11711 North College, Carmel, Indiana 46032 USA

For Amy

© 1990 by SAMS

SECOND EDITION
FIRST PRINTING—1990

International Standard Book Number: 0-672-27329-2
Library of Congress Catalog Card Number: 90-62562

Acquisition Editor: *Richard K. Swadley*
Development Editor: *Marie Butler-Knight*
Manuscript Editor: *Sara Black*
Cover Artist: *Held & Diedrich Design*
Production Coordinator: *Marj Hopper*
Production: *Hilary Adams, Claudia Bell, Jill D. Bomaster, Brad Chinn, Sally Copenhaver, Travia Davis, Tami Hughes, William Hurley, Charles A. Hutchinson, Jennifer Matthews, Joe Ramon*
Indexer: *Sherry Massey*

Printed in the United States of America

Contents

iv

6 *Running Applications with Shell, 147*

V

7 *Backing Up Your Hard Disk Drive, 161*

8 *Recovering Lost Files and Disks, 197*

vi

Introduction

You purchased Central Point Software's PC Tools Deluxe because you have work to do, so let's get right to the point.

This is a book on learning how to use PC Tools Deluxe (from now on, we'll just call it PC Tools). With the information contained in this book, you'll be able to use PC Tools to supervise your computer, manage your hard disk drive, run other applications programs, recover files that have been damaged or erased, inspect your disks for hidden damage, and lots more. *The First Book of PC Tools Deluxe, Second Edition* is a beginner's guide to get you started using PC Tools in your everyday computing.

PC Tools is a complex program, but this book pares it all down to a manageable size. You'll learn everything you need to know to use PC Tools for routine computing chores, including copying files, copying disks, verifying disks, "unerasing" lost files, starting programs, backing up your hard drive, even writing and editing with the PC Tools word processor.

How to Use This Book

The chapters in *The First Book of PC Tools Deluxe, Second Edition* are organized in the same manner that you are likely to use the PC Tools program.

▶ Chapter 1 introduces you to PC Tools and explains its component parts, the concept of its user interface, and the minimum hardware you need to use the program.

▶ PC Tools is composed of several stand-alone programs, yet all follow the same user interface standards. Chapter 2 explains how to use PC Tools interface, including keyboard and mouse control.

▶ Chapter 3 introduces Shell, the main component of PC Tools.

▶ Chapter 4 illustrates how to use Shell to manage files on your floppy and hard disks.

▶ Chapter 5 tells you how you can manage your computer disks, including copying floppy diskettes, verifying and comparing disks, formatting data disks, and managing sub-directories on your hard drive.

▶ Chapter 6 shows you how to run other applications programs directly from PC Tools Shell.

▶ Chapter 7 explains how to use PC Tools for creating backups of the data on your hard drive. You'll learn how to perform quick and easy backups weekly and even daily.

▶ If you've ever accidentally erased a file or even an entire hard disk (or think you might someday), you'll want to read Chapter 8 on using PC Tools to recover lost files and disks.

▶ Chapter 9 details the procedures for maintaining your computer's hard disk drive, including periodically testing the drive for errors (even "hidden" ones), and ways to increase hard drive efficiency.

▶ PC Tools comes with an assortment of handy desk accessory programs, including a word processor and data manager. Chapter 10 introduces these desk accessories, providing quick start help for the word processor, data manager, and communications terminal.

Although you don't have to read this book from cover to cover and in order, at the very least you should start by reading Chapters 1 and 2. These provide an overview of PC Tools and detail how to access its features and capabilities.

Conventions Used in This Book

You need little prior information before you can dive head first into this book. We've used the following conventions to make PC Tools more enjoyable and effective.

▶ This is a beginner's quick start guide to PC Tools, but it assumes you have worked with the IBM PC and its disk operating system. If you are unfamiliar with DOS or how to use your computer, read the instruction manual that came with the computer, or consult one of the many fine books on using the PC and DOS. A good place to start is *Understanding MS-DOS*, published by SAMS.

▶ Many chapters include step-by-step Quick Steps that help you promptly master a particular command or function of PC Tools. The Quick Steps outline only the most commonly used PC Tools commands. Refer to the inside front cover of this book for an alphabetical list of Quick Steps.

▶ PC Tools can be controlled via the keyboard or a mouse. You'll learn how to use both in Chapter 2. For clarity and convenience, instructions for commanding PC Tools do not provide specific steps for using either the keyboard or the mouse. Rather, you'll read "Choose the XYZ command..." and have the choice of using either or both, as you wish.

▶ PC Tools uses an interface similar to the one found on Microsoft Windows. If you're familiar with the Windows interface, you'll be up and running on PC Tools in no time. But if the use of windows, pull-down menus, and dialog boxes is new to you, be sure to read Chapter 2 for a thorough introduction to the PC Tools interface.

ix

Trademark Acknowledgments

All terms mentioned in this book that are known to be trademarks or service marks are listed below. In addition, terms suspected of being trademarks or service marks have been appropriately capitalized. SAMS cannot attest to the accuracy of this information. Use of a term in this book should not be regarded as affecting the validity of any trademark or service mark.

x

dBASE III and dBASE IV are trademarks of Ashton-Tate Corporation.

IBM, IBM PC, and IBM PC AT are registered trademarks of International Business Machines Corporation. IBM PC XT and PS/2 are trademarks of International Business Machines Corporation.

Lotus 1-2-3 is a registered trademark of Lotus Development Corporation.

Macintosh is a trademark licensed to Apple Computer Corporation.

Microsoft Word and Microsoft Windows are trademarks of Microsoft Corporation.

WordPerfect is a registered trademark of WordPerfect Corporation.

WordStar is a registered trademark of MicroPro International.

Chapter 1

An Introduction to PC Tools

In This Chapter

▶ *Component parts of PC Tools*
▶ *Basics of the PC Tools user interface*
▶ *Operating modes of PC Tools*
▶ *Minimum hardware needed*

Some computer programs can be described in a sentence or two. PC Tools needs paragraphs of descriptive prose, because it does so many things. It's a DOS shell, a hard disk backup utility, a data recovery system, a word processor, a data manager, an electronic appointment keeper, a telecommunications program, a data encrypter, and lots more.

PC Tools wears many hats and performs the duty of perhaps a half-dozen software packages.

What PC Tools Provides

PC Tools offers these four basic, core functions:

1. DOS shell, for controlling your computer with easy-to-use menus rather than cryptic DOS commands.

2. Data recovery, for retrieving data from erased or damaged files and disks.
3. Hard disk backup, for storing an archival copy of your hard disk data.
4. Desktop accessories, for providing "pop-up" tools you can use with almost any PC application.

In the following sections we'll take a closer look at each of these important functions. Then we'll discuss the PC Tools user interface, operating modes, and hardware requirements.

DOS Shell

2

The core of PC Tools is a DOS shell, a menu-driven program that not only provides near-instant access to PC Tools commands but also performs many common DOS functions. In addition, the PC Tools Shell can be used to start other programs, like Lotus 1-2-3 or WordPerfect. Instead of starting and ending your programs at the ubiquitous DOS C> prompt, Shell provides a neat and easy-to-use menu interface. With Shell you can:

▶ View files and directories on a floppy or hard disk.
▶ Select any PC Tools function (except Desktop applications, which are run only under Desktop).
▶ Run a stand-alone PC Tools program, such as PC Cache or PC Secure (more about these in a bit).
▶ Run any other DOS or application program.
▶ Perform routine DOS chores, like copying, moving, and comparing files, but with the benefit of menu-driven commands and full-English prompts.
▶ Print, view, and edit document files.
▶ Maintain hard disk directories, including creating, deleting, and even renaming subdirectories.
▶ Restructure the organization of data on a hard disk so that it is more efficient.
▶ Unerase files that have been erased previously.

Shell contains five pull-down menus: File, Disk, Options, Applications, and Special; one of the menus is shown in Figure 1-1. In addition, context-sensitive help is available by pressing the F1 function key or by selecting the Help command with the mouse.

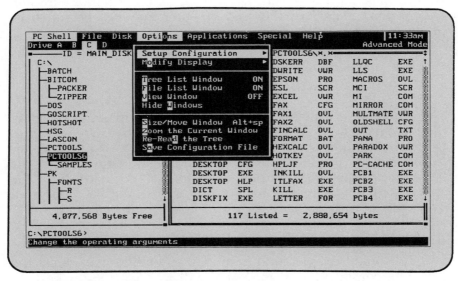

Figure 1-1. A sample PC Tools pull-down menu.

Shell is the main component of PC Tools and is the utility you'll use most often. Because of its versatility and functionality, several chapters of this book are devoted to learning its commands and features.

Data Recovery

One of the most important features of PC Tools is its ability to restore accidentally lost files and disks. The PC Tools data recovery system is composed of five units:

▶ Undelete command.
▶ Mirror program.
▶ Rebuild program.

3

▶ PC Format program.

▶ DiskFix program.

The Undelete command and file restoration programs work separately or together to protect against loss from accidental erasure of files, hard disk "crashes," even reformatting of hard and floppy disks. The four file recovery programs can be run from Shell or directly at the DOS prompt.

Undelete Command

The Undelete command, found in the Shell program, retrieves files that have been erased accidentally using the DOS ERASE or DEL command, or some other delete command within an application. When you delete a file, only it's name is deleted in the file allocation table (file index) of the diskette or hard disk. The actual contents of the file remain on the disk until it is covered over with new data. As long as you don't record any new information on the disk, you can retrieve files that have been erased accidentally.

The undelete operation is mostly automatic: Just select the Undelete command, and PC Tools will take care of the rest. In special situations, you may need to control the undelete process directly, and PC Tools provides a means to retrieve lost files manually.

Mirror Program

The Mirror program (MIRROR.COM) is designed specifically to provide protection against accidental ERASE (like ERASE *.*), RECOVER, or FORMAT of a hard disk. Mirror keeps a clone of the all-important file allocation table (FAT) of a hard disk, along with a mirror image of the root directory recorded on the drive. The FAT tells the computer where to locate previously stored files. If the FAT is somehow damaged or accidentally erased, all of the files on the disk can be lost, because even though they are still contained on the disk, there's no way to retrieve them.

The root directory of a hard disk contains many important files, including CONFIG.SYS and AUTOEXEC.BAT, as well as the first level of subdirectories. Its loss—although not as critical

4

as the FAT—can make reconstruction of your hard disk time consuming and difficult.

Each time Mirror is run (preferably one or more times a day), it resamples the FAT and root directory and stores that information in a backup file. In the case of an accidental ERASE, RECOVER, FORMAT, or damaging hard disk crash, the Mirror backup file can be used to reconstruct the missing data.

Rebuild Program

The reconstruction of the mirrored file allocation table is performed by an adjunct program, Rebuild. Unlike Mirror, which is designed as a preventive maintenance program and should be run often, Rebuild (REBUILD.COM) is used only when needed. In fact, running Rebuild when you don't need to can cause you to lose files you recently created. You can also use Rebuild if Mirror hasn't been taking regular snapshots of the FAT and root directory, but success at data recovery is not ensured.

5

PC Format Program

The PC Format program (PCFORMAT.COM) is a replacement for the DOS FORMAT.COM program. In fact, during installation using PCSETUP, PC Tools automatically replaces the DOS FORMAT.COM program file with PC Format. Your original FORMAT.COM is renamed FORMAT!.COM so that you can still use it, but you must explicitly enter FORMAT! at the DOS prompt to use it.

PC Format differs from the DOS FORMAT command in many important ways. Besides offering more flexibility in formatting (or initializing) floppy and hard disks, PC Format takes special precautions to prevent accidental erasure of data previously placed on the disk.

PC Format is desired over the DOS FORMAT command should you ever accidentally erase a disk you intend to keep (if that hasn't happened to you already, it will sooner or later). When reformatted with PC Tools, you have a much better chance of recovering the entire disk (even a floppy diskette) intact using the PC Tools Undelete functions.

DiskFix Program

The DiskFix program (version 6.0 or later) actually seeks out, reports, and optionally repairs disks automatically. While you have control over the repair process, it is completely automatic, so you don't need to know a thing about how your DOS disks work (although it can help). When DiskFix first starts, it checks the critical portions of the drive you specify (such as floppy disk drive A: or hard disk drive C:). If DiskFix finds errors, it reports them, then asks if you want to repair the damage. The DOS CHKDSK command also offers some of the reconditioning DiskFix provides, but DiskFix is easier to use and offers greater flexibility. Note that not all disk damage can be successfully repaired. Some data may be irretrievably lost, especially if the damage occurred some time ago. You can improve your chances of successful DiskFixing if you run the DiskFix program often.

6

Hard Disk Backup

The movie director often orders a second take, even if the first is perfectly good, as protection or a backup. The information in a hard disk is often treated the same way. Because weeks, months, and even years worth of data can be stored on a hard disk, making an archival copy of it in case of catastrophe is not only common sense but also essential to good computing practice.

If you're a hard disk user (and you probably are if you're running PC Tools), making backups should be a part of your regular routine. In the case of a mishap (the hard disk crashes, you totally corrupt the hard disk using a DOS command like FDISK, or the entire computer is stolen), the data from the hard disk is safely stored on floppy diskettes and can be readily retrieved.

PC Tools provides a handy and capable hard disk backup utility; you can run the backup utility—named PCBACK-UP.EXE—either from within PC Shell or directly from the DOS prompt. The one utility handles both backup and restoration (reclaiming previously stored data back onto the hard disk).

PC Backup, shown in Figure 1-2, allows you full control over the backup process, including selecting subdirectories and files to include in the backup, determining the type of backup media to use, verifying backed up data against the original on disk, and selecting the backup method.

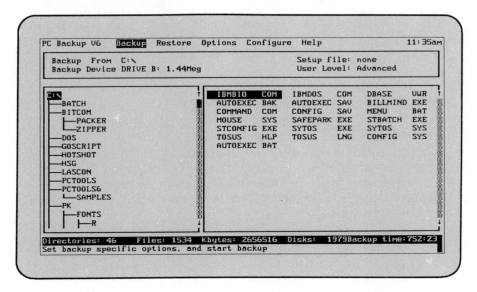

Figure 1-2. PC Tools Backup lets you make archival backups of your hard disk.

PC Backup automatically compresses files so that you need fewer diskettes to hold the archive data. For example, depending on the actual data on your hard disk, you can cram about 20 megabytes of data into just ten or twelve 1.44-megabyte 3 1/2-inch diskettes. Data compression also reduces time, so you're more likely to perform regular backups of your hard disk. It takes about 10—15 minutes to back up 20 megabytes worth of hard disk data.

The first time you use PC Backup, the program asks a number of set-up questions about your computer system and the type of media you'll be using for the backups. The questions aren't repeated on subsequent uses of PC Backup, and you can change and resave your set-up selections at any time.

7

Desktop Accessories

How many times have you needed a calculator, only to find someone walked off with your fancy desktop model? PC Tools contains its own calculator—four different types in fact—plus a number of other useful desktop accessories, including a word processor, a data manager, an appointment book, a telecommunications program, and a macro editor.

As with PC Shell, The PC Tools Desktop Manager (or just plain Desktop) can be loaded into your computer directly at the DOS prompt as a stand-alone program, or it can be loaded into memory and used as a terminate and stay resident (TSR) accessory. Whenever you need the Desktop tools, just press the Desktop hot-keys—Ctrl-Spacebar (but you can change it to almost anything you like).

8

PC Desktop contains the following miniapplications:

▶ *Notepads*, a fairly full-featured word processor (but no match for a WordPerfect or Microsoft Word). Features: opens both ASCII and WordStar files.

▶ *Outlines*, a special-purpose word processor designed to create outlines; it is also called a thought organizer. Features: expands and collapses headings; indents for multiple levels.

▶ *Databases*, an information storage and retrieval system for keeping tabs on moderate amounts of data. Features: data file-compatibility with dBase III and IV; an automatic phone dialer.

▶ *Appointment scheduler*, an electronic diary that keeps track of your appointments and other things you must do. It even sounds an alarm to remind you of lunch breaks or important meetings with the boss. Features: link with macros (see below) for automated control of your computer so you can run programs when you're not there.

▶ *Modem telecommunications*, a "smart" terminal utility that lets you make calls from a modem, communicate with other computer users (or automated computer systems), and send or receive files electronically. Features: Hayes AT-command compatible with full autodial, autoanswer capability.

▶ *Fax communcations*, lets you send and receive fax transmissions while you use your computer for something else.

It requires an Intel (or campatible) fax board in your computer or in a network. Features: selectable resolution (high, standard); delay fax broadcast; autodialing.

▶ *Macro editor*, another specialized word processor designed for writing scripts, this one for automating tasks you routinely do with your computer. Features: wide program compatibility; the macros can be used within Desktop, other PC Tools programs, applications, and DOS.

▶ *Clipboard*, stores bits of text cut or copied from the Desktop applications or from other applications. Features: adds cut-and-paste capabilities to programs that otherwise can't share data.

▶ *Calculators*, a set of algebraic, financial, scientific, and programmer's calculators for use at a moment's notice. Features: algebraic calculator includes memory; all calculators can be programmed with macros to perform complex routines; the algebraic, scientific, and financial calculators include a scrolling tape.

▶ *Utilities*, a collection of miscellaneous tools: select Shell and Desktop hot-keys; view an ASCII character table with IBM graphics characters; change system colors; and unload Desktop from memory (when installed as a TSR).

▶ *Autodialer*, lets you dial the phone using a phone number appearing on your computer screen.

PC Tools Desktop is best used as a memory-resident program, where you can access it from within any application. For example, pop up Desktop while working with Lotus 1-2-3 and access the Appointment scheduler to check the day's events. Or jot down a particularly brilliant thought with Notepads while you're busy putting your company's books in order.

The opening screen for Desktop is simple and clutter-free, as shown in Figure 1-3. Only the main Desktop menu is present, providing access to the miniapplications available under PC Tools Desktop. Desktop employs the same keyboard and mouse conventions as Shell and the other PC Tools programs.

9

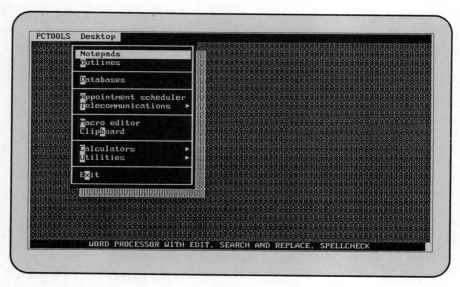

Figure 1-3. The opening screen of Desktop.

10

Miscellaneous Utilities

In addition to the four core functions detailed above, PC Tools comes with three additional utilities—Compress, PC Cache, and PC Secure. You can access as stand-alone programs (through the DOS prompt) or from within PC Shell.

Compress

Imagine the data tracks on a hard disk (or floppy diskette for that matter) uncoiled into a straight line, like a piece of string. As you store information on the hard disk, the string fills up, starting on one end and proceeding to the other. As you fill the disk, each program and document file is stored as a self-contained unit.

Now remove a file or two, and you create a gap in the string. The next program or document you place on the disk will be jammed into the empty slot, with any remainder distributed to other portions of the disk. The more small gaps that are on the disk, the more a particular program or document file might be fragmented throughout the disk.

Over the course of several weeks or months of use, the typical hard disk will consist of hundreds of files, with many of them fragmented in at least one place, as illustrated in Figure 1-4. The separation of individual pieces of the file can impair performance: The heads in the drive must shuttle back and forth over the surface of the disk to pick up all the bits and pieces of the scattered file. Perhaps worse, a fragmented file is harder to retrieve when accidentally erased and is more likely to be corrupted permanently in the event of a DOS or disk error.

11

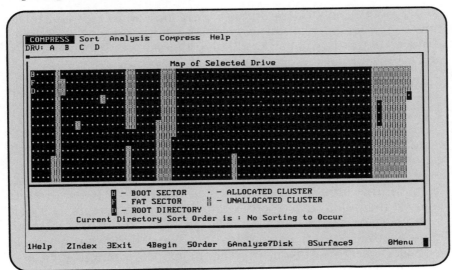

Figure 1-4. File fragmentation causes files to be scattered over the surface of the disk.

The PC Tools Compress utility (called COMPRESS.EXE) examines the files on a hard or floppy disk and rearranges them to eliminate fragmentation. Compress can be started directly at the DOS prompt or within Shell. Although compressing (or "defragmentizing") a large hard disk can take up to several hours—depending on the capacity of the hard disk—the effort is worth the wait in the long run.

PC Cache

PC Cache allows you to partition some of the memory in your computer (either the base 512 or 640 kilobytes of RAM, or expanded) and use it to speed up hard and floppy disk access.

A memory cache works by storing the most frequently used information in the computer's RAM, so that the computer doesn't need to access the hard disk every time it needs a scrap of data. Although the savings in time are but brief flashes—tiny fractions of a second—over a long period, the savings can add up to greatly enhanced efficiency. And, wear and tear on the drive is decreased, because the mechanism isn't being used as often.

The PC Tools Cache is fully programmable: You can tell it how much memory to use as a cache, where to find the memory (base or expanded), even to display the savings it has achieved since first turned on.

12

PC Secure

If you work for the government, or a company manufacturing goods under contract from the government, your computer data may be considered confidential or classified. To prevent the data from falling into the wrong hands, you may be required to encrypt it so that only you, or other authorized persons, are able to read it and use it. Or, you may create or edit sensitive information—like personnel records—that you won't want others to look at. The PC Secure utility scrambles program and data files to an extent that even the largest supercomputers in the world can't crack their code.

PC Secure uses the Digital Encryption Standard (or DES) encoding system, which shuffles the data in an apparent random order. A software key is used to lock and unlock the data. Without the key, it is highly unlikely (but theoretically not entirely impossible) that anyone else will be able to retrieve the file and look at it.

A little-known feature of the PC Secure program (named PCSECURE.EXE) is a file compression command you can use to shrink your program and data files into smaller packets. You don't need to encrypt the file to compress it. You might want to compress a data file, for example, before sending it over the phone lines with a modem. With a size savings of 20 to 60 percent when compressed, your time on the modem will be less—and your phone bills, lower. The receiver needs a copy of PC Tools (or at least PC Secure, which can be run from the DOS prompt or from Shell) to uncompress the data and turn it into a readable form.

The PC Tools Concept

PC Tools is not one huge program but many small ones. In fact, PC Tools consists of about 112 individual files, many of them contributing a small function, application, or subprogram to the PC Tools repertoire. You don't need all these files to take advantage of the basic features of PC Tools, of course. Appendix A details each major PC Tools file: what it does, how it's used, and when it's needed.

13

User Interface

Despite its hodge-podge foundation, the individual files of PC Tools form to create a near seamless integration of DOS power tools. The various PC Tools utilities share a common interface. This interface employs pull-down menus and "point-and-shoot" commands, similar to the interface used in the Apple Macintosh. Because the various components of PC Tools are based on similar operating techniques, once you master one PC Tools application, you can graduate to the others quickly.

Unlike the Macintosh, IBM OS/2 Presentation Manager, or Microsoft Windows, PC Tools doesn't use a graphical interface. Although PC Tools does provide pull-down menus, pop-up dialog boxes, and movable windows, as shown in Figure 1-5, it displays everything as text characters, including the names of files. PC Tools appears in color on a color display (EGA or VGA recommended) or monochrome on a black-and-white display. You don't need a graphics display adapter to use PC Tools.

Mouse Support

PC Tools fully supports a mouse—the Microsoft Mouse, the Logitech/Dexxa Mouse, and any of the many other models compati-

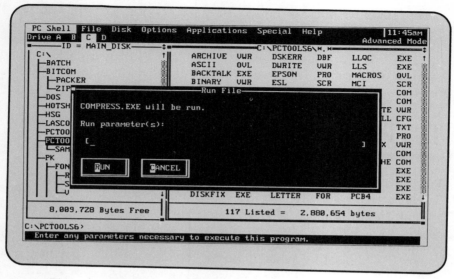

Figure 1-5. Full-English prompts and dialog boxes make PC Tools commands easy to use.

ble with these. Although a mouse is not absolutely mandatory, you'll find PC Tools is best used with a rodentia desktopus (that's "Latin" for desktop rodents). If you don't already own a mouse, you may want to consider purchasing one, even if PC Tools is the only program you use that supports a mouse. You can buy a Microsoft or Microsoft-compatible mouse for under $75 these days (I bought mine for $35 at a computer swap meet), and they connect to your computer through a standard serial port or special mouse expansion board.

Accessing Commands with the Keyboard

Although a mouse is most convenient, PC Tools also offers direct keyboard control. Function keys—F1 through F10—are assigned to the most common commands. A help panel, which appears at the bottom of the screen as in Figure 1-6, reminds you which keys to press to invoke various commands. On-line help is available at any point in PC Tools. The help is context-sensitive: The program determines which command you need help on and provides it in one step. Or you can select a help topic from a master index.

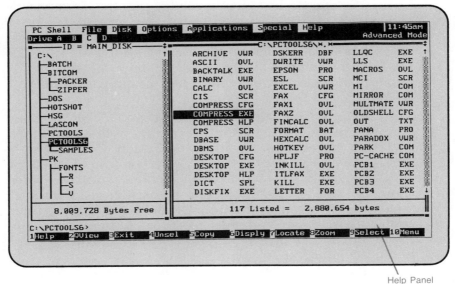

Help Panel

Figure 1-6. The help panel (or message bar) at the bottom of the screen.

Hard Disk or Floppy?

PC Tools is best used with a hard disk. The program comes shipped on several diskettes and requires a great deal of disk space for proper operation. And, most of the PC Tools applications are aimed at hard disk management and administration, so it appears that the program is strictly aimed at hard disk users. However, for those limited to just floppy diskettes, certain PC Tools utilities can run from a 1.2- or 1.44-megabyte floppy disk drive. You cannot use PC Tools from 360-kilobyte drives.

Operating Mode

The PC Tools programs consist of two main applications: PC Shell and Desktop. As detailed later in this chapter, Shell provides a means of accessing the PC Tools and DOS commands under a familiar pull-down menu system. Desktop provides a number of handy miniapplications or desktop accessories, including a word processor and telecommunications terminal program.

Both Shell and Desktop can be loaded into the computer in one of two ways:

▶ *As a stand-alone program.* Shell and Desktop are run like any other ordinary PC software. Enter the name at the DOS prompt, and the program runs. Quit the program, and you are returned to DOS.

▶ *As a terminate and stay resident program.* A TSR or memory-resident program loads into a portion of the computer's RAM and makes room for other applications. You can then access the program by pressing a certain combination of keys, called hot-keys. As a TSR, or "instant-access" program, you can use your computer for regular tasks and call up Shell or Desktop from within DOS or one of your regular applications, such as Lotus 1-2-3 or WordPerfect. This works only if you have a minimum of 512 kilobytes of RAM in your computer.

16

Hardware Compatibility

PC Tools operates with almost any IBM PC or clone. Directly supported are the IBM PS/2 (all models), PC, PCjr, XT, and AT. The program also works with most "100 percent compatibles," which include Compaq, Epson, and Dell. Most generic clones, such as the no-name brand models available at some computer swap meets and mail order, should work as well.

PC Tools needs MS-DOS or PC DOS version 3.0 or higher, although you are advised to use the latest version of DOS that works with your computer. Once you have started PC Tools under a recent version of DOS, you can use the program to work with diskettes formatted under any version of DOS.

Other than an IBM PC or a reasonable clone, you need at least 512 kilobytes of memory in your computer. While PC Tools will work with just 512 kilobytes of RAM, you're better off with the full complement of 640 kilobytes. If your computer is equipped with expanded (LIM 4.0 standard) memory, PC Tools will use it when possible. Expanded memory is particularly handy when using Shell in memory-resident mode, rather than as stand-alone applications run directly from DOS.

You need just one floppy disk drive when using PC Tools with the recommended hard disk, although if you plan on doing diskette-to-diskette copying, a pair of similar media drives (two 5 1/4 inch, for example) is helpful.

Automated Installation

PC Tools is designed for use with a hard disk, and one is strongly recommended. Some of the utilities, such as PC Backup, are expressly designed for hard disk applications.

PC Tools comes with a set-up program, PCSETUP. You must use this program to transfer the contents of the distribution diskettes to your hard disk. The files are compressed (to save space on the distribution diskettes); simply copying the files from the floppy to hard disk does not install the programs properly.

PCSETUP is menu driven, as shown in Figure 1-7, and it needs little explanation to use it. Follow the on-screen prompts until installation is complete.

17

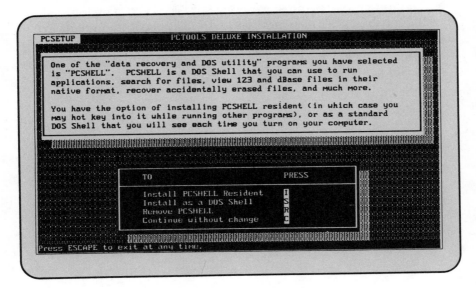

Figure 1-7. A sample screen from the PCSETUP automatic installation program.

Review

This chapter began with an explanation of PC Tools and the menu-driven interface it shares with all its applications and subprograms. The chapter also discussed:

▶ Four core functions of PC Tools are: DOS shell, data recovery, hard disk backup, and desktop accessories.

▶ Shell provides a means of accessing the PC Tools and DOS commands under a familiar pull-down menu system.

▶ Desktop provides a number of miniapplications you can use both independently or with other DOS programs.

▶ Both Shell and Desktop can be loaded into the computer directly from the DOS prompt as a stand-alone application, or as a terminate and stay resident (TSR) "instant-access" program.

▶ You can access on-line help anywhere within PC Tools by pressing the F1 function key.

▶ The program requires MS-DOS or PC DOS version 3.0 or higher, but the latest version of DOS is recommended.

▶ The computer must be outfitted with at least 512 kilobytes of RAM (640 kilobytes is recommended); PC Tools can access LIM 4.0 expanded memory.

Chapter 2

Getting Started with PC Tools

In This Chapter

▶ *Starting PC Tools Shell and Desktop*
▶ *Using either program in memory-resident mode*
▶ *Navigating through PC Tools*
▶ *Using the keyboard and mouse*

It takes but a moment to get started with PC Tools. Installing it is nearly automatic, starting it up is quick and easy, and navigating your way around the program is as simple as pressing keys (or moving a mouse) and watching menus and windows scroll by.

Yet for all its plainness, you'll want to give certain consideration to how you install PC Tools and how to best load the program into your computer's memory. And, if you've never used a pull-down menu system with windows, you may be unfamiliar with the interface used by PC Tools.

This chapter details everything you need to know to get started using the PC Tools utilities. It describes:

▶ The contents of the PC Tools package.
▶ How to run the Shell program.
▶ How to run the Desktop program.
▶ How to navigate through the PC Tools programs, using either the keyboard or mouse.

▶ How to use pull-down menus, windows, and dialog boxes.

▶ Tips on mastering mouse and keyboard control of PC Tools.

▶ How to access the on-line help facility.

Package Contents

PC Tools comes on a series of diskettes and is accompanied by three manuals. The exact composition of the package depends on the specific version of PC Tools and its release date. As of this writing, with version 6.0 of PC Tools, the package comes with both 5 1/4-inch and 3 1/2-inch diskettes.

The three manuals detail different aspect of PC Tools:

20

▶ *Data Recovery and DOS Shell* covers PC Shell, Mirror, Rebuild, PC Cache, Compress, PC Format, PC Secure, and DiskFix.

▶ *Desktop Manager* covers Desktop.

▶ *Hard Disk Backup* covers PC Backup.

Throughout this book, you will be referred to one of these three manuals for additional information on certain advanced topics. Keep this book, and the PC Tools manuals, handy at all times when using the PC Tools program.

> ▶ **Tip:** Last minute updates to the program or corrections to the manual can be found in the README.TXT file located on one of the PC Tools distribution diskettes. Be sure to view or print this file as soon as possible after installing PC Tools. The program includes its own file viewing and printing features, so you don't need a word processor to examine the README.TXT file.

We'll assume the PC Tools programs have already been installed on your computer. The PCSETUP program, provided with PC Tools, makes installation quick and simple. We'll also assume you're using PC Tools with a hard disk.

Running Shell

You can run PC Tools Shell in a number of ways, depending on how you've installed the program in your computer and the AUTO-EXEC.BAT file. There are three ways to run Shell:

▶ As a stand-alone program at the DOS prompt.

▶ As a memory-resident program (loaded manually by you).

▶ As a memory-resident program (loaded automatically by AUTOEXEC.BAT).

As a Stand-Alone Program at the DOS Prompt

Running Shell as a stand-alone program at the DOS prompt assumes you have not installed Shell as a memory-resident program. The PCSETUP program adds a PATH statement to your AUTOEXEC.BAT file so that you can start Shell at any DOS prompt, regardless of the subdirectory you're currently in. You don't need to change the current directory of your hard disk to use PC Tools.

21

Q Running Shell from the DOS Prompt

1. Type c: and press Enter. (If your copy of PC Tools is on another drive, substitute another letter for C.)

   Logs onto the C hard disk drive.

2. Type PCSHELL and press Enter.

   Starts Shell. □

In a few moments, the PC Tools Shell program loads and display a copyright box. Once Shell is loaded, your screen should look like the one in Figure 2-1 (the names of directories and files will be different, reflecting the contents of your hard disk).

```
PC Shell  File  Disk  Options  Applications  Special  Help            11:47am
Drive A  B  C  D                                                 Advanced Mode
┌─────ID = MAIN_DISK─────────┐ ┌──────────C:\PCTOOLS6\*.*──────────────────┐
│C:\                       ↑ │ │ARCHIVE  VWR    DSKERR  DBF   LLQC     EXE ↑│
│ ├BATCH                     │ │ASCII    OVL    DWRITE  VWR   LLS      EXE │
│ ├BITCOM                    │ │BACKTALK EXE    EPSON   PRO   MACROS   OVL │
│ │ ├PACKER                  │ │BINARY   VWR    ESL     SCR   MCI      SCR │
│ │ └ZIPPER                  │ │CALC     OVL    EXCEL   VWR   MI       COM │
│ ├DOS                       │ │CIS      SCR    FAX     CFG   MIRROR   COM │
│ ├HOTSHOT                   │ │COMPRESS CFG    FAX1    OVL   MULTMATE VWR │
│ ├HSG                       │ │COMPRESS EXE    FAX2    OVL   OLDSHELL CFG │
│ ├LASCON                    │ │COMPRESS HLP    FINCALC OVL   OUT      TXT │
│ ├PCTOOLS                   │ │CPS      SCR    FORMAT  BAT   PANA     PRO │
│ ├PCTOOLS6                  │ │DBASE    VWR    HEXCALC OVL   PARADOX  VWR │
│ │ └SAMPLES                 │ │DBMS     OVL    HOTKEY  OVL   PARK     COM │
│ ├PK                        │ │DESKTOP  CFG    HPLJF   PRO   PC-CACHE COM │
│ │ ├FONTS                   │ │DESKTOP  EXE    INKILL  OVL   PCB1     EXE │
│ │ │ ├R                     │ │DESKTOP  HLP    ITLFAX  EXE   PCB2     EXE │
│ │ │ ├S                   ↓ │ │DICT     SPL    KILL    EXE   PCB3     EXE │
│ │ │ └V                     │ │DISKFIX  EXE    LETTER  FOR   PCB4     EXE ↓│
├────────────────────────────┤ ├──────────────────────────────────────────┤
│    8,009,728 Bytes Free    │ │    117 Listed =    2,880,654 bytes        │
└────────────────────────────┘ └──────────────────────────────────────────┘
C:\PCTOOLS6>
1Help 2QView 3Exit 4Unsel 5Copy 6Disply 7Locate 8Zoom 9Select 10Menu
```

Figure 2-1. The basic Shell opening screen.

22

As a Memory-Resident Program (Loaded Manually)

As a memory-resident program, you can load Shell while running another application. (Note: Memory constraints may prohibit you from running Shell within all PC applications.) Manually loading Shell as a memory-resident program means it is not automatically loaded in the computer's memory with the AUTOEXEC.BAT file when the machine is first turned on.

 Manually Loading Shell as a Memory-Resident Program

1. Type c:, then press Enter. (If your copy of PC Tools is on another drive, substitute another letter for C.)

   Logs onto the C hard disk drive.

2. Type PCSHELL /R and press Enter.

   Loads Shell in memory-resident mode. The screen in Figure 2-2 shows available memory.

3. Press Ctrl-Esc.   Activates Shell from
                                      memory.   ☐

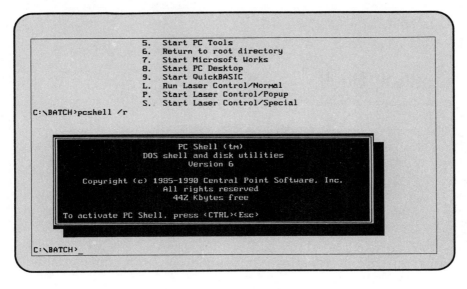

*Figure 2-2. Shell information window when loaded in
memory-resident mode.*

Shell displays a small copyright box when it is loaded and
activated. The box also displays the available memory left in your
computer. You should avoid using Shell if available memory dips
below about 25 kilobytes.

The Control and Escape keys are hot-keys: Pressing them
simultaneously galvanizes Shell from its idle state in memory
and activates it so you see it on the screen. You can change the
hot-keys you use to activate Shell; more about that in Chapter 4,
"Managing Files with Shell."

As a Memory-Resident Program (Loaded with AUTOEXEC.BAT)

The SHELL /R command line in the AUTOEXEC.BAT file loads
Shell into memory when the computer starts, so you don't have to
do it manually at the DOS prompt.

23

Q Running Shell as a Preloaded Memory-Resident Program

1. Press Ctrl-Esc.   Activates Shell from
                                            memory.   ☐

Leaving Shell

The procedure for leaving Shell depends on how it was loaded—as
a stand-alone program started from the DOS prompt or as a memory-resident program:

Stand-Alone Program	Press F3, then type X
Memory-Resident Program	Press Ctrl-Esc

24

If you've loaded Shell as a memory-resident (or TSR) program and want to unload it completely from the computer's
memory, exit the shell, then type

KILL

at the DOS prompt. This removes Shell (as well as Desktop, if it
has also been loaded as a TSR) from the computer's RAM, freeing the space for other programs. Note that KILL.COM is a PC
Tools program and must be on the currently selected drive, or
DOS won't be able to find it.

Running Desktop

You can run Desktop in the same manner as Shell:

▶ As a stand-alone program at the DOS prompt.
▶ As a memory-resident program (loaded manually by you).
▶ As a memory-resident program (loaded automatically by
  AUTOEXEC.BAT).

As a Stand-Alone Program at the DOS Prompt

Running Desktop as a stand-alone program at the DOS prompt assumes you have not installed Desktop as a memory-resident program. The PCSETUP program adds a PATH statement to your AUTOEXEC.BAT file so that you can start Desktop at any DOS prompt.

Q **Running Desktop from the DOS Prompt**

1. Type C: and press Enter. (If your copy of PC Tools is on another drive, substitute another letter for C.)

   Logs onto the C hard disk drive.

2. Type DESKTOP and press Enter.

   Starts Desktop. □

In a few moments, the PC Tools Desktop program loads and presents you with the screen shown in Figure 2-3.

25

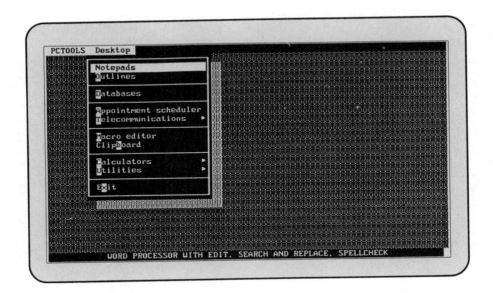

Figure 2-3. The basic Desktop opening screen.

As a Memory-Resident Program
(Loaded Manually)

Manually loading Desktop as a memory-resident program means
it is not loaded automatically in the computer's memory with the
AUTOEXEC.BAT file when the machine is first turned on.

Q Manually Loading Desktop as a Memory-Resident Program

1. Type c: and press Enter. (If   Logs onto the C hard disk
   your copy of PC Tools is on   drive.
   another drive, substitute
   another letter for C.)

2. Type DESKTOP /R and press   Loads Desktop in memory-
   Enter.   resident mode.

3. Press Ctrl-Spacebar.   Activates Desktop from
                                    memory.   ☐

26

As with the hot-keys for activating Shell, the Control and
Spacebar keys trigger Shell from memory. You can change the hot-
keys used to activate Desktop, as described later in this book.

As a Memory-Resident Program
(Loaded with AUTOEXEC.BAT)

The DESKTOP /R command line in the AUTOEXEC.BAT file
loads Desktop into memory when the computer starts; there's no
reason for you to do it manually at the DOS prompt.

**Q Running Desktop as a Preloaded Memory-Resident
Program**

1. Press Ctrl-Spacebar.   Activates Shell from
                                    memory.   ☐

Leaving Desktop

The procedure for leaving Desktop depends on how it was loaded:

Stand-Alone Program   Press F3
Memory-Resident Program   Press Ctrl-Spacebar

If you've loaded Desktop as a TSR program and want to completely unload it from the computer's memory, exit the Desktop, then type

KILL

at the DOS prompt. Note that if Shell is also currently loaded into memory, using the KILL command will remove it also.

27

Working Your Way Through PC Tools

Each of the programs in the PC Tools repertoire follows the same user interface. All embrace pull-down menus, scrollable windows, and dialog boxes, in a similar fashion to the Apple Macintosh.

A typical PC Tools screen is shown, with its component parts identified, in Figure 2-4. These are:

▶ *Menu bar.* The menu bar contains the pull-down menus. Select one of the items in the menu bar, and the menu drops into view.

▶ *Menu.* Menus contain commands, which are selected by highlighting them with the mouse or keyboard.

▶ *Message bar.* The message bar contains messages to guide you through the use of PC Tools, without the need to consult the manual or the on-line help. When no menu or command is selected, the message bar contains a recap of keys you can press to actuate common commands. When a menu command is highlighted, a short single-line description of the command is provided as a reference.

▶ *Application window.* The application window contains the text or data for the PC Tools application, whether it be Shell, Desktop, Compress, or any other application. Some applications, such as Shell, can display more than one window at a time. Each window provides a different view of the data presented by the application.

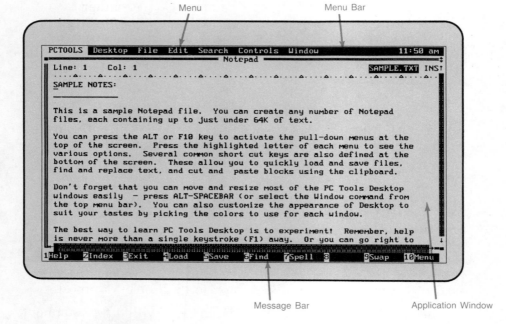

Figure 2-4. Parts of the PC Tools screen interface.

Pull-Down Menus

Pull-down menus offer a convenient and uncluttered method of selecting commands, because you can quickly and easily see the available choices, without having to toggle between menu levels, as with a program such as Lotus 1-2-3 or WordPerfect 5.0. Each menu contains a specific set of commands. The commands are generally grouped by function within the menus so that you can find them more easily.

PC Tool's pull-down menus are the locking type. Once you open the menu, it stays there until you:

28

▶ Select a command.

▶ Select another menu.

▶ Cancel the menu.

While the menu is open, you use the keyboard or mouse to highlight the command you want and the Enter key to select it.

The menus in PC Tools can be controlled by either the keyboard or the mouse (or a combination of the two). Both have their advantages and disadvantages. You'll find, however, that while some commands can be invoked quickly by pressing one or two keys, operating PC Tools goes much faster when you have a mouse by your side.

As shown in Figure 2-5, the way items are written and grouped in menus tells you much about the nature of the commands.

29

▶ *Lines* separating commands act as group boundaries: The commands in one group are generally related to one another, so you can locate them more easily.

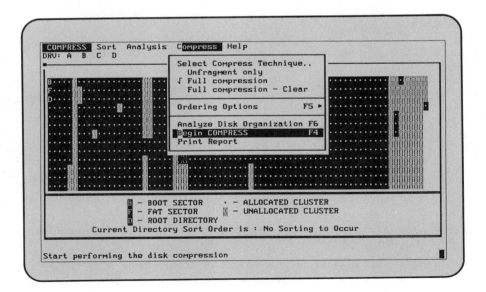

Figure 2-5. A pull-down menu with ellipses (additional information needed after choosing the command) and arrows (additional menu).

▶ An *ellipsis* (...) following a command means that PC Tools provides additional options and selections, presented with a dialog box, as detailed later.

▶ A *right arrow* following a menu item means that selecting the command pops up a submenu.

Windows

The windows in PC Tools are like stacks of paper on a desk. Windows divide the screen into many parts, so you can peer into several computing "portholes" at once. While PC Tools is designed to display windows from just one program at once, the windows provide a convenient and intuitive method for working with files, disks, and subdirectories.

30

PC Tools windows contain many components. Get to know these, and you'll be able to use PC Tools more efficiently. Most of the window features are used exclusively with the mouse, although alternative commands for accomplishing the same tasks are provided for keyboard control. The component parts of PC Tools windows is shown graphically in Figure 2-6.

▶ *Window border.* The border displays the boundaries of the window. Even if the screen displays several windows at once, only one window at a time can be "active," meaning keystrokes and commands affect that window and not the others. The active window is always shown with a double border, as illustrated in Figure 2-7. Many windows can be moved, when using a mouse, by sliding them around the screen by the top border.

▶ *Close box.* The close box closes the window. In some cases, closing the window exits the application; this is especially true when using PC Tools utilities from within Shell.

▶ *Size box.* The size box changes the size of the window, from a small postage size square to full screen.

▶ *Scroll bars.* When the window contains more data than can be shown in one screen, information must be scrolled so you can view the rest of it. Windows can have horizontal scroll bars to scan the text back and forth, vertical scroll bars to move the text up and down, or both.

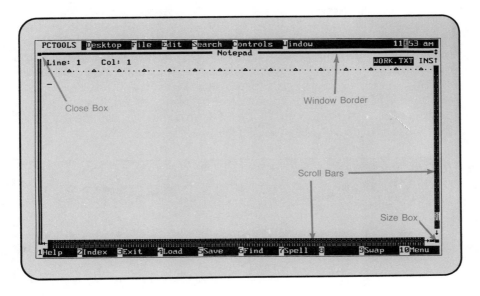

Figure 2-6. The parts of windows.

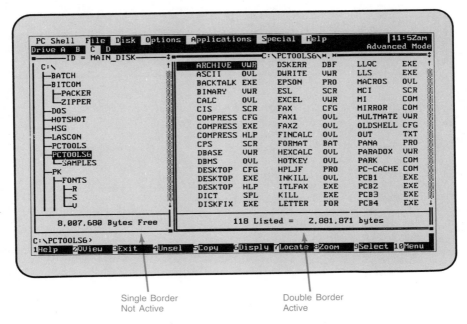

Figure 2-7. Double-bordered windows are currently active.

While all windows have borders, only some windows provide a close box, size box, and scroll bars. The full complement of window controls is generally available only on those windows where you can write and edit text, or select from among a set of directories or files. Information windows, such as the one shown in Figure 2-8, have nothing to select or edit, so the window controls are omitted. Table 2-1 summarizes the features of PC Tools windows and when they are present.

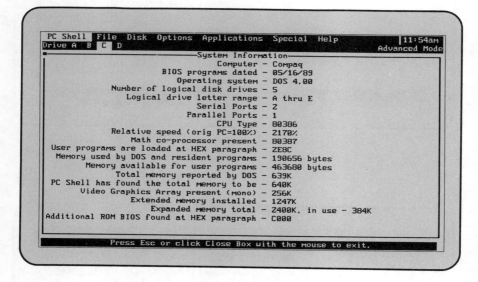

Figure 2-8. An informational window lacks scroll bars, resize boxes, and many other controls.

Table 2-1. Window Features Comparison.

Feature	Present in All Windows
Border	Yes
Close box	No
Size box	No
Scroll bars	No

Dialog Boxes

Working with PC Tools is like carrying on a conversation: You issue commands (via menus) to PC Tools, and it responds with warnings, comments, questions, and messages. These exchanges from PC Tools are displayed in dialog boxes. The boxes are much like windows, except you can't generally move, size, or scroll a dialog box.

The types of dialog boxes vary, but all contain "buttons" you press to indicate your answer or preference. Almost all dialog boxes contain at least two such buttons: OK (or Yes or some other go-ahead command) and Cancel or Exit. You "press" these buttons, as if they were real-life objects, by selecting them with the keyboard or by pointing to them with the mouse.

There are four main types of dialog boxes: prompt, message and warning, option, and list. Two or more of these types may be combined in one composite box.

33

▶ *Prompt boxes.* A prompt asks you to complete some task before the remainder of the command is completed, as illustrated in Figure 2-9. For example, a prompt dialog box may ask you to insert a diskette into drive A: so that data can be recorded on it. PC Tools may sense automatically that you have completed the task, or you may need to acknowledge compliance by pressing a dialog box button.

▶ *Message and warning boxes.* PC Tools is about to do something it thinks you should know about. You read the message and respond (see Figure 2-10).

▶ *Option boxes.* PC Tools wants you to select one or more options, as illustrated in Figure 2-11, before it carries out the command. For example, if you've selected the Sort command, you must indicate the type of sort you want (ascending or descending, for instance) before the actual sorting can begin. The options are checkmarks or "radio buttons"; you select these in a similar fashion to the OK/Exit buttons.

▶ *List boxes.* PC Tools wants you to select from a list of files or subdirectories before it completes the command. The list within the dialog box is like a narrow scroll of paper, as shown in Figure 2-12. If the file or subdirectory you want isn't shown in the list, you can scroll it up or down until it is. List boxes are a fancy way of displaying a directory of files.

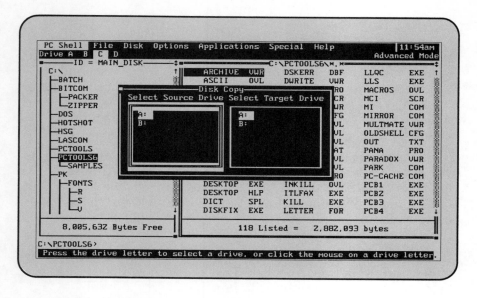

Figure 2-9. A sample prompt dialog box.

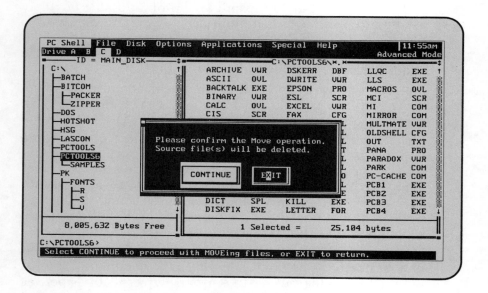

Figure 2-10. A sample message/warning dialog box.

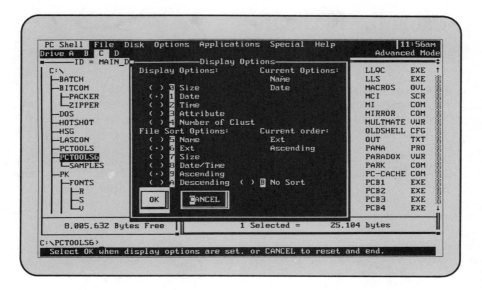

Figure 2-11. A sample options selection dialog box.

35

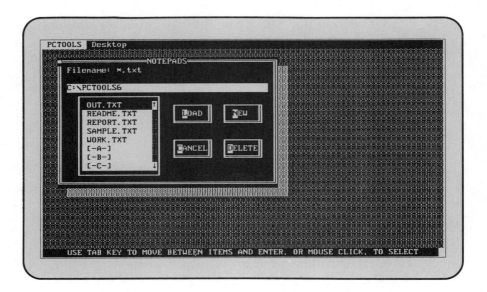

Figure 2-12. A sample list dialog box.

Using the Keyboard

The keyboard offers full control over the PC Tools utilities, although you may need to press several keys in succession to perform a single function. However, the most common PC Tools commands have single-key shortcuts. For example, while in Shell, selecting a file and pressing the F5 function key activates the Copy command.

The procedures that follow pertain to all PC Tools utilities. Specific information on using the various commands within the utilities are provided in the applicable chapters for each program.

Choosing a Pull-Down Menu

36

To pull down a menu when there isn't one visible, press the Alt key and the first letter (the quick-key) of the menu (Alt-F for File, Alt-D for Disk, etc.).

> ▶ **Tip**: Pressing the Alt key or the F10 function key highlights the menus, and their associated quick-key letters, in the menu bar. Once you press the F10 function key, the first menu in the menu bar is highlighted. You can pull the menu open simply by pressing the Enter key, or you can highlight another menu by pressing the Right or Left Arrow key. Cancel the selection by pressing the Escape key.

If a pull-down menu is already in view or you want to look at another one, press the Right or Left Arrow key.

Selecting a Command

You can select a command from within a menu using either of two methods: by pressing the highlighted quick-key associated with the command or by "pointing" with the Up and Down Arrow keys. For instance, to select the Copy command from the File menu (when in Shell), pull open the menu and press the C key (the quick-key for Copy). Or, press the Up and Down Arrow keys until the Copy command is highlighted, then press Enter to select the command.

> ▶ **Tip:** Menus are like endless loops. Pressing the Down Arrow key selects each command in turn down the length of the menu. Continue pressing the Down Arrow key and the highlighting continues back at the top again. To highlight a command at the bottom of a menu quickly, when starting at the top, merely press the Up Arrow key once.

Canceling a Menu

Press the Escape key to close a menu without selecting a command.

37

Selecting Items in a Dialog Box

Dialog boxes require that you provide PC Tools with additional information or affirm an action. Many dialog boxes contain more than one item to select, so you must use the keyboard to highlight the item you want to choose, then press the OK button (or press the Enter key on the keyboard) to make the final selection. The following keys are commonly used in dialog boxes:

▶ *Selecting item groups.* Use the Tab key to move from one set of items to the next. The selected group is shown highlighted or in a different color.

▶ *Selecting action buttons.* Use the Tab key to highlight the action button you want (like OK or Exit), then press Enter or type the highlighted letter in the action button of your choice (the C in Cancel, for instance).

▶ *Selecting options.* After the option group is highlighted (with the Tab key), press the number (or letter) next to the option you want to turn on or off. A dot beside the option means on; no dot means off. You can also select different options by pressing the Up or Down Arrow key to highlight each option in turn and pressing Enter to choose the one you want.

▶ *Selecting option check boxes.* After you select the option check box, place or remove an X in the box by pressing Enter.

▶ *Selecting items in a list.* After highlighting a list (with the Tab key), press the Up and Down Arrow keys to choose the list item you want.

When the desired options in a dialog box are set, continue by pressing Enter. If you want to cancel the dialog box (and therefore cancel the command that brought the box to the screen in the first place), press the Escape key. You can always use the Escape key to investigate a dialog box without the worry of actually making changes.

Selecting the Active Window

38

If more than one window is displayed on the screen at one time, press the Tab key until the window you want to use is shown highlighted—activated. Many of the PC Tools programs have other techniques for selecting the active window. These are detailed throughout this book where appropriate.

Scrolling Through a Window

Windows that provide more information than can be viewed at once usually have scroll bars along the right and bottom edges. (Those windows that don't have scroll bars include buttons that allow you to flip through successive windows like pages in a book.) Even though the scroll bars are intended solely for use with the mouse, you can accomplish the same ends with the keyboard by pressing the cursor movement keys. Table 2-2 summarizes the action of the cursor keys when scrolling through a window.

Closing a Window

For most PC Tools programs, closing the main applications window means quitting the program. To close the window, select the Exit command, usually found in the File menu.

Table 2-2. Cursor Key Scrolling.

Key	Action
Page-Down	Scrolls the contents of the window down one column or window-full
Page-Up	Scrolls the contents of the window up one column or window-full
Down	Scrolls the contents down one line
Up	Scrolls the contents up one line
Home	Scrolls the contents of the window all the way to the top
End	Scrolls the contents of the window all the way to the bottom

▶ **Tip:** The F3 function key serves as a universal exit key. The F3 function key works whether you are closing a window, dialog box, menu, or application. The Escape key also functions as an exit key.

39

Moving a Window

Movable windows can be shuttled around the screen with the Move or Size/Move Window command. After selecting the command, PC Tools displays a small cursor pad window, as shown in Figure 2-13. Press the cursor keys (Up, Down, Left, and Right) until the window is in the position you want.

Resizing a Window

Windows are resized in a similar manner to moving them. Choose the Size command from the Window menu (most applications), and press the cursor keys to expand or contract the lower-left corner of the window.

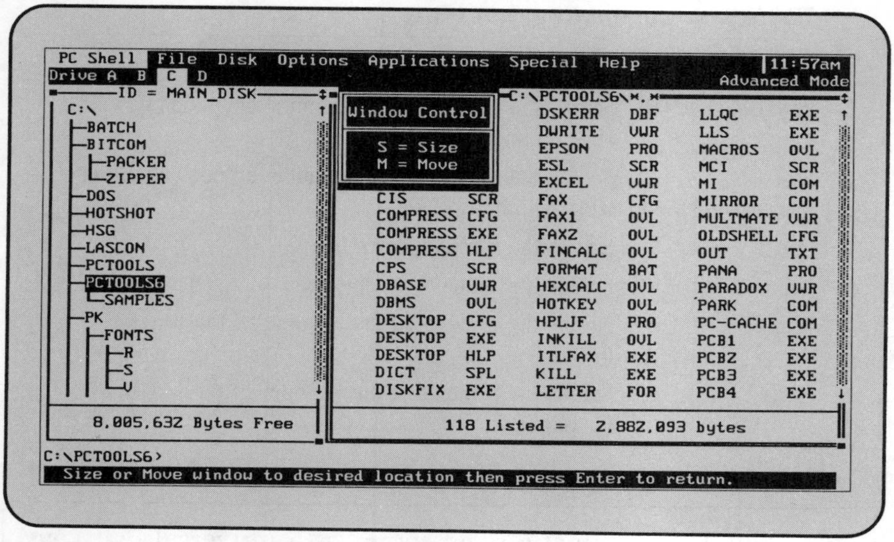

```
 PC Shell  File  Disk  Options  Applications  Special  Help        ┃11:57am
 Drive A  B ▐ C ▌ D                                         Advanced Mode
┌──────ID = MAIN_DISK──────┬─┐   ┌C:\PCTOOLS6\M.M──────────────────────┬─┐
│ C:\                      │↑│   │DSKERR    DBF     LLQC     EXE      │↑│
│ ├─BATCH                  │ │  ┌Window Control┐  DWRITE  VVR  LLS   EXE  │ │
│ ├─BITCOM                 │ │  │              │  EPSON   PRO  MACROS OVL  │ │
│ │ ├─PACKER               │ │  │ S = Size     │  ESL     SCR  MCI    SCR  │ │
│ │ └─ZIPPER               │ │  │ M = Move     │  EXCEL   VVR  MI     COM  │ │
│ ├─DOS                    │ │  └──────────────┘  FAX     CFG  MIRROR COM  │ │
│ ├─HOTSHOT                │ │   CIS      SCR      FAX1    OVL  MULTMATE VVR│ │
│ ├─HSG                    │ │   COMPRESS CFG      FAX2    OVL  OLDSHELL CFG│ │
│ ├─LASCON                 │ │   COMPRESS EXE      FINCALC OVL  OUT    TXT  │ │
│ ├─PCTOOLS                │ │   COMPRESS HLP      FORMAT  BAT  PANA   PRO  │ │
│ ├─PCTOOLS6               │ │   CPS      SCR      HEXCALC OVL  PARADOX VVR │ │
│ │ └─SAMPLES              │ │   DBASE    VVR      HOTKEY  OVL  PARK   COM  │ │
│ ├─PK                     │ │   DBMS     OVL      HPLJF   PRO  PC-CACHE COM│ │
│ │ ├─FONTS                │ │   DESKTOP  CFG      INKILL  OVL  PCB1   EXE  │ │
│ │ │ ├─R                  │ │   DESKTOP  EXE      ITLFAX  EXE  PCB2   EXE  │ │
│ │ │ ├─S                  │ │   DESKTOP  HLP      KILL    EXE  PCB3   EXE  │ │
│ │ │ └─V                  │↓│   DICT     SPL      LETTER  FOR  PCB4   EXE ↓│
│                          │ │   DISKFIX  EXE                              │
├──────────────────────────┴─┤ ├────────────────────────────────────────┤
│    8,005,632 Bytes Free    │ │   118 Listed =    2,882,093 bytes       │
└────────────────────────────┘ └────────────────────────────────────────┘
 C:\PCTOOLS6>
 ▐ Size or Move window to desired location then press Enter to return. ▌
```

Figure 2-13. The window cursor pad, used to change the position of a window.

Zooming a Window

Many PC Tools windows can be zoomed between full size (generally the entire screen, minus the menu and message bars) and one preset size. To zoom a window, press the F8 function key (Shell), or select the Zoom command in the Window menu (this works with most PC Tools applications, but not all).

Specific Keyboard Control

Specific information on using the keyboard with individual PC Tools programs is provided throughout this book.

Using the Mouse

Using the mouse to select commands, manipulate windows, and choose options from a dialog box is easier to learn, and you don't have to remember which keys do what. PC Tools uses both the left and right buttons of the mouse (the center button on a three-button mouse is not used).

Although the left and right buttons do different things under some circumstances, you can normally select commands, control windows, and manipulate dialog boxes using either button. However, in some instances—especially when selecting files from a list or text from within a window—the two buttons behave differently:

▶ The right button scrolls through the list or text.
▶ The left button scrolls through the list or text and highlights (selects) it along the way.

Unlike many other aspects of the PC Tools user interface, the exact nature of the operation of the two mouse buttons differs somewhat between the utilities, so exceptions to this rule are noted in the appropriate chapters throughout this book.

41

If you are left handed, you can exchange the operation of the right and left mouse buttons by starting the desired PC Tools program with the /LE parameter. For example, to start Shell and reverse the mouse buttons, enter

```
PCSHELL /LE
```

at the DOS prompt.

One of the most important concepts to remember when using the mouse is the difference between the cursor and the mouse pointer, as illustrated in Figure 2-14. The cursor displays the spot where text will be entered when you type from the keyboard. Or it appears as a rectangular highlight to show a file you have selected. The mouse pointer appears as a rectangular blip of light that moves when you touch the mouse. The positions of the cursor and mouse pointer may be in separate parts of the screen, so even if the mouse pointer is located over a blank part of the window, it doesn't mean that text you write will appear there. Rather, it will appear at the cursor.

Using the mouse entails its own set of vocabulary and procedures. There are four basic mouse functions used in PC Tools: moving the mouse pointer, clicking, double-clicking, and dragging.

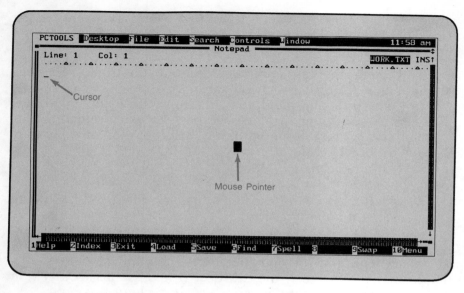

Figure 2-14. The mouse pointer (visible only when using a mouse) is different from the cursor.

42

▶ *Moving the mouse pointer* entails simply pushing the mouse around the table. The mouse pointer will mimic your hand movements.

▶ *Clicking* selects things that are directly under the mouse pointer—things like menu commands and dialog box options. When using a word processor, clicking over a character sets a new cursor point. To click, hold the mouse still, and press the right or left button once.

▶ *Double-clicking* is the same as regular clicking, except that you press the right or left mouse button twice in quick succession, but without moving the mouse. Generally, double-clicking is used to select an item in a list and to activate the default command (such as open the file or copy the file).

▶ *Dragging* involves holding down the right or left mouse button while moving the mouse. In most cases, this selects text or files between the point where you started and finished dragging. Release the mouse button when the selection is complete.

The procedures that follow pertain to all PC Tools programs. Specific information on using the various commands within the utilities are provided in the applicable chapters for each program.

Choosing a Pull-Down Menu

To choose a pull-down menu with the mouse, aim the mouse pointer at one of the menu names in the menu bar and click once. The menu will drop open. To select another menu, click over another name in the menu bar. Or, drag the mouse pointer over to the menu you want.

Selecting a Command

With the menu you want dropped into view on the screen, select the desired command by clicking on it once with the mouse. You can combine menu and command selection in one smooth action.

43

Q **Choosing a PC Tools Command with a Mouse**

1. Click on the menu name in the menu bar; keep the button held down.
Selects the menu.

2. Drag the mouse pointer to the desired menu.
Highlights the command.

3. Lift up on the mouse button.
Invokes the command. ☐

Canceling a Menu

To cancel a menu after you've opened it, click anywhere outside the menu. You may wish instead to press the Escape key or the F3 function key, as clicking may select a portion of the screen you hadn't intended.

Selecting Items in a Dialog Box

You don't need to touch the keyboard to select items in a dialog box with a mouse. Merely point and click at those options you want to engage. To select a dialog box button, for example, position the mouse pointer over it and click once with the right or left mouse button.

Some dialog boxes contain lists of files, disk drives, or directories. These are like miniature windows and have their own scroll bars. See below for more information on using scroll bars.

Selecting the Active Window

Windows are activated with the mouse by clicking anywhere within them, or on one of the borders. The currently active window is shown highlighted with a double border.

44

Scrolling Through a Window

The scroll bars along the bottom and right edges of some windows are for the express purpose of scrolling the contents of windows vertically or horizontally. They're made especially for the mouse.

- ▶ *Scroll arrows* move the display incrementally, usually one line up or down, or one character left or right. Click in the scroll arrow to actuate them, or click and hold the left mouse button to scroll continuously.
- ▶ The *thumb box* shows the approximate location of the cursor within the contents of the window. To view another part, drag the thumb box along the length of the scroll arrow.

> ▶ **Tip:** You can also move to an approximate location within the contents of the window by clicking in the gray area of the scroll bar. For example, to move to approximately two-thirds through a document, click at about the two-thirds mark in the vertical scroll bar.

Closing a Window

To close a window with the mouse, click once in the close box, located in the upper-left corner of the window.

Moving a Window

Not all windows can be moved (for instance, informational windows). Those that can are moved by dragging with the mouse. Position the mouse pointer along the top border of the window, press and hold the right or left mouse button, and drag the window in the direction you want to move it. Release the mouse button when the window is in the proper position.

Resizing a Window

45

Windows with a size box (lower-right corner) can be readily resized with the mouse. Drag the size box with the mouse until the window is the shape you want. A window that's been moved and resized is shown in Figure 2-15.

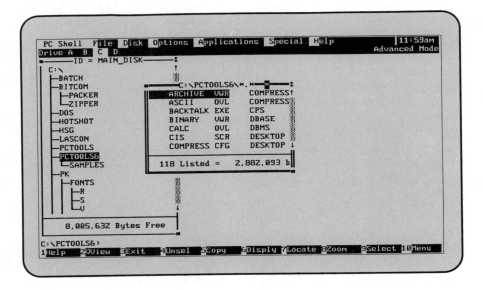

Figure 2-15. A window that's been moved on top of another one.

Zooming a Window

There's no special spot in windows where you can click to zoom
it to full size. If you'd like to zoom a window, use the mouse to
choose the Zoom command in the Window menu (on most PC
Tools applications).

Specific Mouse Control

Specific information on using the mouse with individual PC Tools
programs is provided throughout this book.

Becoming Proficient with the Mouse and Keyboard

46

If you're like most PC Tools users, you'll find a combination of
mouse and keyboard control works best and offers the greatest efficiency. While most functions are more easily and quickly performed
by the mouse, some are better suited to direct keyboard control.

Once you get accustomed to PC Tools and are comfortable with
its interface, take a moment to think about the best course of action
for each function. Do you find it easier to use the mouse or the keyboard for selecting commands from menus? The most common
commands are provided function key equivalents (F3 to exit, for
example), so instead of using the mouse or keyboard to pull down
the File menu and select the Exit command, use the F3 function
key. PC Tools presents two, three, and sometimes four different
approaches for accomplishing the same goals. It's up to you find the
best method that works for you.

This was mentioned in the introduction of this book, but it
bears repeating here. Because of the diverse techniques of accessing
PC Tools commands, you'll be instructed to perform a certain
task—to select a command or to choose an option in a dialog box,
for instance—but without specific mouse or key-by-key instructions
for doing so. That way, you are free to pick your favorite method of
accessing PC Tools commands.

Occasionally, however, you'll have actual instructions for keyboard or mouse shortcuts, as you've seen in this chapter. The shortcuts can differ between PC Tools programs so, unfortunately, it's not possible to group them all here and get them over with.

Getting Help

When you get stuck or forget the meaning of a command or how it works, PC Tools provides a handy on-line system. The help is context-sensitive, meaning the program identifies the command or function you are about to perform and provides help on it. You can also call up a help index and locate the specific information you desire.

Using Context-Sensitive Help

47

PC Tools monitors everything you do with the keyboard or mouse. If you'd like help on a particular command, select it with the keyboard or mouse, then press the F1 function key. Help for that specific command is shown in the Help window, as illustrated in Figure 2-16.

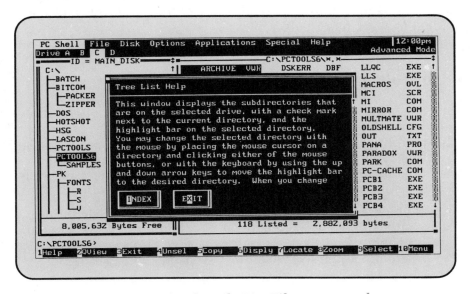

Figure 2-16. Help for the File List Filter command.

The Help window works like any other PC Tools window: If you have a mouse, scroll through the contents with the window's scroll bar. If you're using the keyboard, press the Page Up or Page Down key (or the Up and Down Arrow keys to move one line at a time), and press Enter to select the topic. When you're done with help, press the Escape key, the F3 function key, or the X key (for Exit) or click with the mouse in the close box.

Using the Help Index

If no command is selected, pressing the F1 function key opens the Main Help window, where you have the choice of displaying the help index or closing the Help window. Press the I key for Index, and the index will appear.

48

▶ *For keyboard users*, scroll through the available help topics by pressing the Up and Down Arrow keys.

▶ *For mouse users*, click on the help topic you want (if it's not visible, use the scroll bars to scroll through the list). Then, press Enter to view the help topic.

Read the help screen (scroll the text down if it fills more than one window). Close the Help window if you're finished, or select the Index button (use the mouse or press the I key for Index) to view more help topics.

Variable User Levels

Starting with version 6.0, PC Tools allows you to set one of three user levels: beginning, intermediate, and advanced. You can select the appropriate user level depending on your experience with the program. The higher the user level, the more commands and features the program displays in the menus. The variable user levels feature is found in PC Shell and PC Backup.

If you are new to PC Tools, set the user level to beginning or intermediate. That way, you won't be confused by commands you probably won't have a use for. As you gain experience with the program, set the user level to advanced.

For more information on setting the user level for the PC Shell, see Chapter 3, "Understanding Shell." Refer to Chapter 7, "Backing Up Your Hard Disk Drive," for details on setting the user level in PC Backup.

Review

This chapter explained how to get started with PC Tools and discussed the basic operating procedures for starting the program and using the interface. You also learned:

▶ The PC Tools Shell and Desktop utilities can be run as stand-alone programs at the DOS prompt, as a memory-resident program loaded manually, or as a memory-resident program loaded automatically.

▶ The typical PC Tools screen contains a menu bar, one or more menus, a message bar, and one or more windows.

▶ The most common PC Tools commands are provided single-key shortcuts.

▶ There are four basic mouse functions used in PC Tools: moving the mouse pointer, clicking, double-clicking, and dragging.

▶ Context-sensitive help provides a help screen of the currently highlighted command.

▶ Index help offers a list of available help topics.

49

Chapter 3

Understanding Shell

In This Chapter

51

- ▶ *Loading Shell using special parameters*
- ▶ *Viewing directories and files*
- ▶ *Using the commands in Shell's menus*
- ▶ *Saving your configuration settings*

Shell is the cornerstone of the PC Tools package. It provides the gateway to the PC Tools programs and its functions and offers an easy-to-use alternative to DOS. This chapter provides an overview of the features and capabilities of Shell. This chapter shows you how to run Shell, how to view files and directories, how to move around the directory tree, and more.

In addition, you'll be introduced to Shell's menus and commands, so you know what the program offers.

In Review: Running Shell

In Chapter 2 you learned how to start Shell as either a stand-alone or memory-resident program. For your convenience, we'll quickly review the methods of starting Shell here.

Recall there are three ways to run Shell: as a stand-alone program at the DOS prompt, as a memory-resident program (loaded manually by you), and as a memory-resident program (loaded automatically by the AUTOEXEC.BAT batch file when the computer is first turned on). Throughout this and the remaining chapters, we'll use the terms "memory-resident" and "TSR" (for terminate and stay resident) interchangeably.

The following steps assume that you are using a hard disk drive and that you are currently logged onto the drive that contains the PC Tools programs—usually drive C. You do not need to move to the PC Tools subdirectory unless you have deleted or edited the PCTOOLS directory in the PATH statement in your AUTOEXEC.BAT file.

At the DOS prompt	Type PCSHELL and press Enter
As memory-resident /manual load	Type PCSHELL/R, press Enter, then press Ctrl-Esc to activate
As memory-resident /AUTOEXEC.BAT load	Press Ctrl-Esc to activate

The Control and Escape keys are hot-keys that activate Shell from memory. Under most circumstances, you can activate Shell from within DOS or any application. Some PC programs may require all the memory in your computer, however, and Shell may not load.

You press these same keys to deactivate Shell and return to the DOS prompt or your application. Remember that even though Shell is deactivated, it still resides in your computer's memory, so you can call it back up any time. It also continues to consume a portion of your computer's RAM, so if you need to reclaim that memory for use by another application, type

KILL

at the DOS prompt. This removes Shell (as well as Desktop, if it has also been loaded as memory resident) from the computer's RAM. Note that KILL.COM is a PC Tools program and must be on the currently selected drive, or DOS won't be able to find it.

After Shell is loaded (and activated if you're using it in memory-resident mode), your computer screen should look like that in Figure 3-1. The illustration includes a description of the various components of the Shell display.

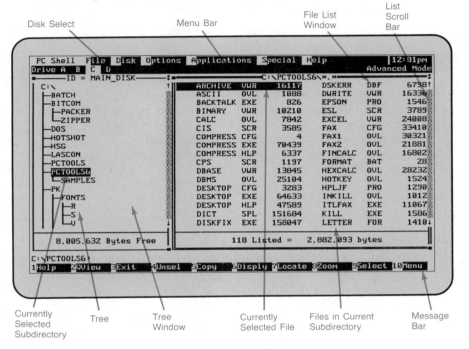

Figure 3-1. The component parts of the Shell screen.

Special Shell Parameters

Parameters are "switches" or options you select when you load a program into your computer. Shell supports about a dozen parameters that control the way the program works and interacts with your computer. To use a parameter, enter it after typing

PCSHELL

at the DOS prompt. You've already learned about one of Shell's parameters already, the /R switch that loads Shell as a memory-resident program instead of a stand-alone program. In most cases, you can combine switches to activate many options.

/BW

Starts PC Shell in black-and-white mode.

/DQ

Disables quick-load feature when activating Shell from the DOS prompt. (Quick-load helps load Shell faster when you activate it; it's used only when Shell is loaded as a TSR.) Use the /DQ switch if you are experiencing problems running Shell as memory resident when activating the program from the DOS prompt.

/FF

Disables screen snow suppression on CGA monitors. Without the /FF switch, screen snow is suppressed when using a CGA monitor, but scrolling takes longer. With the /FF switch, screen snow appears whenever you scroll the contents of a window, but the scrolling goes faster.

/Fn

Changes the default hot-key from Ctrl-Esc to Ctrl-n, where n is one of the function keys (F1 through F10).

/LCD

Allows you to set the "colors" to better show on the monochrome screen of the liquid crystal display (LCD) panel. It is used on laptop computers with LCDs.

/LE

Exchanges right and left mouse buttons, to accommodate left-handed persons.

/IM

Disables the mouse. It is helpful if you are using an older mouse driver that is not supported by PC Tools.

/IN

Used to run Shell in color with a Hercules InColor graphics card (memory-resident mode only).

55

/Od

Selects a different drive to contain the Shell overlay files (these include PCSHELL.OVL, PCSHELL.IMG, and PCSHELL.THM). Ordinarily, Shell places these overlay files in the drive and directory containing the PC Tools files; you can change it if your drive (or RAM disk) gets too full. Replace the d with a drive letter, such as /Oa.

/350

Displays Shell in 350 line resolution; used only with VGA monitors.

/PS2

Resets the mouse on IBM PS/2 computers upon entering Shell. Use this switch if the mouse cursor does not appear properly.

/R

Loads Shell memory resident. You can control the amount of memory consumed by Shell when it is loaded (but not actually activated) as a TSR. The more RAM consumed, the faster Shell operates, but the less room you have for other applications.

▶ /R or /RT or /RTINY consumes about 9 kilobytes of RAM.
▶ /RS or /RSMALL consumes about 70 kilobytes of RAM.
▶ /RM or /RMEDIUM consumes about 90 kilobytes of RAM.
▶ /RL or /RLARGE consumes about 170 kilobytes of RAM.

/Annn

Allocates a certain amount of RAM when Shell is activated (called up from memory) when loaded as a TSR. The minimum setting for the /A switch is 180 kilobytes; the maximum is approximately the total amount of RAM in your computer, minus 200 kilobytes (for example, if your computer has 640 kilobytes, the maximum /A setting is about 440 kilobytes). Enter a memory amount after the /A switch, such as /A360, for 360 kilobytes. The default setting of /A is 200 kilobytes.

/TRn

Rebuilds the tree (directory hierarchy) every n number of days. Normally, this is set to 1, but you can increase it if you like to force Shell to examine and rebuild the three every 2 days, every 3 days, whatever. With a setting of 0 (/TR0), Shell rebuilds the tree every time it is run. Tree rebuilding takes some time—about 5–10 seconds for the average hard disk.

Table 3-1 offers a quick reference guide to using the parameter switches with Shell running as a stand-alone program from the DOS prompt, or as a TSR.

Table 3-1. Parameter Switches for Shell Operating Modes.

Parameter	Shell Loaded from DOS Prompt	Shell Loaded as a TSR
/BW	X	X
/DQ		X
/FF	X	X
/Fn		X
/LCD	X	X
/LE	X	X
/IM	X	X
/IN		X
/Od	X	X
/350	X	X
/PS2	X	X
/R		X
/Annn	X	X
/TRn	X	X

Viewing Directories and Files

When Shell is first started, it displays the screen shown in Figure 3-1. (Your directory and file listing will be different, reflecting the contents of your hard disk.) Unless you've used Shell before and changed its configuration (using the Save Configuration File command, introduced later in this chapter), the display will be divided into two windows.

The window on the left contains the tree of the hard disk drive. The tree represents the organization and layout of the subdirectories. The tree begins at the root directory, listed at the top. Subdirectories are listed alphabetically under the root.

You might consider the first hierarchy of subdirectories as the main trunk of the tree. Subdirectories under the main subdirectories are shown as limbs branching off the trunk. Shell displays the complete hierarchy of subdirectories, even if you have created many subdirectory levels. You may have to use the scroll bars in the Tree window to view the entire hierarchy. The root or a subdirectory is always selected (shown highlighted) in the Tree window. This represents the currently active directory.

The window on the right contains the files within the currently active directory. For example, if the root directory is selected in the Tree window, as shown in Figure 3-2, the File List window displays the files contained within the root directory. As you make other subdirectories active, the files in the File List window change.

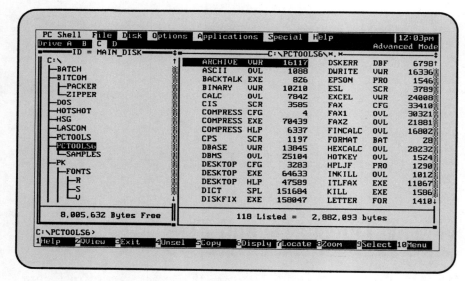

Figure 3-2. The root directory (shown as C:\) is currently selected in the Tree window.

Moving Around the Tree and File List Windows

The Tree and File List windows behave like any other PC Tools window. You can control with the keyboard or mouse, as detailed in Chapter 2. Remember that only one window can be active at any time. The active window is shown with a double border. Press the Tab key to activate a different window.

Selecting Subdirectories

You select a subdirectory simply by scrolling through the contents of the Tree window.

▶ When using the keyboard, press the Up or Down Arrow key to move through the directory list. Table 3-2 lists some shortcut keys you can use to move through the Tree window quickly.

▶ When using the mouse, press the left mouse button to select a new subdirectory. Or, press and hold the right mouse button and drag up or down to scroll through the tree.

Table 3-2. Shortcut Keys Used in Tree Window.

Key	Action
Page Up	Moves selection up eight subdirectories
Page Down	Moves selection down eight subdirectories
End	Moves selection to end of tree
Home	Moves selection to beginning of tree

Selecting Files

You will often select a file within the File List window, for such tasks as deleting, renaming, or copying the file. To select a single file, highlight it with the cursor keys or click on it once with the mouse, using the left button.

Shell allows you to select multiple files for ganged operations (deleting an entire set of files, for instance). Follow these steps to select a series of files.

 Selecting a Series of Files; Keyboard Control

| 1. | With the cursor keys, highlight the first file you want to select. | Selects the file for the next operation. |

2. Press Enter.   Highlights the file and places a number to the left of it.

3. Repeat selecting and entering for each file in the series.

☐

To deselect a file, highlight it again with the cursor keys and press Enter. The number will disappear.

Ⓠ Selecting a Series of Files; Mouse Control

1. Using the left mouse button, click on the first file of the series.   Actuates the first file.

60

2. Repeat the procedure for other files in the list.

☐

To deselect a file, click on it again with the mouse.

> ▶ **Tip:** You can select two or more contiguous (adjacent) files quickly by using a novel drag—select technique. However, the drag—select technique does take some time and practice to master. To drag—select, position the mouse pointer over the first file you want to select, press and hold the right mouse button, then press and hold the left mouse button. Finally, drag over the other files in the series. Release the mouse buttons when all the desired files are selected. You can deselect the files in the same manner.

As with the Tree window, you can use the Page Up, Page Down, Home, and End keys to move through the file list quickly, as detailed in Table 3-3.

If you're using a mouse, you can scroll through the files quickly: Press and hold the right mouse button, then drag up or down to scroll through the file list.

Table 3-3. Shortcut Keys Used in File List Window.

Key	Action
Page Up	Moves selection up one column or window-full
Page Down	Moves selection down one column or window-full
End	Moves selection to end of files
Home	Moves selection to beginning of files

Automatic Quick File Display and Selection

Shell offers other means for displaying and selecting groups of files quickly.

▶ You can display a list of only those files that match the name or extension you've provided (with and without wildcards) using the File List Filter command in the Modify Display submenu.

▶ You can retain the entire list, with the files you chose highlighted and numbered, using the File Select command.

▶ You can select only those files that match the name or extension you've provided (with and without wildcards) using the File Select Filter command under the Options menu.

61

> ▶ **Tip:** Press the F9 function key then press Enter twice to select all files quickly. Conversely, press the F4 function key to deselect all files quickly.

Q List File Filter

1. Select the subdirectory that contains the files you wish to view.

2. Choose the Modify Display command from the Options menu.

   The Modify Display submenu appears on the screen.

3. Choose the File List Filter command from the submenu.

   A dialog box like the one in Figure 3-3 appears.

4. Define the name and/or extension of the files you want. For example, to view only .EXE files, enter EXE in the Ext field. You may use the * and ? DOS wildcards: Enter SHOW?.EXE to find SHOW1.EXE, SHOW2.EXE, SHOWA.EXE, etc.

Selects the "filter" for the list display.

5. Press the Select button.

Displays the newly defined list.

Redisplay all files by entering asterisks (the * character) in both the Name and Ext fields or by pressing the Reset button in the File Select Filter dialog box.

62

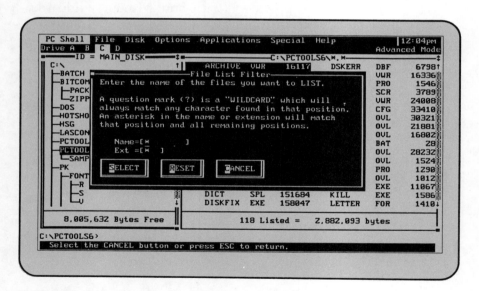

Figure 3-3. The File List Filter dialog box.

Activate to Select File Filter

1. Select the subdirectory that contains the files you wish to view.

2. Choose the Modify Display command from the Options menu.

The Modify Display submenu appears on the screen.

3. Choose the File Select Filter command from the submenu.

Opens the File Select Filter dialog box.

4. Define the name and/or extension of the files you want to display.

Sets the display to your file name critera.

5. Press the Select button.

Activates the newly defined display. □

Return File List to its original state by entering asterisks (the * character) in both the Name and Ext fields or by pressing the Reset button in the File Select Filter dialog box. A sample of selected files (all with the .EXE extension) is shown in Figure 3-4.

63

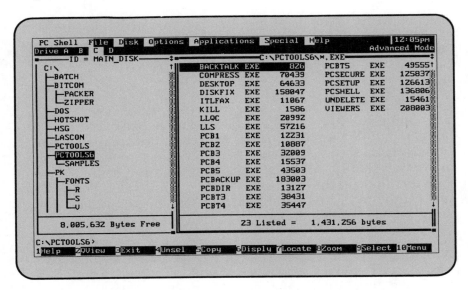

Figure 3-4. File List display showing only .EXE files.

Changing the Current Drive

The current drive (with directory and files shown in the Tree and File List windows) is indicated immediately under the Shell menu bar. The available drives—as detected by Shell or indicated with the LASTDRIVE command in your CONFIG.SYS file—are listed as A, B, C, etc.; the currently active drive is highlighted.

▶ To change the current drive with the keyboard, hold down the control key and type the letter of the drive you want to activate (such as Ctrl-A or Ctrl-B).

▶ To change the current drive with the mouse, click on one of the drive letters under the menu bar. For example, to activate drive D, click on D.

64 Viewing Two Lists

Shell normally presents a single set of Tree and File List windows, but you can readily add another set of windows to view two trees and file lists at a time. This comes in handy, for example, when copying or moving files between two directories or drives.

To add another set of windows, choose the Two List Display command from the Modify Display submenu (under the Options pull-down menu). Now, four windows are displayed on the screen, as shown in Figure 3-5. To revert to one list display, choose the One List Display command from the Options menu. Note that the current list display setting (either One List or Two List) can be recording for subsequent sessions with Shell. More on saving the configuration of Shell later.

> ▶ **Tip:** To open a second set of windows quickly and read the directory on another drive, press Ctrl-Alt-Drive Letter, where "Drive Letter" corresponds to the drive you want to view (A, B, etc.). Press Tab to move highlight between windows.

```
┌──────────────────────────────────────────────────────────────┐
│  PC Shell  File  Disk  Options  Applications  Special  Help        12:07pm │
│  Drive A  B  C  D                                      Advanced Mode │
│  ──ID = MAIN_DISK──────╪═          ──C:\PCTOOLS6\*.*──────────────╪ │
│    └─ZIPPER              ↑  │  ARCHIVE  VWR    16117    COMPRESS  EXE   70439↑│
│    ─DOS                     │  ASCII    OVL     1088    COMPRESS  HLP    6337▓│
│    ─HOTSHOT                 │  BACKTALK EXE      826    CPS       SCR    1197▓│
│    ─HSG                     │  BINARY   VWR    10210    DBASE     VWR   13845▓│
│    ─LASCON                  │  CALC     OVL     7842    DBMS      OVL   25104▓│
│    ─PCTOOLS                 │  CIS      SCR     3585    DESKTOP   CFG    3283▓│
│    ─PCTOOLS6             ↓  │  COMPRESS CFG        4    DESKTOP   EXE   64633↓│
│  ───────────────────────   │                                               │
│      8,005,632 Bytes Free  │    118 Listed  =   2,882,093 bytes            │
│  ──ID = ALT_DISK───────╪═  │          ──D:\GOSCRIPT\*.*──────────────╪ │
│    ─WP50                 ↑  │  CANBJ130 DRV     1935    EPSONFX   DRV    1967↑│
│      ─DOCS                  │  DEMO1    PS       891    EPSONLQ   DRV    1855▓│
│      ─LIBRARY               │  DEMO2    PS       477    EPSONLQ5  DRV    1983▓│
│      ─MACROS                │  DEMO3    PS       658    FONTDEMO  PS     4480▓│
│    ─UTIL                    │  DEMO4    PS       619    FUJITDL   DRV    1871▓│
│    ─GOSCRIPT            ↓   │  DESKJET  DRV     2239    F_3000    GSF   44646↓│
│  ───────────────────────   │                                               │
│     25,362,432 Bytes Free  │     67 Listed  =   1,911,751 bytes            │
│  D:\GOSCRIPT>                                                              │
│  1Help   2QView  3Exit  4Unsel  5Copy  6Disply 7Locate 8Zoom  9Select 10Menu │
└──────────────────────────────────────────────────────────────┘
```

Figure 3-5. Two List display.

65

Shell Menus

Shell offers five pull-down menus where you can access the program's commands. (Additionally, you can access the most common
commands using the shortcut keys, as displayed in the message bar
at the bottom of the Shell screen.) These menus are:

▶ File.

▶ Disk.

▶ Options.

▶ Applications.

▶ Special.

These menus, and the commands contained within them,
are described here. This section provides just an introduction to
the PC Tools Shell commands and does not explain how to use
them in actual practice. Subsequent chapters detail, according to
function, the use of Shell commands.

The Shell File Menu

The File menu, shown in Figure 3-6, contains those commands used for running an applications program, exiting the PC Tools Shell, or managing individual files.

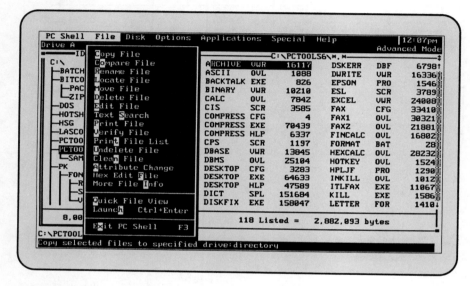

| PC Shell | File | Disk | Options | Applications | Special | Help | | 12:07pm |

Figure 3-6. The File menu.

▶ *Copy File* creates a duplicate of a file. Copies can be made anywhere—in the same disk or directory as the original or in another disk or directory.

▶ *Compare File* matches two files to see if they are the same or different. Each dissimilarity can be viewed individually.

▶ *Rename File* changes the DOS name of a file.

▶ *Locate File* hunts through all or portions of your disks to find specified files.

▶ *Move File* transplants a file to another directory or disk.

▶ *Delete File* erases a file from a disk.

▶ *Edit File* lets you view a file (program or document in ASCII form) and edit it character by character.

▶ *Text Search* hunts through a selected file and looks for a specified string of characters.

► *Print File* makes a paper copy of a document in your printer.

► *Verify File* checks the integrity of a file—either a program file or data document.

► *Print File List* makes a paper copy of the current DOS directory on your printer.

► *Undelete File* reclaims accidentally erased files.

► *Clean File* erases a file and also wipes away all data on the disk. This prevents reclaiming the erased file or viewing the remnants of an erased file.

► *Attribute Change* alters certain information attached to each file created by DOS, including the time and date of creation or last edit and whether or not the file can be erased or edited.

► *Hex Edit File* lets you view a file (program or document) in hexadecimal form and edit it byte by byte.

► *More File Info* provides a run-down of important facts about a particular file, such as its size and the actual amount of space it takes up on a disk.

67

► *Quick File View* displays the contents of a document file. If PC Tools has a file viewer filter (special disk file) for the document you have selected, it will display the file formatted as it would appear in the original application.

► *Launch* starts any program or batch file from within PC Shell.

► *Exit PC Shell* leaves PC Shell.

Some of the PC Shell commands under the File menu are duplicates of ones DOS provides, as detailed in Table 3-4.

Table 3-4. Equivalent File Menu DOS Commands.

PC Shell Command	Equivalent DOS Command
Copy	COPY
Move	No direct command
Compare	COMP or FC
Find	FIND
Rename	REN
Delete	DEL or ERASE
Verify	VERIFY
View	TYPE

By using the PC Tools Shell file commands instead of the DOS commands, you are provided with convenient "fill-in-the-blanks" prompts, such as the one shown in Figure 3-7. You don't have to remember the special syntax DOS requires of its commands or worry about the effects of entering a command incorrectly.

68

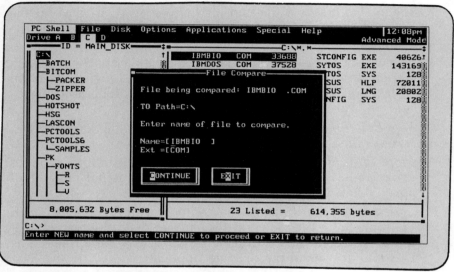

Figure 3-7. The dialog box provides prompts for entering additional information.

The PC Shell Disk Menu

The File menu manages files; conversely, the Disk menu governs operations that apply to entire disks or disk directories. The Disk pull-down menu is shown in Figure 3-8 and contains these commands:

► *Copy Disk* duplicates the entire contents of one disk onto another disk. The copy includes visible and hidden files.

► *Compare Disk* matches two disks and indicates whether they are the same or different. You can optionally view the differences, if any.

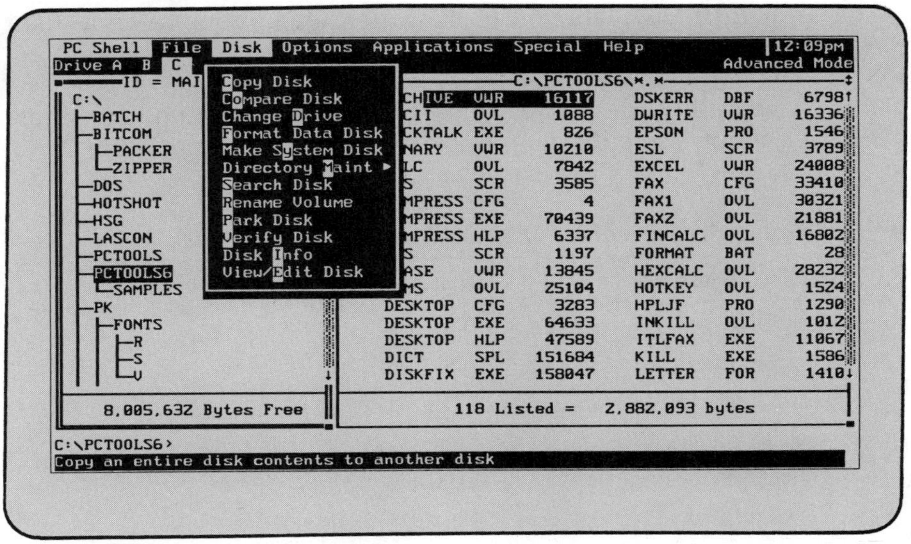

```
 PC Shell File  Disk  Options  Applications  Special  Help        12:09pm
Drive A  B  C                                                 Advanced Mode
    ID = MAI  Copy Disk                  C:\PCTOOLS6\*.*
C:\           Compare Disk       CHIVE    VWR    16117    DSKERR   DBF    6798↑
 ─BATCH       Change Drive       CII      OVL     1088    DWRITE   VWR   16336
 ─BITCOM      Format Data Disk   CKTALK   EXE      826    EPSON    PRO    1546
  ─PACKER     Make System Disk   NARY     VWR    10210    ESL      SCR    3789
  └ZIPPER     Directory Maint ►  LC       OVL     7842    EXCEL    VWR   24008
 ─DOS         Search Disk        S        SCR     3585    FAX      CFG   33410
 ─HOTSHOT     Rename Volume      MPRESS   CFG        4    FAX1     OVL   30321
 ─HSG         Park Disk          MPRESS   EXE    70439    FAX2     OVL   21881
 ─LASCON      Verify Disk        MPRESS   HLP     6337    FINCALC  OVL   16802
 ─PCTOOLS     Disk Info          S        SCR     1197    FORMAT   BAT      28
 ─PCTOOLS6    View/Edit Disk     ASE      VWR    13845    HEXCALC  OVL   28232
  └SAMPLES                       MS       OVL    25104    HOTKEY   OVL    1524
 ─PK                             DESKTOP  CFG     3283    HPLJF    PRO    1290
  ─FONTS                         DESKTOP  EXE    64633    INKILL   OVL    1012
   ─R                            DESKTOP  HLP    47589    ITLFAX   EXE   11067
   ─S                            DICT     SPL   151684    KILL     EXE    1586
   └U                            DISKFIX  EXE   158047    LETTER   FOR    1410↓

     8,005,632 Bytes Free           118 Listed =   2,882,093 bytes

C:\PCTOOLS6›
Copy an entire disk contents to another disk
```

Figure 3-8. The Disk menu.

▶ *Change Drive* changes the currently active drive (for viewing other drives and directories).

▶ *Format Data Disk* initializes or renews the format of a floppy diskette, preparing it for new data.

▶ *Make System Disk* produces a bootable floppy diskette.

▶ *Directory Maint* pops up a secondary menu for handling subdirectories. Among the available commands are *Add* a new subdirectory, *Rename* a subdirectory, *Delete* a subdirectory, *Prune and graft* a subdirectory, and *Modify Attributes* (change the DOS attributes of a directory).

▶ *Search Disk* hunts through the entire disk and looks for a specified string of characters.

▶ *Rename Volume* changes the name that you (or someone else) previously gave to a disk.

▶ *Park Disk* places the heads of a hard disk drive in a normally unused portion of the disk surface. Once placed there, the computer can be safely turned off and moved.

▶ *Verify Disk* quickly scans the disk and determines if all the data on it is readable.

▶ *Disk Info* provides a run-down of important facts about a disk, such as its capacity, number and size of bad sectors, and number of files.

▶ *View/Edit Disk* lets you look at the data anywhere on a disk and, optionally, edit it.

As with the File menu, some of the Shell commands under the Disk menu are similar to ones DOS provides (see Table 3-5).

Table 3-5. Equivalent Disk Menu DOS Commands.

PC Shell Command	Equivalent DOS Command
Copy Disk	DISKCOPY
Compare Disk	DISKCOMP
Search Disk	FIND
Rename Volume	None
Verify Disk	CHKDSK
View/Edit Disk	No direct command
Format Data Disk	FORMAT
Make System Disk	FORMAT /S
Disk Info	CHKDSK (only partial information as that given with Disk Info command)
Park Disk	SHIPDISK (can cause damage to some non-IBM hard disk drives)
Directory Maint	
Add	MKDIR
Rename	None
Delete	RMDIR
Prune and graft	None
Modify Attributes	None

70

The Shell Options Menu

The Options menu (see Figure 3-9) lets you control the presentation of Shell's windows and the data contained within them. The Options menu also lets you prepare a list of applications you can quickly launch from the Applications menu.

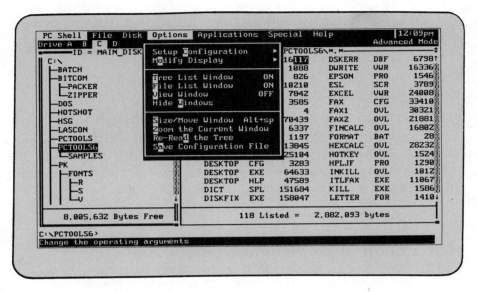

Figure 3-9. The Options menu.

71

▶ *Setup Configuration* allows you to set a number of configuration parameters for the appearance of the PC Shell display. The Setup Configuration command presents a submenu where you can *Change User Level*, turn the *Short Cut Keys* on or off, turn the *DOS Command Line* on or off, *Wait on DOS Screen* when running applications, turn the *Background Mat* on or off, alter the *Viewer Cfg* (configuration) to view files/directories in a vertical or horizontal orientation, change the *Default Viewer* for files between TEXT and BINARY, alter the *Screen Colors*, set the *Date/Time*, and define new keys with *Define Function Keys* (you can always use the ones PC Tools comes with, of course).

▶ *Modify Display* allows you to select how files and directories are displayed on the screen. The Modify Display command presents a submenu where you can alternate between windows with *Tree/Files Switch*, show two sets of files/directories with *Two List Display*, show one set of files/directories with *One List Display*, change to a new list of files with *Active List Switch*, list only certain files with *File List Filter*, select only certain files with *File Select Filter*, change the information displayed with files with *File Display Options*, and *Unselect Files*.

▶ *Tree List Window* hides/displays the tree list window(s).

▶ *File List Window* hides/displays the file list window(s).

▶ *View Window* hides/display file viewer windows.

▶ *Hide Windows* hides/displays all windows.

▶ *Size/Move Window* moves and resizes the active window.

▶ *Zoom the Current Window* zooms the active window.

▶ *Re-Read the Tree* forces PC Shell to reexamine the directories and files on the currently active disk.

▶ *Save Configuration File* records the changes you make in the Options menu for the next time you use Shell.

The PC Shell Applications Menu

72

The Applications menu lists programs (as well as batch files) you want to run directly from Shell. Depending on how you installed the PC Tools programs and what software is already contained in your hard disk, the menu will already be filled with a number of applications, as shown in Figure 3-10.

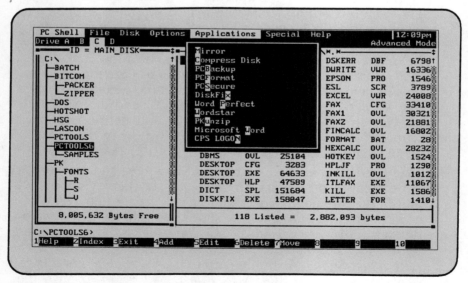

Figure 3-10. The Applications menu.

The Applications menu automatically includes the following programs:

▶ Mirror.
▶ Compress Disk.
▶ PCBackup.
▶ PCFormat.
▶ PCSecure.
▶ DiskFix.

These programs are discussed more fully in later chapters.

During initial installation of PC Tools (as performed by the PCSETUP program contained on the PC Tools distribution disks), the software searches for common programs such as Lotus 1-2-3, dBase, Microsoft Word, WordPerfect, and WordStar, automatically adding these to the Applications menu. You can readily add, remove, or edit the listed programs.

73

Note that each of the six PC Tools programs (Mirror, Compress, Backup, Format, Secure, and DiskFix) are really stand-alone applications you can run without Shell. You may use these programs, as listed in Table 3-6, by entering their name at the DOS prompt or by initiating them from the Applications menu.

Table 3-6. Applications Menu Name and Actual Program Name.

Applications Menu Name	PC Tools Stand-Alone Program
Mirror	MIRROR.EXE
Compress Disk	COMPRESS.EXE
PCBackup	PCBACKUP.EXE
PCFormat	PCFORMAT.COM
PCSecure	PCSECURE.EXE
DiskFix	DISKFIX.EXE

As with any command in a Shell menu, you can select any of the programs in the Applications menu either with the keyboard or with the mouse. (The exact procedure for using the keyboard and mouse with the PC Tools programs is explained fully in Chapter 2, "Getting Started with PC Tools.")

The PC Shell Special Menu

The Special menu, illustrated in Figure 3-11, contains many of Shell's most useful features, including the all-important file Undelete command. If you own PC Tools for one purpose, Undelete alone is worth the cost. In exchange for the importance of the commands, the menu contains relatively few entries.

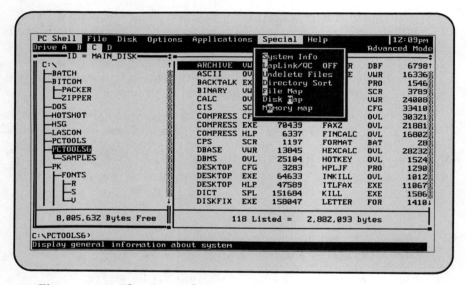

Figure 3-11. The Special menu.

▶ *System Info* checks the hardware configuration of your computer—regardless of switch settings in an IBM XT or XT clone—and shows the information in a window.

▶ *LapLink/QC* turns LapLink on or off.

▶ *Undelete Files* attempts to unerase files accidentally erased from your disks (using either the DOS DEL or ERASE command, or a delete command from within PC Tools or another application). Shell provides numerous methods for retrieving previously tossed files successfully.

▶ *Directory Sort* rearranges the file entries in a directory. Sorting can be temporary or permanent.

▶ *File Map* displays a map of the currently selected file, as it resides on a hard or floppy disk.

▶ *Disk Map* displays a map of the current disk, showing parts used and still available, along with important areas like bad sectors.

▶ *Memory Map* displays a list of programs loaded into memory and how much RAM is taken up by each.

▶ *Remove PC Shell* dislodges Shell from active memory in your computer, assuming you previously loaded Shell in instant-access memory-resident mode. If you started Shell from the DOS prompt as a regular program, the Remove PC Shell command isn't listed.

Variable User Levels

75

PC Tools Shell lets you select one of three user levels, either beginning, intermediate, or advanced. These user levels determine the contents of the pull-down menus. Only a handful of the most critical commands are listed in the menus under the Beginner Mode user level. The number of commands increases as you select Intermediate Mode and Advanced Mode.

Table 3-7 shows the commands provided in each of the three modes. After you become proficient with Shell, you'll probably want to select Advanced Mode, as it allows you to use all of the commands PC Tools offers.

Table 3-7. PC Shell User Level Commands.

Menu/Command	Beginner	Intermediate	Advanced
File Menu			
Copy File	X	X	X
Compare File	X	X	X
Rename File	X	X	X
Locate File	X	X	X
Move File		X	X
Delete File		X	X

continued

Table 3-7. *(continued)*

Menu/Command	Beginner	Intermediate	Advanced
Edit File		X	X
Text Search		X	X
Print File		X	X
Verify File		X	X
Print File List		X	X
Undelete File		X	X
Clean File			X
Attribute Change			X
Hex Edit File			X
More File Info			X
Quick File View	X	X	X
Launch	X	X	X
Exit PC Shell	X	X	X
Disk Menu			
Copy Disk	X	X	X
Compare Disk	X	X	X
Change Drive	X	X	X
Format Data Disk	X	X	X
Make System Disk	X	X	X
Directory Maint			
Add	X	X	X
Rename		X	X
Delete		X	X
Prune & Graft			X
Modify Attributes			X
Search Disk		X	X
Rename Volume		X	X
Park Disk		X	X
Verify Disk		X	X
Disk Info			X
View/Edit Disk			X

76

Table 3-7. *(continued)*

Menu/Command	Beginner	Intermediate	Advanced
Options Menu			
Setup Configuration			
Change User Level	X	X	X
Short Cut Keys			X
DOS Command Line	X	X	X
Wait on DOS Screen	X	X	X
Background Mat	X	X	X
Viewer Cfg	X	X	X
Default Viewer	X	X	X
Screen Colors	X	X	X
Date/Time	X	X	X
Define Function Keys	X	X	X
Modify Display			
Tree/Files Switch	X	X	X
Two List Display	X	X	X
One List Display	X	X	X
Active List Switch	X	X	X
File List Filter	X	X	X
File Select Filter	X	X	X
File Display Options	X	X	X
Unselect Files	X	X	X
Tree List Window	X	X	X
File List Window	X	X	X
View Window	X	X	X
Hide Windows	X	X	X
Size/Move Window	X	X	X
Zoom the Current Window	X	X	X

77

continued

Table 3-7. *(continued)*

Menu/Command	Beginner	Intermediate	Advanced
Re-Read the Tree	X	X	X
Save Configuration File	X	X	X
Special Menu			
System Info	X	X	X
LapLink/QC	X	X	X
Undelete Files		X	X
Directory Sort		X	X
File Map			X
Disk Map			X
Memory Map			X
Remove PC Shell	X	X	X

78

To change the user level,

1. Choose the Setup Configuration command under the Options menu.
2. In the pop-up menu that appears, choose the Change User Level command.
3. Select one of the three user levels, Beginning, Intermediate, or Advanced. You also have the option of forcing Shell to pull down the Applications menu each time you start the program.
4. Press Enter to accept your changes.

The currently set user level is shown in the upper-right corner of the PC Shell screen.

Using the DOS Command Line

PC Tools version 6.0 allows you to enter a DOS command directly while in Shell. Note: You must have DOS Command Line set to on and Short Cut Keys set to off (as set with the Setup Configuration command under the Options menu), or the DOS command line won't appear at the bottom of the Shell display.

To enter a command, simply begin typing. Press Enter, and Shell will temporarily exit to DOS, where your command will be executed. After the command is finished, press any key to reenter Shell. Shell automatically restarts if you have the Wait on DOS Screen option (under the Setup Configuration command) set to off.

User-Definable Function Keys

PC Tools version 6.0 lets you define your own shortcut function keys. You may wish to define your own if you want to modify the Shell interface for some reason—for example, to make Shell behave more like some of the other applications you use.

Shell lets you redefine seven of the ten function keys. Function keys F1, F3, and F10 are not redefinable. To redefine a function key:

1. Choose the Setup Configuration command from the Options menu.
2. In the pop-up submenu that appears, select the Define Function Keys command.
3. On the left side of the dialog box that is shown, select a function key to redefine (choose any except for F1, F3, and F10).
4. On the right side of the dialog box, select an action, such as Print File or Park Disk.

Repeat steps 3 and 4 for each function key you want to redefine. When done, press the F3 function key, then press Enter to accept the changes.

Running Shell on a Network

PC Tools can be used on a network as long as certain measures are followed.

▶ The PC Tools programs should be installed in a write-protected directory on a Novell NetWare, IBM Token Ring, or compatible network server.

▶ The PC Tools server directory should be included in the PATH statement executed with the system administrator's AUTO-EXEC.BAT file.

▶ The AUTOEXEC.BAT file for each user should include an environment variable specifying where the program should place all user-specific files. The variable should indicate a directory where the individual user has read and write privileges, such as:

`SET PCTOOLS=C:\MYTOOLS`

for a directory called MYTOOLS on drive C:.

▶ All of the drives on the network (real and virtual) that can be accessed by the user will appear on the drive line above the file and directory list windows.

▶ All of PC Shell's commands are available on the network except for Directory Sort, Disk Info, Disk Map, File Map, Rename Volume, Search Disk, Undelete File, Verify Disk, and View Edit Disk.

The PC Tools manual includes additional specifics on setting up the program on network systems. Refer to the Data Recovery DOS Shell manual for more details.

Saving the Shell Configuration

The Save Configuration command (in the Options pull-down menu) lets you save certain changes you've made to Shell and its windows. The settings are stored in the file PCSHELL.CFG. If this file is damaged or erased, Shell will return to its original defaults. You can purposely erase the PCSHELL.CFG file if you want to return to the factory settings and start over.

To save a new configuration, choose the Save Configuration File command from the Options menu. Shell pauses a moment while it updates the PCSHELL.CFG file. If you don't manually save the configuration, Shell will remind you to do it when you exit the program.

Review

What you learned in this chapter:

- ▶ The /R parameter loads Shell in memory-resident mode.
- ▶ Shell displays the root directory and subdirectories of the currently selected disk in a Tree window.
- ▶ Shell displays the files contained within the currently selected directory in a File List window.
- ▶ If you have a mouse, you can select multiple contiguous files with the drag–select technique.
- ▶ To change the current drive, press Ctrl-Drive Letter or click on the drive letters with the mouse.
- ▶ The File menu contains those commands used for running an applications program, exiting the PC Tools Shell, or managing individual files.
- ▶ The Disk menu controls operations that apply to entire disks or disk directories.
- ▶ The Options menu lets you control the presentation of Shell's windows and the data contained within them.
- ▶ The Applications menu lists programs you want to run directly from Shell.
- ▶ The Special menu contains miscellaneous PC Tools commands and features.

81

Managing Files with Shell

In This Chapter

▶ *Copying one or more files, without typing*
▶ *Safely renaming and deleting files*
▶ *Using Shell commands for DOS functions*
▶ *Viewing, editing, and printing files*
▶ *Locating any file, anywhere*

The PC Tools Shell program performs all of the file functions offered by DOS, but Shell is far easier and quicker to use. Shell actually helps you to work faster, and because you can see exactly what you're doing at every instant, you're less likely to make mistakes (and even if you do, PC Tools can help you fix them!).

This chapter discusses file management using Shell; chapters 5 and 6, respectively, detail how to manage disks and run applications with Shell.

List Files Display

In Chapter 3, "Understanding Shell," you learned how Shell displays the files within a subdirectory in the File List window. This window is the main gateway to Shell's file management functions. (If you haven't read Chapter 3 yet, do so now and learn how to move around inside Shell and select files and directories with the keyboard or mouse.)

Normally, Shell displays just the file name in the File List window. Assuming the File List window is full size, you can view about 48 files at one time, or roughly 16 files each in three columns. The three columns wrap from left to right, as shown in Figure 4-1.

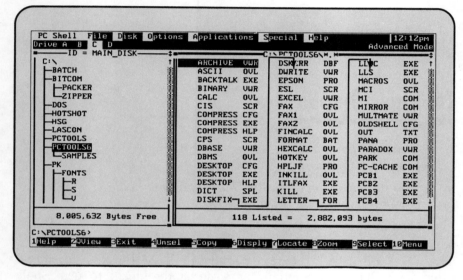

Figure 4-1. When displaying more than one row of files at a time, the file list wraps from the row on the left and continues to the one on the right.

Extra files that won't fit in the one screen scroll into view from the lower-right corner of the File List window. Take note that the entire three-column listing does not scroll in synchronization. That is, when you scroll the contents of the window, new files appear in the right-most column only, not in all three columns. This may confuse you at first until you understand how file scrolling works. Shell functions this way so that files are always shown as specified in the Display Options menu. When you scroll, the first files in the alphabetical list disappear as new ones come into view.

You are not limited to just file names in the File List window. Shell allows you to display a number of informational tidbits about each file, including file size and time/date of creation or last edit. The more information you display, the fewer files you can see in one window. Use the File Display Options command in the Options menu to select how you want the files to appear in the window.

Q Setting File Display Options

1. Choose Modify Display command from the Options menu.

2. Choose the File Display Options command from the pop-up menu that appears.

The dialog box shown in Figure 4-2 appears. The currently selected display and sort options are shown in the dialog box.

85

3. Using the keyboard or the mouse, select those display options you want to show.

Sorts by size, date, time, attribute, and/or number of disk clusters (a disk cluster is a single storage module and is the smallest amount of space on a disk). The file name is always displayed.

4. Optionally, set the sorting option for the files. Set sorting order, either ascending (starting from A or 1) or descending. You can also set no sort, in which case the files will appear in the same order as they are found in the disk directory.

Sorts by extension, by size, or by date/time (you can set only one).

5. With the display and sorting options set the way you want them, click the OK button. Or, click Cancel.

OK sets the new sorting criteria. Cancel cancels all changes you've made.

□

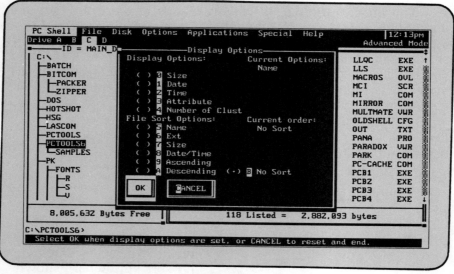

Figure 4-2. The Display Options dialog box.

Figure 4-3 shows a File List window displaying the file name, size, attribute, and ascending order. (See later in this chapter for more on file attributes.)

> ▶ **Tip:** The order in which Shell displays its file is entirely independent of the order in which files are recorded on the disk, or the order in which files are displayed when you ask for DIRectory while in DOS. PC Tools provides additional features and commands for physically sorting files on a disk (the Compress program) and for sorting directories (the Directory Sort command in the Special menu).

Changes you make in the Display Options dialog box are recorded in the PCSHELL.CFG configuration file. Should this file be damaged or erased, Shell will revert to the factory display setting, which is file name and extension only, with no sorting.

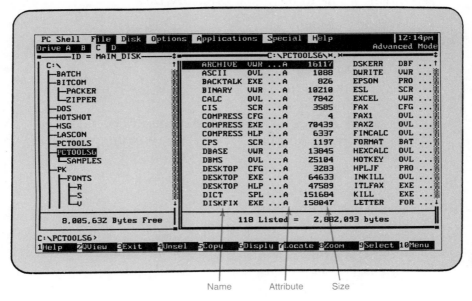

Name   Attribute   Size

Figure 4-3. File display with attributes.

Copying Files

One of the most common duties of operating a computer is copying files. Shell lets you copy files to any disk or directory quickly and easily. And because the available drives and directories are displayed on screen, you never have to worry about typing the wrong path.

Shell handles file copying differently depending on whether you are copying files within a single disk and directory or to a different disk and/or directory. We'll discuss both of these techniques separately.

Copying to the Same Directory and Disk

Making a copy of a file in the same directory and disk is no more difficult than the other techniques, but the copy must be given a different name from the original.

Q **Copying a File to the Same Directory/Disk**

1. If you haven't done so already, select the disk and directory that holds the file you want to copy.

2. Highlight the file to copy from the File List window.

   Selects the file to copy.

3. Choose the Copy File command from the File menu.

   Activates Copy File. The dialog box in Figure 4-4 appears.

4. Select the same drive that contains the source file.

5. Select a subdirectory for the copy, if any. In this case, it will be the same subdirectory that contains the original file.

88

6. Enter a new name for the copied file.

   Shell provides the original file name, so you can edit it or merely add a distinguishing character (like BUDGET1 to a file named BUDGET) to supply the new name. The new name, as in Figure 4-5, prevents you from erasing the existing file.

7. Press Continue when you're done renaming the file.

   Verifies the copy.

8. Press Copy if everything looks good.

If you select more than one file for copying, Shell will ask that you provide a new name for each one. Unfortunately, you cannot perform "wildcard copies" where you indicate a group of files to copy with a wildcard character (? or *) and include the wildcard in a "group destination" file. For example DOS allows

`COPY REPORT?.DOC REPORT?1.DOC`

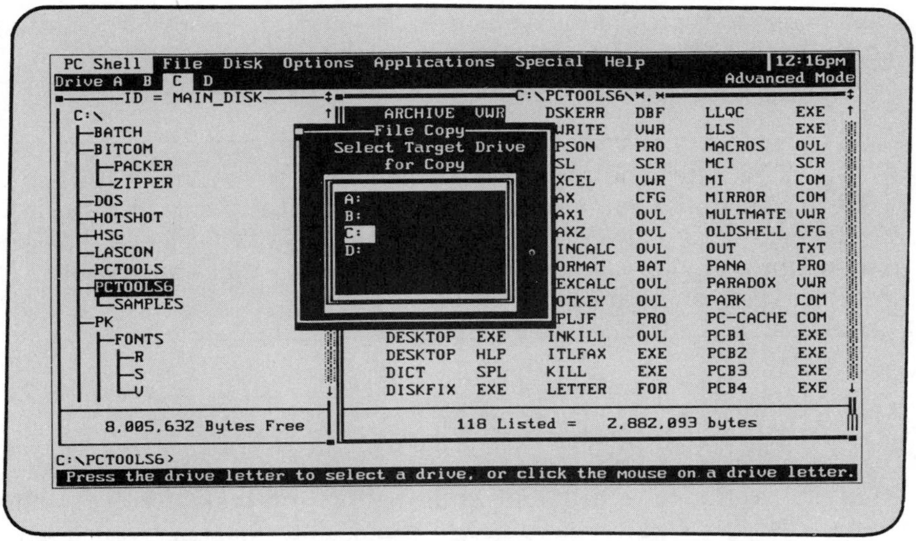

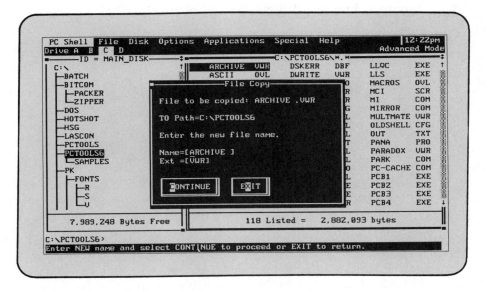

Figure 4-4. *The File Copy dialog box prompting you to enter the target drive.*

Figure 4-5. *PC Tools lets you rename the copied file in case a disk or directory already contains a file with the same name.*

but Shell doesn't. Should you need to perform a copy procedure such as this (it's not that common, in any case), you can always leave Shell temporarily and do it directly in DOS.

> ▶ **Tip:** After you copy a file, Shell remembers the destination disk you selected, so it automatically selects it for the next copy. However, Shell always asks you to select a destination directory. If you plan on making copies of several files, it's best if you do them all at once.

Copying to a Different Subdirectory or Disk

90 Copying a file to a different subdirectory or disk involves the same basic procedures as those outlined above, except you don't need to provide a new name for the copy.

Ⓠ Copying a File to a Different Subdirectory or Disk

1. If you haven't done so already, select the disk and directory that holds the file you want to copy.

2. Select the file to copy from the File List window.   Identifies the source file.

3. Choose the Copy File command from the File menu.   Starts Copy File.

4. Select a drive that will contain the copied file.

5. Select a subdirectory that will contain the copied file.   Copies the file into the new disk/subdirectory.   ☐

Shell flashes a dialog box that informs you that the file is being copied. If your computer is equipped with a fast hard disk drive, the dialog box will remain on the screen only momentarily.

Fast Mouse File Copying

If you have a mouse, you can quickly copy one or more files by dragging them from directory to directory. File copies with the mouse are best performed with the Two List Display, as set with the Two List Display command in the Options menu.

Q **Fast Mouse File Copying**

1. In one list, select the directory disk that contains the file you want to copy.	Sets the source directory.
2. In the other list, select the subdirectory that you want to copy the file to.	Sets the destination directory.
3. Highlight the file (or files) to copy with the mouse.	Selects the file(s) to copy.
4. Holding down the left mouse button, drag the mouse pointer into the destination File List window.	As you drag, a copy message box appears, as shown in Figure 4-6, telling you that X number of files will be copied.
5. Release the mouse button.	Copies the files for you automatically.

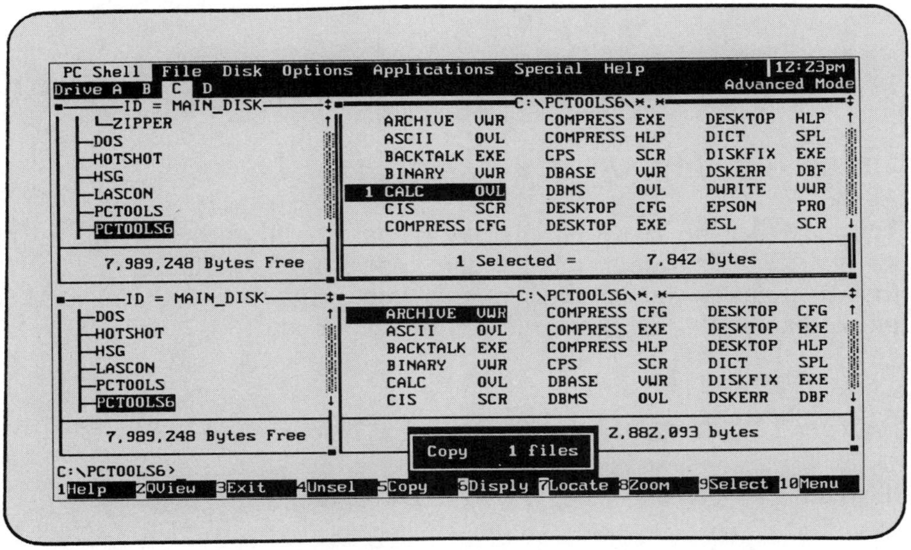

91

Figure 4-6. Two List Display file copying using the mouse.

> ▶ **Tip:** You can also drag the files directly into a subdirectory in the Tree window, as shown in Figure 4-7. This requires that you copy the files within the same drive and that both source and destination subdirectories are visible in the Tree window.

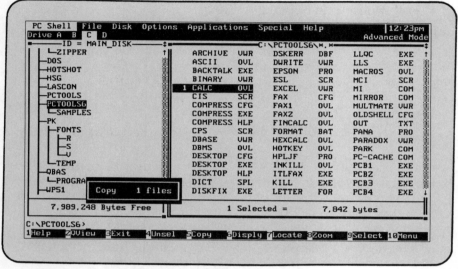

Figure 4-7. Copying files from the File List window directly into a subdirectory.

Using the Keyboard with the Two List Display

You may use the Two List Display when operating Shell from the keyboard. The procedure is the same as a One List Display, except that Shell asks you to confirm that you want to use the second path (second list) as the target. Press the Yes button to go on.

Name Conflicts

If you try to copy a file to a disk or directory that already contains a file with the same name, Shell asks if you want to replace it or quit. Shell displays the same dialog box whether you are copying one file or many.

▶ Press the Replace File button to replace just the indicated file.
▶ Press the Replace All button if you are copying many files and want to replace them all at once.
▶ Press the Next button if you are copying many files and want to skip the current one.
▶ Press the Skip All button to skip all files.
▶ Press Exit to cancel the copy.

Moving Files

93

Moving a file is similar to copying a file, except that the original is erased and only the copy remains. As with Copy File, Shell lets you move files to any disk or directory. But unlike Copy File, you cannot move a file within the same subdirectory on the same disk (what use would that be?), so we need only concern ourselves with moving between subdirectories and disks.

Q **Moving a File to a Different Subdirectory or Disk**

1. If you haven't done so already, select the disk and directory that holds the file you want to move.

2. Highlight the file to move from the File List window.   Selects the file to move.

3. Choose the Move File command from the File menu.   Confirms the Move File operation, and reminds you that the original file will be erased.

4. Select a drive that will contain the moved file.

5. Select a subdirectory that will contain the moved file.   Moves the file to the designated disk and directory.

Shell flashes a dialog box that informs you that the file is moved. If your computer is equipped with a fast hard disk drive, the dialog box will remain on the screen only momentarily.

Fast Mouse File Moving

If you have a mouse, you can quickly move one or more files by dragging them from one subdirectory to another. File moves with the mouse are best performed with the Two List Display, as set with the Two List Display command in the Options menu.

Q Fast Mouse File Moving

1. In one list, select the subdirectory that contains the file you want to move.	Sets the source directory.
2. In the other list, select the subdirectory that you want to move the file to.	Sets the destination directory.
3. Highlight the file (or files) to move with the mouse.	Selects the file(s) to move.
4. Press and hold the Control key.	Indicates a Move File operation.
5. Holding down the left mouse button, drag the mouse pointer into the destination File List window.	As you drag, a message box appears, as shown in Figure 4-8, telling you that X number of files will be moved.
6. Release the mouse button.	Confirms the Move File operation, and reminds you that the original file will be erased. □

> ▶ **Tip:** You can also drag the files directly into a subdirectory in the Tree window. This requires that you move the files within the same drive and that both source and destination subdirectories are visible in the Tree window.

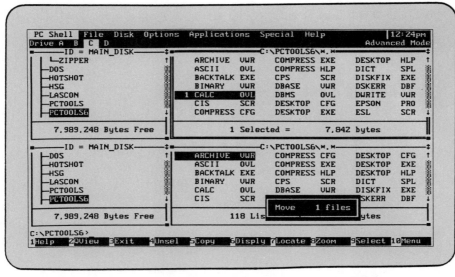

Figure 4-8. Two List Display file moving using the mouse.

95

Name Conflicts

If you try to move a file to a disk or directory that already contains a file with the same name, Shell asks if you want to replace it or quit. Shell displays the same dialog box whether you are moving one file or many.

▶ Press the Replace File button to replace just the indicated file.

▶ Press the Replace All button if you are moving many files and want to replace them all at once.

▶ Press the Next button if you are moving many files and want to skip the current one.

▶ Press the Skip All button to skip all files.

▶ Press Exit to cancel the move.

Renaming Files

The Rename File command in the File menu functions the same as the DOS REN (or RENAME) command. But, as usual with PC Tools, the Shell command is a lot easier to use. Shell makes it fairly easy to rename groups of files at one time, even if the file names are greatly dissimilar.

Q Renaming a File

1. Highlight the file (or files) you wish to rename.

   Selects the file to rename.

2. Choose the Rename File command from the File menu.

   The File Rename dialog box appears, as shown in Figure 4-9.

3. Enter the new name for the file in the File Rename dialog box.

4. Press the Rename button when you are done, or press the Cancel button.

   Rename completes the command; Cancel cancels the file rename operation.

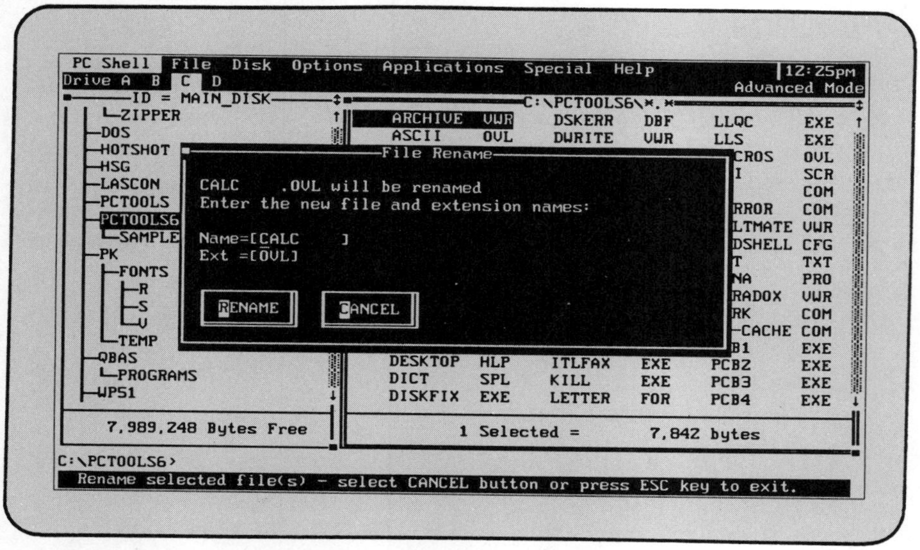

96

Figure 4-9. The File Rename dialog box.

If you select more than one file, Shell asks you if you want to perform a Global or Single file rename:

▶ *Global rename* changes the names of files using wildcard characters (? and *) in place of one or more character in the file name. Selecting Global displays the dialog box in Figure 4-10. To use the Global rename feature, type the name and/ or extension you want to change. For example, if you want to add the .TXT extension to all selected files, enter the * wildcard in the Name field and DOC in the Ext field.

▶ *Single rename* changes the names of files one at a time. You are prompted for the new name for each file in turn, as illustrated in Figure 4-11.

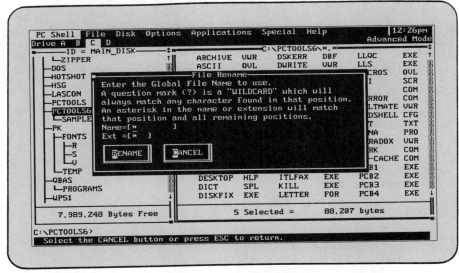

Figure 4-10. The dialog box shown when renaming many files all at once (the Global option).

Deleting Files

Files you no longer need should be deleted so that they don't take up precious disk space. (This is true whether your hard disk has 10 megabytes of storage space or 100; sooner or later, you'll need that room.)

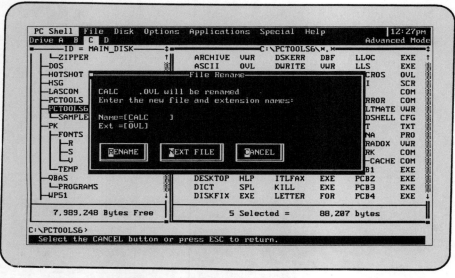

Figure 4-11. *The dialog box shown when renaming many files one at a time.*

Q Erasing a File

1. Highlight the file (or files) you want to delete.

   Selects the file to delete.

2. Choose the Delete File command from the File menu. Carefully check that you've selected the right file (the name of the file in the dialog box).

   Verifies that you want to delete the file.

3. Press the Delete button, or press Cancel.

   Delete erases the file; Cancel voids the Delete File operation. □

If you have selected more than one file, Shell presents the dialog box shown in Figure 4-12. You can:

▶ Press the Delete button to erase the indicated file.

▶ Press the Next File button to keep the indicated file and move to the next one.

▶ Press the Delete All button to erase all files. (Be careful!)
▶ Press the Cancel button to stop.

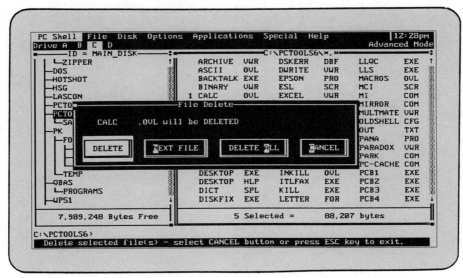

Figure 4-12. When more than one file is selected, PC Tools displays this dialog box so you can selectively delete files, or erase them all at once.

99

Verifying Files

The Verify File command checks the integrity of a file and makes certain that the entire file can be read from the disk. Verify works on one file or many.

To verify a file:

1. Select the file (or files) you want to verify.
2. Choose the Verify File command from the File menu. Shell checks the file and looks for possible problems.

If Shell can't find anything wrong with the file, it displays the dialog box shown in Figure 4-13 (when verifying many files, each of the selected files that passed the test will be displayed).

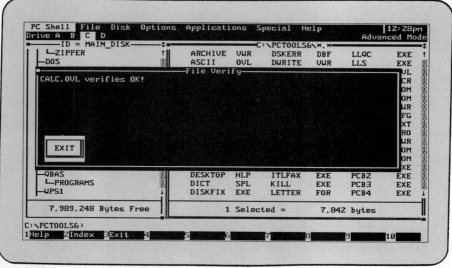

100

Figure 4-13. A File verified as OK.

However, if Shell detects a problem with a file, it will indicate the error and the logical sector that contains the error. You may be able to repair the file using the advanced file restoration techniques outlined in Chapter 8, "Recovering Lost Files and Disks."

Comparing Files

You may have occasion to compare two files to see if they are the same. The Compare File command in the File menu does this for you quickly and painlessly.

There are many ways to use the Compare File command, depending on whether you are checking files that are in the same directory or in separate directories or disks. The steps that follow describe the two most straightforward methods of using the Compare File command in these two contexts.

Comparing Files on the Same Directory

Follow these steps for comparing two files contained in the same directory. To compare two files in the same directory:

1. Select the two files you want to compare.
2. Choose the Compare File command from the File menu.
3. Select the drive that contains the file to compare (choose the current drive).
4. Press the Matching Names button (even though the names of the two files are different).
5. Locate the subdirectory (if any) that contains the files you are comparing.

   Shell now checks the two files against one another and determines whether the two are the same or different.

101

Comparing Files on Different Disks and/or Directories

Follow these steps for comparing two files contained in different directories or on different disks. To compare two files on different disks or in different directories:

1. Choose the Two List Display command in the Options menu.
2. In the first list, select the first of the two files to compare.
3. In the second list, select the second of the two files to compare.
4. Choose the Compare File command from the File menu.
5. Press the Different Names button if the file names are different; press the Matching Names button if the file names are the same.
6. Verify that you are using the second path (the second list) as the target by clicking the Yes button.

   For Different Names only:

7. Enter the name of the second file in the name and extension editing fields provided.

8. Press the Continue button.
9. Verify that the file names for the comparison are correct, and press the Compare button.

Shell now checks the two files against one another and determines whether the two are the same or different.

Viewing, Editing, and Printing Files

102

DOS users have long suffered with the TYPE command, which quickly scrolls a text document on the computer screen. TYPE provides no means to freeze the display, then go forward or back one line at a time. Likewise, printing and editing files require some arcane DOS commands (like COPY FILENAME.DOC PRN:) or using (horrors!) the DOS EDLIN file editor.

Relax. Shell offers its own features for viewing, editing, and printing files. While you'll most likely use these abilities to work with text documents, you can also perform editing functions on any file type, including program files. (Be careful!) What's more, you can directly view dBase and Lotus 1-2-3 documents in their proper format.

Viewing a File

Viewing a file lets you see its contents, but not all files are easy to decipher. There are three basic types of files you'll encounter on the PC:

▶ *ASCII text documents.* Straight text documents without control codes or other special characters. They are created by some word processors, as well as the capture files generated by telecommunications programs. "Readme" files distributed with many programs are formatted in straight ASCII. Shell displays these in the same manner as a word processor displays text in its editing screen, as illustrated in Figure 4-14.

▶ *Binary text documents.* Documents that have been stored with control codes and special formatting codes. These are created by most applications programs, including word processors, electronic spreadsheets, and data managers. With the exception of the document file listed in the next section, you see the text of the document interspersed among unintelligible codes when viewing a binary document, as shown in Figure 4-15.

▶ *Program files.* Files that consist almost entirely of binary characters, and little—if any—intelligible text can be seen (refer to Figure 4-16).

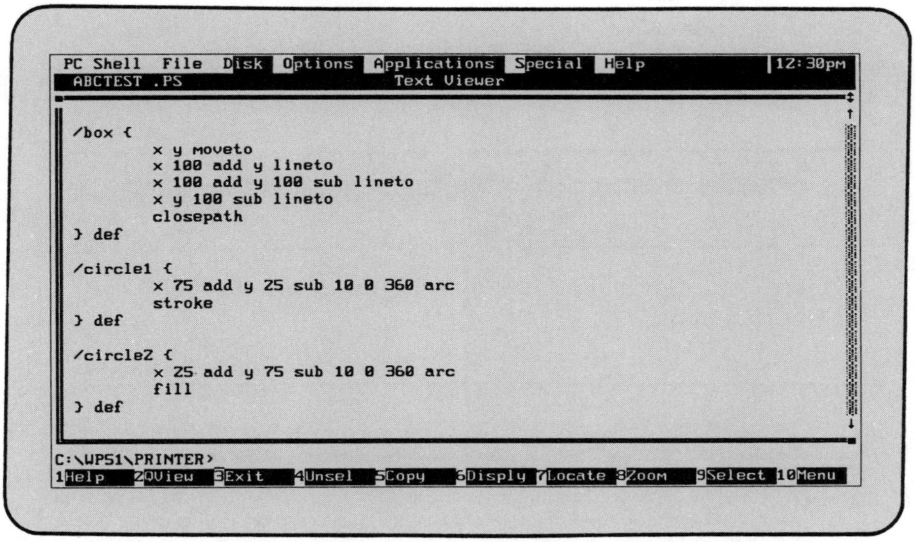

103

Figure 4-14. Sample ASCII text file as seen with the File View command.

Follow these steps to view a file.

Q Viewing a File

1. Highlight the file you want to view.	Selects the file to view.
2. Press the F2 function key.	The view window appears.

Use the cursor keys to scan forward and backward through the file. When you are finished, close the window. (Press the Escape key or the F3 function key, or click in the window's close box with the mouse.)

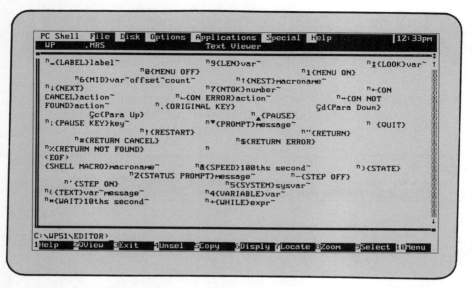

Figure 4-15. Sample binary text file as seen with the File
View command.

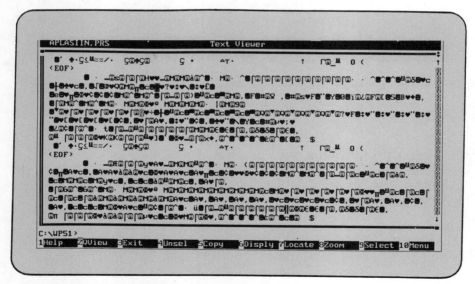

Figure 4-16. Sample binary-only file as seen with the File
View command.

The view window provides some shortcuts and options:

▶ Press the Home, End, Page Up, and Page Down keys to move through the document quickly.

▶ If you have selected two or more files, select Next File (click on it or press the F9 function key) to view the next file.

Special View Filters

PC Shell version 6.0 incorporates "filters" to display the contents of over 30 different types of document files in their original format. Shell automatically senses that you are using one of these document files and selects the appropriate filter for you. An example of a viewed Lotus document is shown in Figure 4-17. Note the message bar at the bottom of the screen. It indicates keys you can use to move around the document.

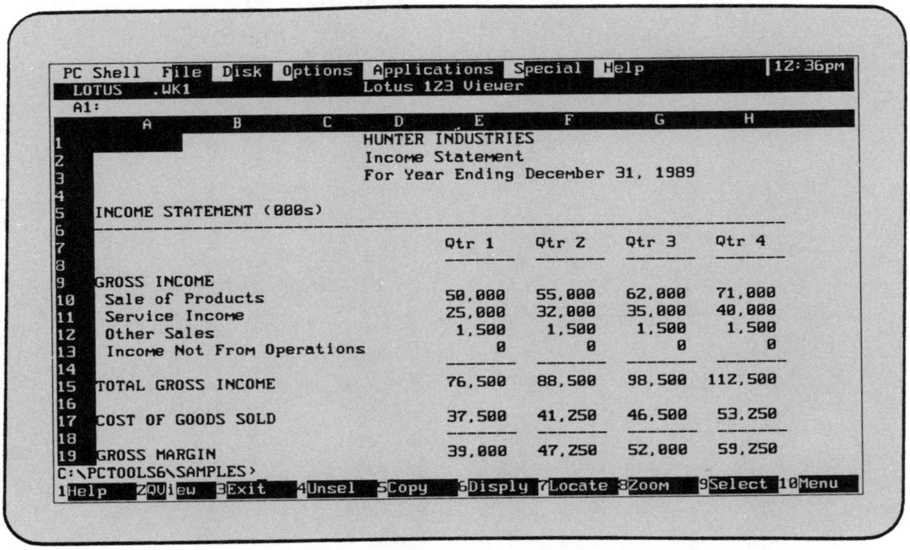

105

Figure 4-17. A Lotus 1-2-3 worksheet displayed in proper format using File View.

Shell comes with the following file filters (additional filters may be packaged with later releases of PC Tools Deluxe; check the README.TXT file).

Viewers for Word Processing Programs	Text (default)
	DisplayWrite
	Microsoft Word Microsoft Works
	Microsoft Windows Write
	MultiMate
	PC Tools Desktop
	WordPerfect
	WordStar (3.3, 4.0, etc.)
	WordStar 2000
	XyWrite
Viewers for Database Programs	Clipper
	dBase
	BXL
	FoxBase
	Microsoft Works
	Paradox
	R:Base
Viewers for Spreadsheet Programs	Borland Quattro
	Lotus 1-2-3
	Lotus Symphony
	Microsoft Works
	Microsoft Excel
	Mosaic Twin
	MultiPlan
	VP Planner
	Words and Figures
Viewers for Miscellaneous File Types	ARC
	Binary
	LHARC
	PAK
	PKZIP
	PXC
	ZOO

106

Shell will display the file in binary format if the file has a .COM, .EXE, .OBJ, .BIN, or .SYS file extension. If the file is in one of the formats listed above and has an extension of .TXT or .BAT, Shell will display it in text mode. You can indicate the default file view mode for all other files—either binary or text—in the Setup Configuration menu.

1. Choose the Setup Configuration command from the Options menu.

2. Highlight the Default Viewer command from the pop-up menu that appears.

3. Press Enter to toggle the default between TEXT and BINARY.

4. Press the F3 function key when you are done.

Editing a File

If you feel so inclined, you can edit files—even binary documents and programs—with Shell. Of course, changing the contents of files can lead to disastrous consequences if you don't know exactly what you're doing. It is not the purpose of this book to explain program editing, hexadecimal code, and other technical topics. If you'd like to learn more about these subjects, check out the many programming books now available and refer to the PC Tools Data Recovery and DOS Utilities manual.

107

Shell offers two methods of editing files: Hex Edit and File Edit.

▶ *The Hex Edit File command* (in the File menu) displays the contents of a file in hexadecimal format. You see everything contained in the file, including nulls (hex 00) and special characters. You can use the Hex Edit command to change each byte of a file.

▶ *The Edit File command* (in the File menu) displays just the printable ASCII characters of a file (these include the special IBM characters at ASCII positions 128 and higher).

As hexadecimal file editing is most helpful when resurrecting damaged files, a more thorough description of using the Hex Edit command appears in Chapter 8, "Recovering Lost Files and Disks."

Following are two procedures for editing an existing file and for creating a new file. To edit an existing file:

1. Select the file you want to edit.

2. Choose the Edit File command in the File menu.

3. Shell asks if you want to edit the file or create a new one. Press the Edit button.

4. The contents of file appears in the Edit File window. Use the cursor keys to move around. (The mouse does not function in the editing portion of this window.)

5. To make changes, position the cursor at the point where you want to edit and begin typing. Use the Delete and Backspace keys to remove characters you don't want. If you wish to overwrite existing characters, press the Insert key so that the INSERT indicator in the window goes out.

6. Save the document when you are done with the changes (click on Save with the mouse or press Alt-S).

The Shell file editor works like almost any other word processor and is fairly self-explanatory. That is, press a key to enter it at the cursor, press the Tab key to add a tab, press Enter to start a new line, and so forth. Table 4-1 lists the editing keys you can use in the file editor.

108

Table 4-1. File Edit Editing Keys.

To	Press
Delete a character under the cursor	Delete
Erase a character to left of cursor	Backspace
Move down one line	Down Arrow
Move up one line	Up Arrow
Move left one character	Left Arrow
Move right one character	Right Arrow
Move to beginning of line	Home
Move to end of line	End
Move to start of file	Ctrl-Home
Move to end of file	Ctrl-End
Move to start of window	Home, Home
Move to end of window	End, End
Move up one window	Page Up
Move down one window	Page Down

The Shell file editor contains rudimentary word processing features, including search and replace and clipboard cut and paste. You access these commands (as listed in the message bar at the bottom of the screen) by pressing the Alt key and the associated quick-key (such as Alt-C for Cut).

The Cut and Copy commands require that you first select the text you want to place in the clipboard.

If you're using the keyboard, position the cursor at the start of the block, choose the Select command (Alt-L), then move the cursor to the end of the block. The selected text is shown highlighted.

To create a new file:

1. Click on any file to select it.
2. Choose the Edit File command in the File menu.
3. Press the Create button in the dialog box that appears.
4. Shell presents a new window for you to write in. You may write and edit text as you would with almost any other word processor.

Printing a File

109

The Print File command makes a paper copy of one or more selected files. Shell does not provide elaborate printing features, however; you are limited to printing to the LPT1: device only (unless you've redirected LPT1: to another port using the DOS MODE command). Document formatting is also limited. Still, the Print File command serves its duty well in making quick copies of text and binary documents.

Q Printing a File

1. Highlight a file to print. (You may also select multiple documents if desired; the remaining steps are the same for single or multiple files.)	Selects a file to print.
2. Choose the Print File command in the File menu.	
3. Select a printing format, as shown in Figure 4-18.	Formats the document as straight text, as text with special print options, or as a "sector dump" in ASCII and hex format.
4. Press the Print button when you are done making your selection.	Initiates printing.

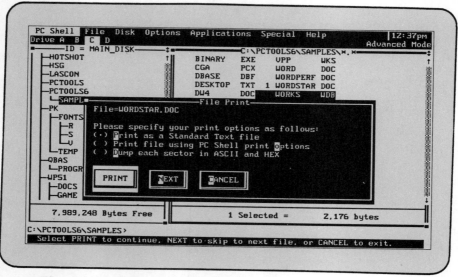

Figure 4-18. The File Print dialog box.

If you selected the "Print file using PC Shell print options," an additional dialog box, illustrated in Figure 4-19, appears. Here, you may select the number of lines per page, the margins, and other formatting variables. The options are self-explanatory. Make the desired changes, and press the Print button.

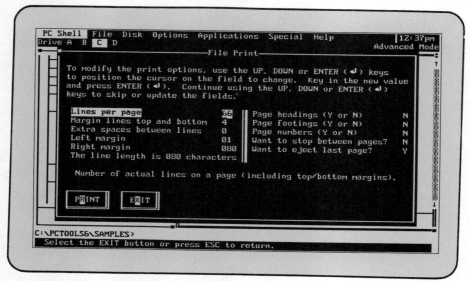

Figure 4-19. The File Print Options dialog box.

> ▶ **Tip:** If you are using a laser printer, such as the Hewlett-Packard LaserJet Series II, you should select Yes for the "Want to eject last page?" option. This ensures that the last page of the document is ejected from the laser printer, thus saving you the hassle of using the printer's front panel control.

Changing File Attributes

Each file created on the PC carries with it certain attributes, special characteristics that the computer can use during some of its operations. These attributes are:

111

- ▶ *Read only.* Indicates whether the file can be both read and written to (read only off) or just read (read only on).
- ▶ *Hidden.* Indicates whether the file is visible (hidden off) in a normal DOS DIRrectory or invisible (hidden on). Note that Shell lists hidden files.
- ▶ *System.* Indicates whether the file is reserved for system use (system on) or regular application use (system off).
- ▶ *Archive.* Indicates if file has not been recently backed up using any of several types of disk backup programs, including PC Tools and DOS Backup. When archive is on, the file is new or has been edited and should be backed up in the next backup session. When archive is off, the file has already been backed up and needn't be again.
- ▶ *Time of creation or last edit.* Indicates the time of day the file was created or last edited.
- ▶ *Date of creation or last edit.* Indicates the date the file was created or last edited.

To change the attributes of a file:

1. Select the file (or files) you want to change.

2. Choose the Attribute Change command in the File menu. Shell presents the dialog box shown in Figure 4-20 (yours will look different depending on the file or files you have selected).

3. To change the read-only, hidden, system, or archive attributes press R, H, S, or A, respectively.

4. Or, to change the time, position the cursor at the beginning of the time field (keyboard or mouse) and enter a new time from the keyboard.

5. Or, to change the date, position the cursor at the beginning of the date field (keyboard or mouse) and enter a new date from the keyboard.

6. When you are done changing the attributes, click the Update button. Or, press Exit to cancel all changes.

112

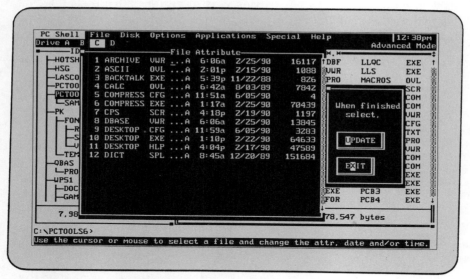

Figure 4-20. File attributes for selected files (only those files currently selected are shown).

Getting File Information

Shell provides some interesting tidbits about files in its File Information dialog box. To look at information about a file:

1. Select a file.
2. Choose the More File Info command from the File menu. A dialog box like the one in Figure 4-21 appears.

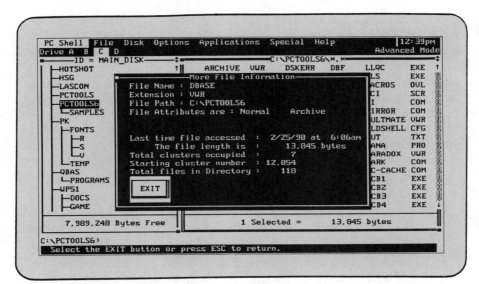

Figure 4-21. Interesting tidbits about the file in the More File Information dialog box.

Here's what the information in the More File Information box means:

▶ *File name.* The name of the file.

▶ *Extension.* File extension, if any.

▶ *File Path.* Location of file in directory tree.

▶ *File Attributes are.* Indicates if file is read only, hidden, system, and/or archive.

▶ *Last time file accessed.* Time of day and date of creation or last edit. (Note: The word "accessed" is misapplied here, as you can access—but not change—a file, and it won't be updated.)

▶ *The file length is.* Actual size of file, in bytes.

▶ *Total clusters occupied.* The number of disk clusters consumed by the file.

▶ *Starting cluster number.* The physical disk cluster containing the first bytes of the file.

113

▶ *Total files in Directory.* Total number of files contained in the subdirectory holding the selected file.

Locating Files

How many times have you created a file, safely recorded it on your hard disk, then promptly forgotten which subdirectory you saved it in? If you're like most PC users, this has happened plenty of times. Shell offers a nifty way to search for files by file name or extension and to view the location of all the matches it finds. Once a file has been located, you can open it, delete it, copy it, and more.

Follow these steps to find a file:

114

1. Select a disk to search. (Normally, this will be your hard disk, but it can also be another floppy diskette or an auxiliary hard disk.)

2. Choose the Locate File command from the File menu. The Located Files window appears as shown in Figure 4-22.

3. With the mouse or Right and Left Arrow keys, highlight the type of file you want to find in the list that appears. Shell lets you search for any type of file (the Specify File Names selection) or document files prepared by your applications (the applications listed are those that PC Tools found during installation). Press Enter to choose the file type.

4. If you selected an application file, skip to step 5. If you chose Specify File Names, enter the file or group of files you want to locate. You can search through an entire disk or just a directory. Here are some examples:

LETTER.TXT	Searches for the file LETTER.TXT.
*.TXT	Searches for all files that end with the .TXT extension.
\WP51\LETTER.TXT	Searches only through the WP51 directory for the file LETTER.TXT.

Press Enter when done.

5. You can optionally ask Shell to find a certain string of text in the file or file group. Fill in the Search For blank, and press Enter. For example, to search for the word "BILL," (upper- or lowercase), enter BILL at the blank, and press Enter. You don't have to ask for string search. Press Enter without filling in the blank. Note: This will cause Shell to search for the indicated file(s) much faster.

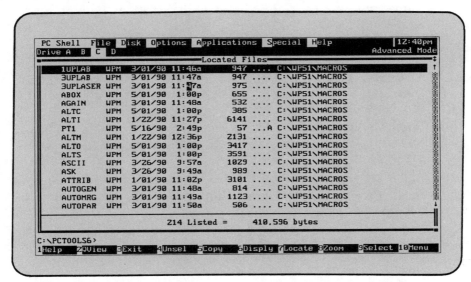

Figure 4-22. Found files that contain the extension .WPM indicated in the Located Files window.

115

Shell locates all occurrences of the file or file group the file groups and directories you specified and displays them in a window.

If you're not sure about the file name, but are sure of the text string to search for, you can do wildcard searches when indicating the file name, as in:

.	Searches through all files in the disk.
.	Searches through all files just in the root directory.
\WP51*.EXE	Searches only through files with extension .EXE in WP51 directory.
. -.BAT	Searches only through files in current directory with any extension except .BAT.

Review

This chapter discussed using Shell to manipulate and maintain the files on your hard disks and floppy diskettes. You also learned:

116

▶ The default setting of List Files window displays just the file name, but you can add auxiliary information, including file size and attributes.

▶ You can copy one or more files from disk to disk or directory to directory using the Copy File command.

▶ Shell warns you if you attempt to copy or move one or more files into a disk or directory that already contains files with the same name.

▶ Shell always double-checks that you want to delete a file by presenting a warning dialog box before completing the command.

▶ The Verify File command checks the integrity of a selected file.

▶ Shell lets you change file attributes, including read-only, hidden, system, and archive settings.

▶ You can locate any file on a hard disk with the Find File command (from the Disk menu).

Chapter 5

Managing Disks with Shell

In This Chapter   117

▶ *Displaying the contents of disks*
▶ *Copying floppy diskettes*
▶ *Verifying and comparing disks*
▶ *Formatting data and program disks*
▶ *Maintaining directories*

Program and document disks are no longer obscure entities with lives of their own. PC Tools Shell helps you tame your disks and puts you in control. Rather than use arcane DOS commands, you'll use Shell's pull-down menus to format and copy disks, verify the contents of disks, maintain subdirectories in your hard disk, and more.

Disk Display

Shell can display the contents of either one or two disks at a time. With One List Display, you can view the contents of just one disk. With Two List Display, you can view the contents of two disks at the same time. You change displays with the appropriate commands in the Options menu.

Q To View the Contents of One Disk

1. Choose the Modify Display command from the Options menu.

2. In the pop-up menu that appears, select the One List Display command.

3. When using the keyboard, press Ctrl-Drive Letter to activate the drive you want. (Substitute the drive you want to view for "Drive Letter," such as Ctrl-A for Drive A.)

   OR

   When using the mouse, click on the desired drive letter in the drive list under the menu bar (see Figure 5-1).

Displays the drive you want to view.

Displays the drive you want to view.

□

118

The contents of the drive you selected is now shown in the Tree and File List window.

Q To View the Contents of Two Disks

1. Choose the Modify Display command from the Options menu.

2. In the pop-up menu that appears, select the Two List Display command.

3. If the top set of windows isn't already selected, as illustrated in Figure 5-2, choose the Tree/Files Switch command from the Options menu and Modify Display submenu (or press Tab).

Selects the top set of windows.

Drive List

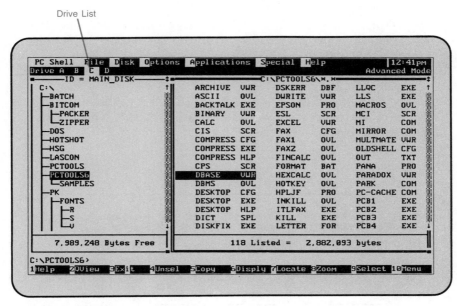

Figure 5-1. The drive list indicates the currently selected drive.

4. When using the keyboard, press Ctrl-Drive Letter to activate the drive you want. (Substitute the drive you want to view for "Drive Letter," such as Ctrl-A for Drive A.)

Displays the first drive in the top set of windows.

OR

When using the mouse, click on the desired drive letter in the drive list under the menu bar.

Displays the first drive in the top set of windows.

5. Choose the Tree/Files Switch command from the Options menu and Modify Display submenu (or press Tab).

Makes the bottom set of windows active.

6. Press Ctrl-Drive Letter or click with the mouse to activate the drive you want.

Displays the second drive in the bottom set of windows.

> ▶ **Tip:** As a shortcut, press the Insert key to activate Two List Display. Conversely, press the Delete key to activate One List Display.

The contents of the first drive you selected is shown in the top Tree and Files List windows; the contents of the second drive is shown in the bottom Tree and Files List windows.

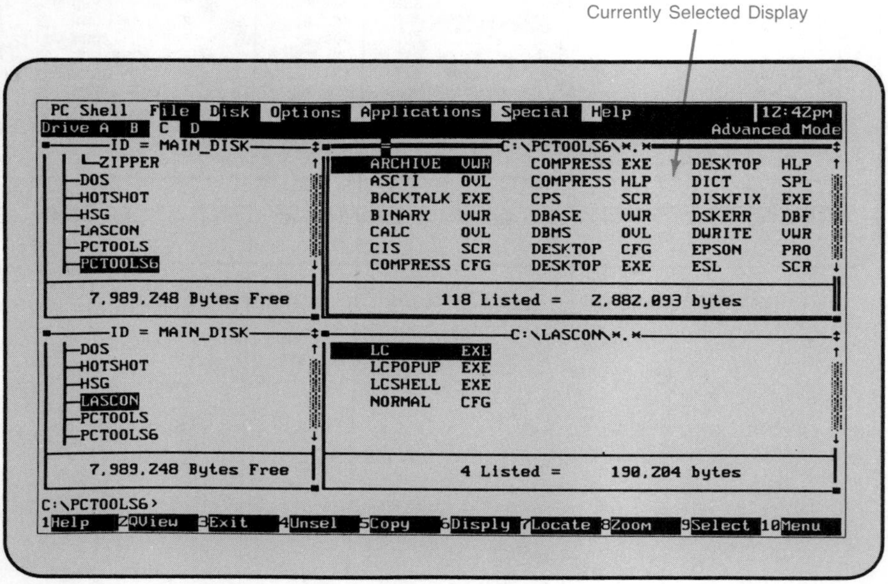

Figure 5-2. Two List Display with top list currently selected.

Re-Reading the Tree

Recall that the tree is the directory path on a given disk (usually a hard disk). The tree starts at the root directory, displayed as the first item in Shell's Tree window and branches out into many subdirectories.

It takes a few moments for Shell to register the organization of the tree and present it in the Tree window, so the program doesn't do it all the time. Normally, Shell re-reads the tree every day, unless you've set a new option for the /TRn parameter, as described in Chapter 2, "Getting Started with PC Tools."

This can become a problem when you've added or deleted subdirectories, because Shell won't immediately recognize the change. If you suspect that you are viewing an old rendition of the directory tree, choose the Re-Read the Tree command from the Options menu. This command forces Shell to examine the tree structure and update the Tree window.

Similarly, the effect of copying and moving files between directories and disks may not be immediately updated in the File List window. For example, you may copy a set of files to a new disk, but the File List window won't immediately show the added files. You can counter this problem in one of two ways: Choose the Re-Read the Tree command, or momentarily select another directory (or disk), then reselect the old one. The files should now be updated.

121

Copying Disks

Even if your computer is equipped with a hard disk drive, you'll still need to make copies of floppy diskettes occasionally. You may need to make a clone of a data disk for distribution to the branch offices in your company, for example, or you may need to make a set of backup copies of a new application program you purchased.

Shell offers a convenient and nearly foolproof method of copying disks (especially compared to the DOS DISKCOPY command). You can use Shell to copy disks using one drive or two. When using two drives, both must be the same size and type. You can't copy from a 5 1/4-inch drive to a 3 1/2-inch drive, for example.

The instructions that follow assume you are using Shell from a hard disk drive.

 Copying with One Disk Drive

1. Place the diskette you want to copy in the drive (such as drive A or B).

2. Choose the Copy Disk command from the Disk menu.

Presents the Disk Copy dialog box, as displayed in Figure 5-3.

3. Choose the same drive for both the Source and the Target (you'll be copying from and to the same drive).

Indicates a one drive copy. Press Enter when done.

4. Shell does not assume you've placed the original diskette in the drive already and asks you to do it now.

5. Press the Copy button to go on.

Reads the contents of the disk.

6. After the source diskette is read, Shell prompts you to insert the target diskette (the target diskette can be formatted or unformatted). Do so, and press the Continue button to go on.

Copies the data to the target diskette.

122

Depending on the available memory in your computer, the capacity of the diskette, and how you've loaded Shell, the program may not be able to read the entire contents of the disk in one pass. If necessary, swap the source and target diskettes in and out of the drive as requested by Shell.

> ▶ **Tip:** You don't need to preformat diskettes before you copy files to them. Shell will automatically sense whether the disk is properly formatted and will format it during the copying process. However, if you are using diskettes of questionable quality, you may want to preformat them using Shell before copying files to them. Shell will report any errors during disk formatting.

During copying, Shell provides a progress indicator, as illustrated in Figure 5-4. During the copy operation, Shell indicates the current status of each sector of the disk.

► F means formatting track.
► R means reading track.
► W means writing track.
► E means an error reading or writing the track.

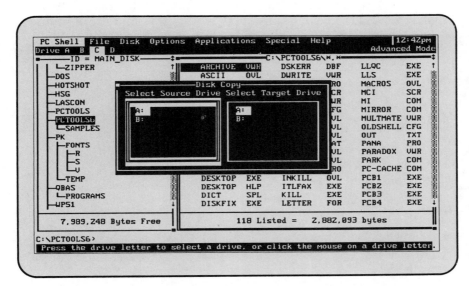

Figure 5-3. *Choose the source and target drives in the Disk Copy dialog box.*

123

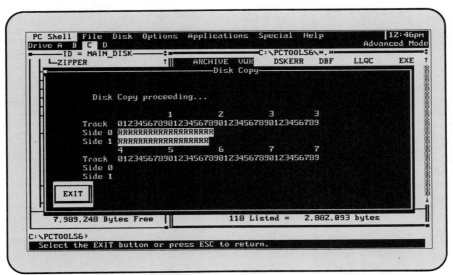

Figure 5-4. *During copying, Shell provides a progress status report.*

> ▶ **Tip:** When using Shell in memory-resident mode, you
> may want to provide a little more memory to the pro-
> gram so that single-drive copies go faster and with fewer
> disk swaps. When loading Shell into the computer, use the /
> RL (resident, large) parameter, as described more fully in
> Chapter 2. Using this parameter won't consume more mem-
> ory when Shell is not active, but it will minimize disk
> swapping.

124

Ⓠ Copying with Two Disk Drives

1. Place the source diskette
   (the one you want to copy)
   in one drive.

2. Place the target diskette
   (the one you want to copy
   to) in the other.

   We'll assume the source is placed in drive A, and the target
   in drive B.

3. Choose the Copy Disk   Presents the Disk Copy
   command from the Disk   dialog box.
   menu.

4. Choose drive A for the   Sets source and destination
   source and drive B for the   drives.
   target.

5. Press Enter when done.

6. Press the Copy button   Verifies that the source and
   twice.   target diskettes are in their
                                 respective drives.   □

   Shell now copies the contents of the source diskette to the
target diskette. Disk swapping is not required.

Verifying and Comparing Disks

Although Shell does a good job in ensuring that copies it makes of diskettes are error-free, you may want to verify the integrity of your copied disks with the Verify Disk and Compare Disk commands. You don't need to limit these commands to when you've copied disks. You can (and should) routinely verify your data disks to be sure the information contained within them is still reliable. Likewise, you may need to compare two disks against each other occasionally to determine if they are exact duplicates.

Verifying a Disk

The Verify Disk command in the Disk menu scans the entire contents of the disk—including files, subdirectories, and unused space—to make sure the data is readable.

125

To verify a disk:

1. Insert the disk you want to verify in the desired drive.
2. Activate the drive (press Ctrl-Drive Letter or when using a mouse click on the desired drive in the drive list).
3. Choose the Verify Disk command from the Disk menu.
4. After Shell pauses to inform you that the disk is about to be verified, press Verify to continue or Cancel to quit.

If Shell finds an error in a sector not previously marked as "bad," it displays the sector number containing the error, as shown in Figure 5-5. Shell will also indicate if the error is within the data portion of the disk or occurs within the DOS system area (which represents a greater danger, as the entire contents of the disk may be threatened).

In the lucky instance when the error occurs in a formatted but unoccupied (unused) portion of the disk, Shell marks the spot as "bad" so data will never be written there. If the error occurs in a used portion of the disk, Shell asks if you want to mark the sector as bad so that data can be rerouted around the problem.

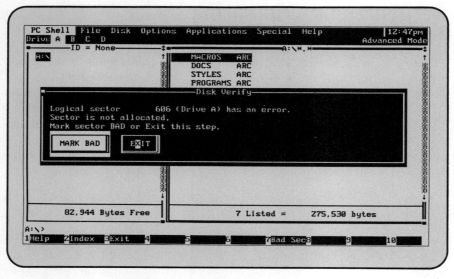

Figure 5-5. Shell has found sector 606 contains an error, as shown in the Disk Verify dialog box.

Comparing Two Disks

The Compare Disk command in the Disk menu checks two disks against one another. You can compare disks using one disk drive or two. When using two drives, both must be the same size and type. For example, you can compare two 5 1/4-inch 360-kilobyte diskettes, but not a 5 1/4-inch disk against a 3 1/2-inch disk.

To compare disks with one disk drive:

1. Choose the Compare Disk command from the Disk menu.
2. In the dialog box that appears (as shown in Figure 5-6), select a source and a target drive. In this case, set both drives the same (such as A:).
3. Insert the source diskette in the appropriate drive, and press Enter to start, then press the Compare button to go on.
4. Next, you will be prompted to insert the target diskette. Do so and press the Compare button to go on.
5. Depending on the available memory in your computer, the capacity of the diskette, and how you've loaded Shell, the

program may not be able to read the entire contents of the diskette in one pass. If necessary, swap the source and target diskettes in and out of the drive as requested by Shell.

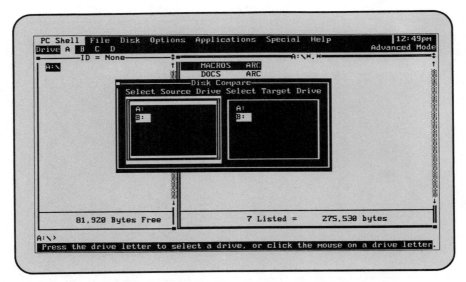

Figure 5-6. Choose the source and target drives in the Disk Compare dialog box.

During the comparison, Shell provides a progress indicator, as illustrated in Figure 5-7. Shell indicates the current status of each sector of the disk.

▶ R means reading track.
▶ C means comparing track.
▶ A dot means the track has been compared successfully.

To compare disks with two disk drives:

1. Place the first (source) diskette in one drive and the second (target) diskette in the other. We'll assume the source is placed in drive A, and the target in drive B.
2. Choose the Compare Disk command from the Disk menu.
3. Shell presents the Disk Compare dialog box. Choose drive A for the source and drive B for the target. Press Enter when done.

4. Verify that the source diskette is in drive A, and press the Compare button. Do the same for the target diskette.

5. Shell now compares the two diskettes. Disk swapping is not required.

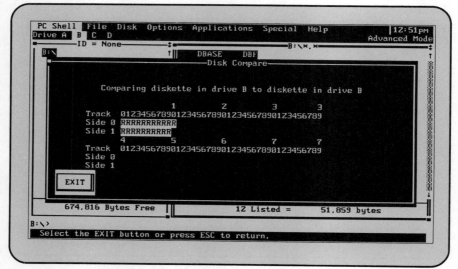

128

Figure 5-7. During Compare, Shell provides a progress status report.

Performing a Surface Scan

Another method of verifying a disk is performing a surface scan using the PC Tools Compress program. Compress analyzes the surface of the disk in a similar manner to the Verify Disk command, but it provides more in-depth reporting.

The following quick steps detail how to perform an in-depth surface scan analysis of a specified disk. Surface scanning is only one of several features built into Compress. For more about using the PC Tools Compress program, refer to Chapter 9, "Maintaining Your Hard Disk Drive."

Here's how to scan a disk with Compress. Note that Compress is a stand-alone program separate from Shell, so you can't run it when using Shell in memory-resident mode. You can, however, run Compress as a stand-alone program: Just type

COMPRESS

at the DOS prompt and the program starts.

1. Within Compress, select the drive you want to check. You can select a hard or a floppy disk drive.
2. Choose the Surface analysis command from the Analysis menu.
3. Indicate the number of passes you want Compress to perform. One pass is the default. You can also set continuous, where the surface analysis continues until you manually stop it.
4. Indicate where you want the exception report sent to. The exception report lists problems Compress found with the disk. Press the Printer or Disk button, as desired, or press No Report. If you send the exception report to a disk file, Compress asks you to indicate a drive for the exception report file (named SCANEXCP.RPT). You can't save the report to the same drive being tested.
5. Compress now scans the disk looking for problems. Scanning takes 2 to 4 minutes for floppy diskettes and up to an hour or more for large hard disks. Compress shows how much of the disk it has processed.

129

The legend at the bottom of the screen tells how to interpret the surface analysis symbols. To recap:

▶ B means boot sector.
▶ F means FAT sector.
▶ D means root directory.
▶ X means bad cluster.
▶ * means unreadable cluster.
▶ A dotted block means allocated cluster.
▶ A shaded block means unallocated cluster.

If an X appears in the boot or FAT sectors or in the root directory, it means the disk may be severely damaged. Refer to

Chapter 8, "Recovering Lost Files and Disks," for more information on reclaiming out-of-order disks.

Formatting Disks

Diskettes must be formatted before you can use them to hold data. Shell provides its own menu-driven formatter for floppy diskettes that is considerably easier (and safer) to use than the DOS FORMAT command.

The Format Data Disk command in the Disk menu operates separately from the PC Format program, which is part of the PC Tools collection. PC Format is intended primarily as a command-line substitute for DOS FORMAT. Its main benefits are that it offers additional features and safety nets over the standard DOS FORMAT command. See Chapter 9, "Maintaining Your Hard Disk Drive," for more information on using PC Format.

Shell's Format Data Disk command automatically senses the type of floppy disk drives contained in your computer and—depending on the drive type—allows you to select from among several possible media formats. Table 5-1 lists the drive types and formats supported by Shell.

Table 5-1. Drive Types and Formats Supported by Shell.

Media Size	No. of Sides	Capacity	No. of Sectors	No. of Tracks
5-1/4″	1	160K	8	40
5-1/4″	1	180K	9	40
5-1/4″	2	320K	8	40
5-1/4″	2	360K	9	40
5-1/4″	2	1.2M	15	80
3-1/2″	2	720K	9	80
3-1/2″	2	1.44M	18	80

130

Table 5-1. *(continued)*

▶ The 1.2- and 1.44-megabyte drive capacities require an AT class or higher computer.

▶ MS-DOS 3.3 (or PC DOS 3.2) or higher required for 3 1/2-inch media.

▶ DRIVER.SYS in CONFIG.SYS file required for DOS 3.X when used with 3 1/2-inch media. (The driver file is not required for DOS 4.0 or later.)

Ⓠ Formatting a Data Disk

131

1. Place a blank diskette in one of the floppy disk drives. (Note: You can also use a previously formatted floppy diskette, but, of course, its contents will be erased when it is reformatted.)

    We'll assume that you're using drive A.

2. Choose the Format Data Disk command from the Disk menu. — Activates Format Data Disk command.

3. Select a drive to use (drive A in this example). — Selects drive to use for the disk formatting.

4. Select a format type according to the drives you have in your computer. — Determines the format options possible with the selected drive, as shown in Figure 5-8 (your drive may not show these same options).

5. Press the Format button. — Starts disk formatting.

    Shell provides a status report during formatting. Sectors formatted correctly are shown as a dot; uncorrectable errors are shown as an E. Shell will attempt to format and verify troublesome sectors several times before it assigns an error. Unlike the DOS FORMAT command, Shell's Format Data Disk command continues with the formatting process even when errors occur.

6. After formatting is complete, Shell asks you to provide a volume name for the diskette. Enter a name.

7. Press Continue.　　　　　　Accepts the new name.

8. Indicate whether you want to make the formatted disk bootable. If you must, also use the Make System Disk command to complete the boot disk process. Otherwise, press Exit to stop formatting, or press Skip to go on to the next step.

Records the necessary system files at the beginning of the disk.

132

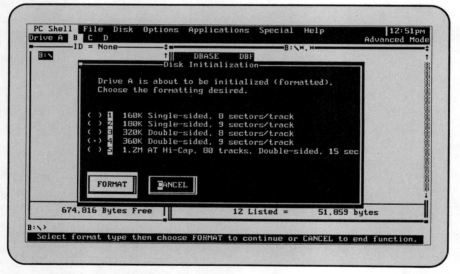

Figure 5-8. Shell displays the media capacities possible with your floppy disk drive. Select the one you want before formatting.

 Tip: At any time during the format process you can stop Shell by pressing the Escape key.

After formatting is complete, Shell provides you with some important information about your disk, including total bytes of disk space and bytes in bad sectors. If you want to format another diskette, remove the one that's in the drive, replace it with a fresh one, and press the Next Disk button. Otherwise press the Exit button to quit.

▶ **Tip:** Did Shell report an error during disk formatting? Is it time to throw the disk away and try another? Not yet. Although Shell may uncover a bad sector or two on a disk, it's not totally unusable. The bad sectors are "locked out" from use, so your computer won't accidentally try to access them. The disk won't have as much free space on it, but at least you won't have to throw the whole thing away. However, you should avoid using a disk with sector errors to hold hard disk backup data or to store a backup copy of another diskette.

133

Making a Bootable Disk

A bootable disk is one that can be used to start your computer. During disk formatting, Shell asks if you want to make the disk bootable; answering yes to the prompt only reserves the required space on the disk for the boot files. To complete the process, you must use the Make System Disk command (also in the Disk menu).

The instructions that follow assume you've already formatted the data disk, as described above, and that you indicated that you want to make the disk bootable. You should not attempt to make a bootable disk using a disk that already contains data.

To make a previously formatted disk bootable:

1. With the diskette in the proper drive, choose the Make System Disk command from the Disk menu.
2. Indicate the drive that contains the disk.
3. Shell asks that you confirm you want to make the disk bootable. Press the System button if you do; press Exit if you don't.

4. Shell will report any errors it encounters in making the disk bootable. After boot initialization is complete, you may wish to try the disk to be sure it works properly.

Renaming a Disk

The PC considers disks "volumes" and allows you to name the volumes for record-keeping purposes. Both Shell and DOS permit you to provide the name when you format the diskette; Shell goes one step further and lets you easily add or change the name at any time.

Here's how to rename a disk:

134

1. Place the diskette you want to rename in a disk drive.
2. Select the drive you want to rename in the drive list.
3. Choose the Rename Volume command from the Disk menu.
4. Shell provides you with a dialog box for entering a new name, as shown in Figure 5-9. The old name, if any, is displayed above the new volume label entry box. Type in a new name (up to 11 characters). Acceptable characters are the same as those used in a DOS file name.
5. Click the Rename button when you're done.

> ▶ **Tip:** Get into the habit of naming your disks, but exercise care to use different and descriptive names. For example, if one of your data diskettes is used to store backups of your Lotus 1-2-3 worksheets, call it something like LOTUS_1, with the anticipation that you'll be creating other Lotus worksheet diskettes in the future. Better yet, store like worksheets on separate diskettes, and use more descriptive names, such as LOT_89_SALE or LOT_90_SALE. Disk names are handy when you prepare a catalog of your disks or when you print disk directories.

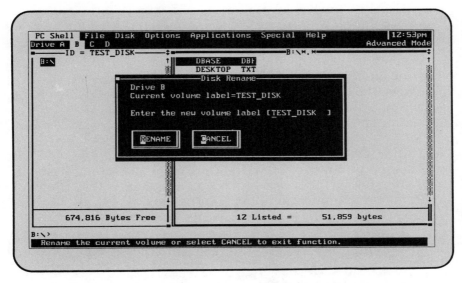

```
PC Shell  File  Disk  Options  Applications  Special  Help        12:53pm
Drive A  B  C  D                                              Advanced Mode
├──ID = TEST_DISK──────┤•─                     ─B:\*.*─
  B:\                              DBASE    DBF
                                   DESKTOP  TXT
                        ─────Disk Rename─────
                       Drive B
                       Current volume label=TEST_DISK

                       Enter the new volume label [TEST_DISK  ]

                        ┌─────────┐   ┌─────────┐
                        │ RENAME  │   │ CANCEL  │
                        └─────────┘   └─────────┘



        674,816 Bytes Free              12 Listed =      51,859 bytes

B:\>
  Rename the current volume or select CANCEL to exit function.
```

Figure 5-9. The Disk Rename dialog box.

135

Directory Maintenance

While subdirectories allow you to store files in centralized locations
on a hard disk, they can be difficult to manage. Take, for example,
the seemingly simple task of renaming a subdirectory. Unfortunately, DOS doesn't currently allow it, so if you want to rename a
subdirectory, you have to create a new one. Once that's accom-
plished, you have to move the files from the old directory to the
new one.

Shell offers a series of directory maintenance tools to help
smooth your trials with DOS subdirectories. You can:

▶ Add a new subdirectory.
▶ Rename a subdirectory.
▶ Delete a subdirectory.
▶ Prune and graft subdirectories.
▶ Modify certain attributes of a subdirectory.

> ⃠ **Caution:** With the exception of adding a new subdirectory, you should avoid using the directory maintenance commands when using Shell in memory-resident mode while another DOS application is loaded into memory. Otherwise, the application may not be able to track the changes you make, leading to possible loss of data.

All of the directory maintenance commands are located in a separate pop-up menu under the Disk menu, as shown in Figure 5-10. To access this secondary menu, select the Directory Maint(enance) command under the Disk menu.

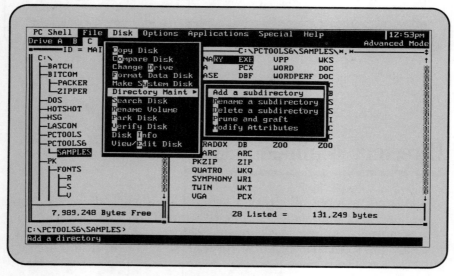

Figure 5-10. The Directory Maintenance pop-up menu.

Adding a New Subdirectory

You can add a new subdirectory anywhere in the directory tree of your hard disk. (Of course, you can also add subdirectories to a floppy diskette, although few PC users do so.)

To add a new subdirectory:

1. Choose the Add a subdirectory command from the Directory Maint(enance) pop-up menu.

2. On the directory tree (within the Tree window), indicate the location you want to add the new subdirectory to. Press the Continue button to go on. If the disk you're working with lacks subdirectories, Shell won't ask you to select a location on the directory tree for adding the new subdirectory. Instead, proceed directly to step 3.

3. Shell provides a naming box for creating the new subdirectory.

4. Enter a name and an optional extension, and press the Continue button to complete the subdirectory creation process.

The new subdirectory may not be immediately visible in the directory tree until you force Shell to re-read the tree. See the section above entitled "Re-Reading the Tree" for more information.

137

Renaming a Subdirectory

You can rename any subdirectory using the Rename a subdirectory command. To rename a subdirectory:

1. Choose the Rename a subdirectory command from the Directory Maint pop-up menu.

2. Indicate the subdirectory (within the Tree window) you want to rename.

3. Shell provides a naming box for renaming the subdirectory, as shown in Figure 5-11.

4. Enter a name and an optional extension, and press the Continue button to complete the subdirectory renaming process.

The renamed subdirectory may not be immediately visible in the directory tree until you force Shell to re-read the tree. See the section above entitled "Re-Reading the Tree" for more information.

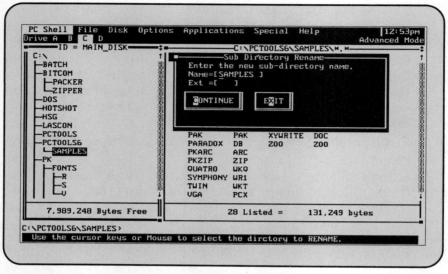

Figure 5-11. The Sub Directory Rename dialog box.

Deleting a Subdirectory

Delete subdirectories you no longer need so that they don't clutter up your hard disk. Before you can delete a subdirectory, you must empty it of all files and additional subdirectories. For obvious reasons, you cannot delete the root directory. You also cannot delete the currently logged directory. To delete a subdirectory:

1. Choose the Delete a subdirectory command from the Directory Maint pop-up menu.
2. Indicate the subdirectory (within the Tree window) you want to delete.
3. Shell asks that you confirm the deletion. Press the Continue button to go ahead; otherwise, press Exit to quit.

The deleted subdirectory may remain in the directory tree until you force Shell to re-read the tree. See the section above entitled "Re-Reading the Tree" for more information.

Prune and Graft

Prune and graft lets you move the contents of a subdirectory—
including all files and any additional subdirectories contained
within it—to another subdirectory.

Here's how to prune and graft a subdirectory:

1. Choose the Prune and graft command from the Directory
   Maint pop-up menu.
2. Indicate the subdirectory (within the Tree window) you
   want to prune (take items from). Press the Continue button
   to go on. The subdirectory to prune is marked with a greater
   than symbol (>), as shown in Figure 5-12.
3. Indicate the subdirectory you want to graft to (add the items
   to). Press the Continue button to go on.
4. Confirm that the prune and graft subdirectories are properly
   identified, and press the Continue button to verify your
   choices.

139

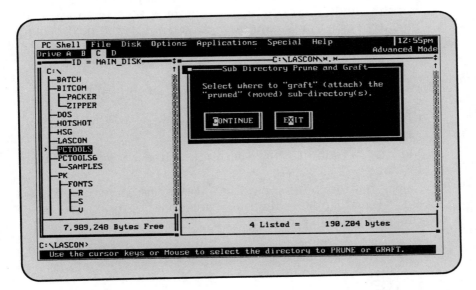

*Figure 5-12. The greater than symbol (>) indicates the
directory that will be pruned.*

Modify Subdirectory Attributes

Like files, subdirectories have certain attributes that describe important characteristics about them. Shell allows you to modify the read-only, hidden, system, and archive attributes of selected subdirectories.

▶ *Read only.* Indicates whether the subdirectory can be both read and written to (read only off) or just read (read only on).

▶ *Hidden.* Indicates whether the subdirectory is visible (hidden off) in a normal DOS DIRrectory or invisible (hidden on). Note that Shell lists hidden subdirectories.

▶ *System.* Indicates whether the subdirectory is reserved for system use (system on) or regular application use (system off).

140

▶ *Archive.* Indicates whether the directory has not been backed up recently using any of several types of disk backup programs, including PC Tools and DOS Backup. When archive is on, the subdirectory is new or contains files that have been recently edited and should be backed up in the next backup session. When archive is off, the subdirectory and its contents have already been backed up and needn't be again.

Follow these steps to modify subdirectory attributes:

1. Choose the Modify Attributes command from the Directory Maint pop-up menu.
2. Indicate the subdirectory (within the Tree window) you want to modify.
3. Select the attributes you want to set, as shown in Figure 5-13. Press Update when you are done, or press Cancel to cancel any changes.

Disk Info

The Disk Info command, under the Disk menu, provides information about the currently selected drive, including size, number of

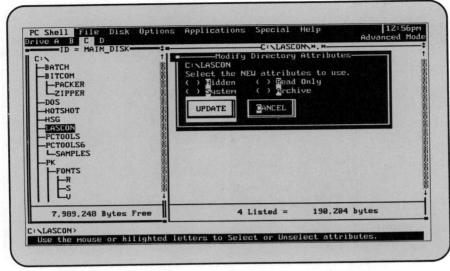

PC Shell **File** Disk Options Applications Special Help ┃12:56pm
Drive A B **C** D   Advanced Mode
━━ID = MAIN_DISK━━ ╪ ━━━━━━━━━━C:\LASCON*.*━━━━━━━━━━
C:\   ┌────Modify Directory Attributes────┐
 ┣BATCH   │C:\LASCON   │
 ┣BITCOM   │Select the NEW attributes to use. │
 ┃ ┣PACKER   │( ) **H**idden   ( ) **R**ead Only │
 ┃ ┗ZIPPER   │( ) **S**ystem   ( ) **A**rchive   │
 ┣DOS   │ ┌──────────┐ ┌──────────┐   │
 ┣HOTSHOT   │ │ UPDATE │ │ **C**ANCEL │   │
 ┣HSG   │ └──────────┘ └──────────┘   │
 ┣**LASCON**   │   │
 ┣PCTOOLS   │   │
 ┣PCTOOLS6   │   │
 ┃ ┗SAMPLES   │   │
 ┣PK   │   │
 ┃ ┣FONTS   │   │
 ┃ ┃ ┣R   │   │
 ┃ ┃ ┣S   │   │
 ┃ ┃ ┗U   │   │
━━
    7,989,248 Bytes Free   4 Listed =   190,204 bytes

C:\LASCON>
 Use the mouse or hilighted letters to Select or Unselect attributes.

Figure 5-13. The Modify (Sub) Directory Attributes dialog box.

141

files, number of directories, sectors per track, and more. The Disk Information dialog box, shown in Figure 5-14 (yours will be different, depending on the drive you select), is intended mainly to keep you abreast of the condition of your disks. You can also use it when recovering damaged disks, as described in Chapter 9, "Maintaining Your Hard Disk Drive."

Q Getting Disk Information

1. Select a drive to check.

2. Choose the Disk Info command from the Disk menu.

   Invokes the Disk Info command.

3. When you're done looking at the Disk Info box, press the Exit button.

   Returns you to Shell.

   □

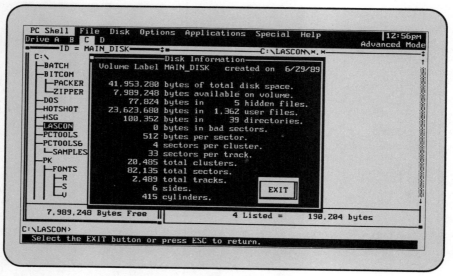

PC Shell File Disk Options Applications Special Help   12:56PM
Drive A B C D   Advanced Mode
       ID = MAIN_DISK   C:\LASCOM*.*
C:\
   BATCH   ┌────────Disk Information────────┐
   BITCOM   │ Volume Label MAIN_DISK   created on 6/29/89 │
      PACKER   │   │
      ZIPPER   │ 41,953,280 bytes of total disk space.   │
   DOS   │   7,989,248 bytes available on volume.   │
   HOTSHOT   │   77,824 bytes in   5 hidden files.   │
   HSG   │ 23,623,680 bytes in 1,362 user files.   │
   LASCON   │   100,352 bytes in   39 directories.   │
   PCTOOLS   │   0 bytes in bad sectors.   │
   PCTOOLS6   │   512 bytes per sector.   │
      SAMPLES   │   4 sectors per cluster.   │
   PK   │   33 sectors per track.   │
   FONTS   │   20,485 total clusters.   │
      R   │   82,135 total sectors.   │
      S   │   2,489 total tracks.   │
      U   │   6 sides.   ┌────────┐   │
                    │   415 cylinders.   │ EXIT │   │
                    │   └────────┘   │
     7,989,248 Bytes Free   │   4 Listed =   190,204 bytes
C:\LASCON>
 Select the EXIT button or press ESC to return.

Figure 5-14. *Useful information about a disk drive. The information contained in the sample illustration is for a 42-megabyte hard disk drive using nonstandard 33 sectors per track formatting.*

Sorting Files

Nothing's worse than a jumble of files. The Directory Sort command, found under the Special menu, helps you put your files in order. You can sort by any of five fields, in either ascending or descending order. The sorting procedure also sorts directories.

To sort a disk or directory:

1. Select the drive and/or directory you want to sort.
2. Choose the Directory Sort command from the Special menu.
3. Select a field for sorting, either name, extension, size, date/time, or select number (works only with files you previously selected).
4. Indicate whether you want the sorting to be in ascending or descending order.

5. Press the Sort key when you are done.

6. Shell asks how you want to review the results of the sort, as illustrated in Figure 5-15. The View option sorts the files in the Shell window only and does not make the sorting permanent. The Update option sorts the file on the disk. The Resort option returns you to the previous dialog box, where you can select another sorting field.

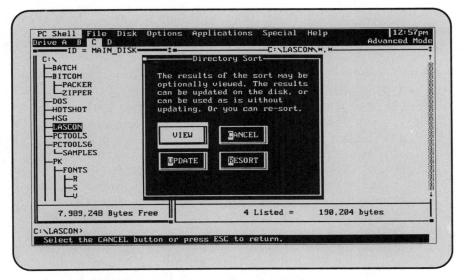

Figure 5-15. The Directory Sort dialog box.

143

If you've resorted the root directory of your hard disk or floppy diskettes, the order of the files and directories will be updated until you force Shell to re-read the drive. Simply reselect the drive you sorted, and the changes are updated.

Printing Disk and Directory Contents

The Print File List command, in the File menu, lets you create hard-copy printouts of the files in your disks and subdirectories. You can use the Print File List command to build a master disk/subdirectory catalog, to help you easily find files stored on archive disks. You can also print just those files that are currently selected. Use the file selection techniques you learned about in Chapter 4, "Managing Files with Shell."

Before printing a directory, make sure that your printer is on and that it is on-line. To print a directory:

1. Select the drive and/or subdirectory you want to print.
2. Choose the Print File List command from the File menu.

Shell informs you that printing is in progress. If an error occurs (the printer wasn't ready, for instance), you have the option of quitting or trying again.

144

> ► **Tip:** Shell doesn't offer a means to send the listing to a file, rather than directly to the printer. But with a separate utility, such as PRN2FILE (available through PCMAGNET on CompuServe), you can intercept data sent to a printer and capture it in an ASCII text document. Once the data is captured, you can format and edit it with any word processor or with the Notepads editor in the PC Tools Desktop. Make a text-file copy of all your directories or disks and save them in a master catalog file. You can then use the file (with the proper formatting, of course) with a data management program to pinpoint quickly the location of a particular document. This technique is particularly handy when cataloging a collection of floppy diskettes.

Review

In this chapter you learned how to use Shell to maintain your hard and floppy disks. You also learned:

► Shell can display the contents of either one or two disks at a time, using the One List Display or Two List Display commands.

► From time to time, you may need to choose the Re-Read the Tree command to force Shell to recognize changes in the directory structure.

► Shell provides a progress report while copying and formatting diskettes.

► The Verify Disk command scans the entire contents of the disk to make sure the data is readable.

► Shell can format any PC standard floppy diskette size and capacity.

► The Make System Disk command places the DOS system files on a freshly formatted diskette. It is similar to using the FORMAT /S DOS command.

► You can sort files in the disk directory using the Directory Sort command.

145

Running Applications with Shell

In This Chapter

▶ *Using the Launch command*
▶ *Selecting PC Tools programs from a menu*
▶ *Adding your own "instant-run" programs*
▶ *Launching documents with programs*

Imagine the convenience of running a program at the touch of a key. Or how about choosing a document and automatically launching the program that created it? Using Shell takes the place of typing program names at the DOS prompt, making it easy to start all your PC applications. You can even choose to open a selected document when you start a program, saving you the trouble of doing it manually yourself. You can use Shell as a way station for all your programs, or you can reserve it for just special occasions.

Shell as a Way Station

Shell is a substitute for starting your PC programs from the DOS prompt. Instead of returning to DOS when you quit your applications, you are returned to Shell, where you can start another program or perform some file and disk maintenance with Shell's other functions.

If you want to make Shell your permanent applications launcher, you should have it automatically load when you start your computer. Add the command

PCSHELL

as the last line in your AUTOEXEC.BAT file. That way, whenever you start or reset your computer, Shell automatically loads.

For all the things Shell does, it isn't a 100 percent replacement for DOS. Sometimes you must access DOS directly. You have two choices:

▶ Exit Shell, using the Exit Shell command (in the File menu). Shell is removed from memory; you can restart it by typing PCSHELL at the DOS prompt.

148

▶ Type a command at the DOS prompt while in Shell. The DOS prompt is normally visible near the bottom of the Shell display. Note: The DOS prompt is not visible if you have turned it off using the DOS Command Line option in the Setup Configuration command (under the Options menu). The DOS prompt also does not appear if you have turned on the Short Cut Keys (also in the Setup Configuration command).

The Launch Command

The Launch command, located in the File menu, lets you start any program or batch file located on a hard or floppy disk. Follow these simple procedures to use the Launch command.

Q Launching a Program in Shell

1. Highlight the program or batch file (.COM, .EXE, or .BAT extension) you want to run in the File List window.

   Selects the program to run; changes drives and directory, if necessary.

2. Choose the Launch command from the File menu.

   Invokes the Launch command.

3. Enter any run-time parameters required by the program or batch file. A run-time parameter is a file name or options switch the program or batch file needs to operate properly. For example, if you're running a graphics conversion program that needs to be told what type of graphics mode you want to use, you might enter /EGA or /VGA in the parameters entry box. Of course, the parameters are optional and required only when the program or batch file needs it.

Indicates run-time parameters, as shown in Figure 6-1.

149

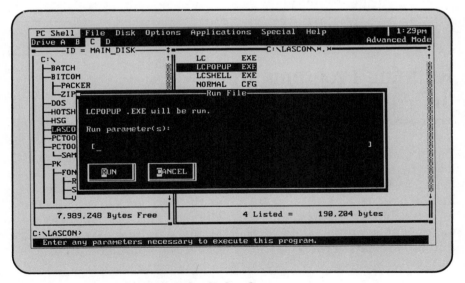

Figure 6-1. The Run File dialog box.

The Launch command has several shortcuts:

▶ Pressing Ctrl-Enter is the same as choosing the Launch command.

▶ If you're using a mouse, double-clicking (with the left button) on the desired program or batch file is the same as choosing the Launch command.

▶ **Tip:** Although the Launch command is designed to launch programs and batch files, you can also use it to start a program and load a document at the same time. Normally, Shell won't let you launch a nonprogram or non-batch file (for example, a .TXT document file created by a word processor), unless you've "attached" the document type to one of your programs on your hard disk. Shell monitors the file extensions of documents, so when you launch a document, it finds the application that goes with it, starts the application, and loads the document. See the section in this chapter entitled "Attaching Documents to Applications" for more information.

150

Running Programs from the Applications Menu

When you first installed PC Tools, the PCSETUP program automatically inserted the PC Tools ancillary programs (Compress, PC Format, PC Backup, etc.) in the Shell Applications menu. During installation, PCSETUP also searched through your hard disk for recognizable programs and inducted them into the Applications menu. For example, if PCSETUP found WordStar, WordPerfect, Microsoft Word, PKunzip, and LOGON on your hard disk, the Applications menu would look like the one in Figure 6-2.

Table 6-1 lists the applications PCSETUP looks for and installs automatically in the Applications menu. (This program list may change; you can check the PCSETUP.CFG file for additions and deletions.)

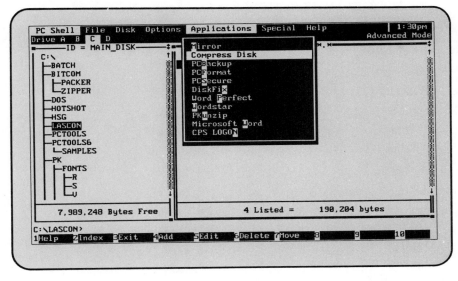

Figure 6-2. Listed programs under the Applications menu.

Notice in Figure 6-2 that one of the letters in each of the programs is highlighted. Like the rest of Shell's menus, these highlighted letters represent quick-keys you can use to select one of the programs from the menu quickly. Table 6-1 lists the letter used for the quick-key highlight, as well as the program name and associated document file name extensions.

The Applications menu is meant to store the most commonly used programs on your hard disk, thus freeing you from hunting them down in the File List window and starting them manually with the Launch command. Shell keeps track of the location and other important tidbits (as explained in the next section) of each program listed in the Applications menu.

To use the Applications menu, merely choose a program listed on it. There's no need to indicate any run-time parameters; these are coded with the program entry in the menu and are provided for you automatically.

Table 6-1. List of PCSETUP Identified Applications.

Program Name	Quick-Key	File Name	Associated Document
PC Tools Programs			
Compress Disk	C	COMPRESS.EXE	
PCBackup	B	PCBACKUP.EXE	
Mirror	M	MIRROR.COM	
PCFormat	F	PCFORMAT.COM	
PCSecure	S	PCSECURE.EXE	
DiskFix	X	DISKFIX.EXE	
Additional Applications			
Agenda	A	AGENDA.EXE	.AGB .AGA
Copy II PC	Y	COPYIIPC.EXE	
dBase III	D	DBASE.COM	.DBF
dBase IV	D	DBASE.EXE	.DBF
DisplayWrite 4	4	DW4PG.COM	
Excel	E	EXCEL.EXE	.XLS .XLM .XLW .XLC
First Publisher	I	FP.EXE	.PUB
FoxBase	X	FOXPLUS.EXE	.DBF
Framework III	R	FW.EXE	.FW3
Freelance Plus	E	FL.COM	
Generic Cadd	N	CADD.EXE	.DWG
Grammatik III	I	GMK3.EXE	
GraphWriter II	G	GW.COM	.CHT
Harvard Graphics	H	HG.EXE	.CHT
Lotus 1-2-3	L	123.COM	.WK1 .WKS
Lotus 1-2-3	L	123.EXE	.WK1 .WKS
Lotus 1-2-3, V3	L	123.EXE	.WK3 .WK1 .WKS
Manuscript	N	MS.EXE	.DOC
Microsoft Works	T	WORKS.EXE	.WKS .WDB .WPS
Microsoft Word 5	W	WORD.EXE	.DOC
Microsoft Word	W	WORD.COM	.DOC
MS Windows 386	O	WIN386.EXE	
MS Windows	O	WIN.COM	
Multimate	T	WP.EXE	
Multiplan	U	MP.EXE	

Program Name	Quick-Key	File Name	Associated Document
Option Board	A	TE.EXE	
PageMaker 3	K	PM.COM	.PM3
Paradox 3	X	PARADOX3.EXE	
PFS: 1st Choice	:	FIRST1.COM	
Professional File	O	PF.EXE	
Professional Write	W	PW.COM	
Q&A	&	QA.COM	
Quattro	Q	Q.EXE	.WKQ
Reflex	X	RELEX2.EXE	.RRD
RightWriter	R	RIGHT.EXE	
SuperCalc 5	S	SC5.COM	.CAL
Symphony	Y	SYMPHONY.EXE	
VP Planner	V	VPP.COM	.WKS
Windows Write	R	WRITE.EXE	.WRI
WordPerfect	P	WP.EXE	.DOC
WordStar 2000	W	WS2.EXE	.DOC
WordStar	W	WS.EXE	.DOC
XYWrite 3+	+	EDITOR.EXE	.DOC

153

Adding Programs to the Applications Menu

You are free to add more programs to the Applications menu or to edit and delete ones already there.

 Adding or Editing a Program in the Applications Menu

1. Pull down the Applications menu (click on it with the mouse, or press Alt-A).

2. To ADD a new program to the menu, press the F4 function key. To EDIT an existing program entry, press the F5 function key.

3. If you are adding a new program indicate where you want it in the Applications menu list, then press Enter. If you are editing a program entry, highlight it, then press Enter.

A dialog box like that in Figure 6-3 appears. If you are adding a new program entry, the fields in the box will be empty.

4. Provide Shell with the name and path of the program in the appropriate editing fields.

154

5. Press the Tab key to move to the next editing field (or click there with the mouse).

6. When you are done adding or editing the program list, press the F4 function key to accept.

Makes the changes permanent.

You can also delete an entry by pulling down the Application menu and pressing the F6 function key. Highlight the entry you want to delete, then press Enter. Confirm the deletion. If you don't like the position of one of the entries, pull down the Application menu and press the F7 function key. Highlight the entry to move, then press Enter. Indicate a new location for the entry, and press Enter one more time. You can continue moving entries this way until you press the F3 function key to exit the Application menu.

Here's what the editing fields in the Application Editor dialog box mean:

▶ *Application.* The name of the program as it will appear in the Applications menu. Enter a caret character (^) immediately before the letter you want to use as the highlighted quick-key. This letter can be used to start the program from the keyboard. Be sure that no two programs share the same quick-key.

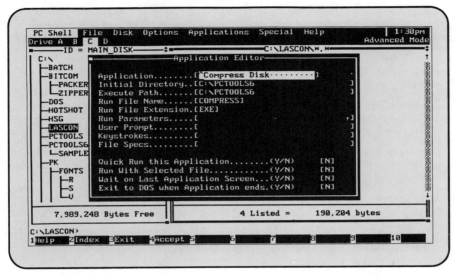

Figure 6-3. The Application Editor dialog box contains the entries for the Applications menu.

▶ *Initial Directory.* The path (including, when necessary, the drive letter) where the application and its files are found.

▶ *Execute Path.* The path where the application executes. For most applications, enter the same path for the Initial directory and Execute Path entries.

▶ *Run File Name.* The exact name and extension of the program.

▶ *Run Parameters.* Optional. Run-time options the applications expect. When Shell starts the program, it will automatically append the parameters you've specified. For instance, if you've added the parameter /h for a program called CONVERT, Shell will start the program as if you entered CONVERT /h at the DOS prompt.

▶ *User Prompt.* Displays a prompt of your choice immediately before executing the selected application. Fill in the user prompt (up to 128 characters) as desired. Leaving this field blank skips the user prompt, and Shell immediately runs the application after it is selected from the Applications menu.

▶ *Keystrokes.* Keys that Shell automatically "presses" for the selected application when you first start it. This field is helpful if you need to press a series of keys to start an application all the way or load a document. This is an advanced topic; see the PC Tools Deluxe Data Recovery/DOS Shell manual for more details on how to program with keystrokes.

▶ *File Specs.* A file spec is a document file associated with an individual application. You can indicate one or more file specs in the field (up to 128 characters). Most file specs will be documents with particular name extensions, such as *.TXT and *.DOC. Selecting one of these files from within PC Shell will automatically run the application these files are associated with.

▶ *Quick Run this Application.* Answering Y(es) to this option causes Shell to run the application without freeing up memory. Normally, answer N(o) so that Shell frees up some of its memory for use by your applications.

156

▶ *Run With Selected File.* Runs the application using a file you have selected in the Files List window. Answer Y or N accordingly.

▶ *Wait on Last Application Screen.* Pauses the program at the last screen before restarting Shell. This is necessary for most DOS programs, like CHKDSK, where the programs runs and stops without using special screens. Answer Y or N accordingly.

▶ *Exit to DOS when Application ends.* Goes to DOS when the application is terminated instead of going back to Shell. Answer Y or N accordingly.

You can enter a specific file name in the Run Parameters field if you want to load a particular document when you start a program. Suppose, for example, that you always run dBase with the file ADDRESS.DBF. Enter the file name ADDRESS.DBF in the Run Parameters line, and dBase will automatically load it when you start the program. If you're using other command-line parameters, be careful of where you place the file name. Some programs expect it in a certain location if other parameters are included.

Another approach: You can also select a file in the File List window, then choose the program you want to run. For example, to load the file REPORT.DOC into WordPerfect, select REPORT.DOC in the File List window, and choose WordPerfect from the Applications menu. If you select more than one document, Shell will pick the first one you chose and ignore the others, unless the program can open multiple documents.

Shell records the programs contained in the Applications menu in the PCSHELL.CFG file. If this file is erased or damaged, your list of programs will be lost. It's, therefore, a good idea to keep a backup (on a floppy diskette) of the PCSHELL.CFG file, in case something should ever happen to the original.

After a program has run, you will be returned to Shell. You will probably be requested to press a key to reenter Shell. If you're using the mouse, just press one of the mouse buttons to reactivate Shell.

Attaching Documents to Applications

157

One of the most useful features of Shell is automatically launching an application when you select a document in the File List window. Let's say, for instance, that you can select a file named BUDGET.WK1 in the File List window. Choose the Launch command from the File menu, and Shell will start Lotus 1-2-3 and automatically load the BUDGET.WK1 document.

Launching a file and loading a document requires that you provide a file extension association in the Application Editor dialog box, as detailed in the previous section entitled "Adding Programs to the Applications Menu." When you run a file with a particular extension, Shell automatically launches the associated program and loads the document.

Note that this technique doesn't work with all programs. The application you're running must be able to accept a file name as a command-line parameter. For example, if you type

```
PROGRAM FILENAME.TXT
```

at the DOS prompt to launch the application and automatically load the file, you can use the File Specs feature of Shell.

Figure 6-4 shows an Application Editor dialog box for a Shareware program called PICEM, which allows you to look at various types of graphics files. The File Specs entries include several of the file types PICEM can handle. In use, you merely select a graphic file and choose the Launch command, and PICEM automatically loads, displaying the picture.

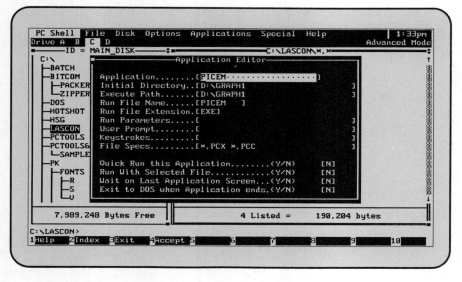

Figure 6-4. Sample entry in the Application Editor dialog box.

> ▶ **Tip:** Some of the programs in your Applications menu may share the same file specs. While no harm will come to your computer or files if this occurs, Shell will associate a given document spec only with the first program it finds in the menu that recognizes the extension. For example, suppose you have WordStar, WordPerfect, and Microsoft Word on your hard disk. During installation, PCSETUP will enter the .DOC extension in the file spec fields for all three programs. Regardless of what program created the file in the first place, Shell will start the first program in the list when you select a .DOC document. If you want to launch another program when you select a certain file, change the order of the applications in the menu, or use a unique file extension.

Review

In this chapter you learned how to use PC Tools Shell to run your applications. You also learned:

▶ Shell must be loaded as a stand-alone program (as opposed to a memory-resident program) if you want to use it for launching applications.

▶ The Launch command runs any application or batch file you select.

▶ A keyboard shortcut for the Launch command is: Select a program or batch file to run, and press Ctrl-Enter.

▶ A mouse shortcut for the Launch command is: Double-click on the program or batch file you want to run.

▶ The Applications menu is for programs you often use.

▶ The Application Editor allows you to change the programs listed in the Applications menu.

▶ The file spec feature lets you automatically launch programs and load document files at the same time.

159

Backing Up Your Hard Disk Drive

In This Chapter

161

▶ *Configuring Backup for your computer*
▶ *Backing up an entire hard disk*
▶ *Backing up a portion of a hard disk*
▶ *Restoring files in case of data loss*

Consider the following nightmare: You finished a week-long project, saving the files on your computer's hard disk. The next day, when you return to print the files, you find the hard disk has "crashed": The contents of the disk, the files, everything is gone. Not only must you recreate a week's worth of data, you have to rebuild your hard disk and reinstall all your programs, a task that in itself can take several days.

This type of scenario is often repeated as a means to promote the benefits of making backups—an archival copy of your hard disk. The scenario is a common one because it occurs, often. In fact, odds are that something like it will happen to you sooner or later.

The PC Tools Backup utility makes it easy to store an archive of your hard disk for safe keeping. Should a problem occur, you can use the backup to restore your data to its original form and content.

Backup Strategy

Backup programs are worthless if you don't have a strategy for making archival copies of your hard disk. For best results, you should back up your hard disk drive at least once a week, and preferably once a day.

PC Tools Backup, which is a stand-alone program you can access from within Shell or directly at the DOS prompt, lets you make partial archives, meaning you can back up just a portion of the hard disk drive, or just those files that have been changed or created since the last archive. That makes daily backups much more palatable. Instead of spending 10 to 30 minutes to back up an entire 30-megabyte hard disk drive, you spend only a few minutes archiving the work you've done for that day.

162

Backup Types

PC Tools Backup offers five types of backups. Understanding these methods helps you prepare your own backup strategy. Depending on the backup method used, PC Tools Backup relies on the "archive bit," one of the file attribute characteristics stored along with the contents of the file. The archive bit tells the computer (and PC Tools Backup) if the file has been archived since it was created or edited. If the archive bit is on (set), the file has not been backed up since it was created or edited. Conversely, if the archive bit is off (not set), the file has been backed up.

The setting of the archive bit is automatic as you create and edit files. But as you learned in Chapter 4, "Managing Files with Shell," you can manually change the archive bit using Shell.

▶ *Full.* Archives all the files on the hard disk or, optionally, just those files and subdirectories you've manually selected. During a Full backup, PC Tools Backup ignores the setting of the archive bit. (It archives everything, no matter how the archive bit is set.) After the backup is complete, the program resets the archive bit to off to indicate that the files have been backed up.

▶ *Full Copy.* Functions the same as Full, except that the settings of the archive bit are not changed after the backup is complete.

▶ *Incremental.* Backs up only those files with the archive bit set (recently edited or created). When the backup is complete, the program resets the archive bits. If you have previously performed a Full backup, files archived with Incremental will be appended to the end of the Full backup.

▶ *Separate Incremental.* Functions the same as Incremental, except that the archive is not appended to the Full backup.

▶ *Differential.* Archives only those files that have been changed since the last Full backup. The archive bit is not reset after the backup is complete.

The setting and resetting of archive bits between the different methods can get confusing. Table 7-1 lists the settings of the archive bits for files backed up with the five archival methods.

Table 7-1. Setting of Archive Bits by Backup Method.

163

Archive Method	Before Backup	After Backup
Full	N/A	OFF
Full Copy	N/A	UNCHANGED
Incremental	ON	OFF
Separate Incremental	ON	OFF
Differential	ON	UNCHANGED

Note again that Full and Full Copy backup methods back up all selected files regardless of the setting of the archive bit. Also note that with the exception of the Incremental backup option, all other options create a new backup (containing the archive of your hard disk) set each time they are run.

Establishing a Backup Policy

A backup policy is a consistent routine you keep for yourself for backing up your hard disk. Without an effective backup policy, you might as well not even make archival copies of your hard disk. For example, if you back up the hard disk drive only occasionally, the archive will be of little use to you because it will probably be seriously out of date. The files in the archive may be weeks, if not months, old and may not reflect any changes you've made in the interim.

An ideal backup policy is one full backup every week—say every Friday before you go home for the weekend—plus a partial backup at the end of each day. While that may seem like a lot of extra work, it really isn't. Few hard disks are over 40 megabytes (under DOS 2.X and 3.X hard disk partitions are limited to 32 megabytes), and few hard disks are filled to capacity. On average, it will take you between 15 to 20 minutes to archive your hard disk using the Full backup method. That's required only once a week. The incremental backups, using the Archive method, take only a few minutes.

If you don't use your computer daily, then there's no reason to archive its hard disk every day. As a rule of thumb, though, if you use your computer on any particular day, back up your work.

164

Estimating Diskette Requirements

PC Tools Backup crams hard disk data onto diskettes. The number of diskettes you need to archive your hard disk depends on several variables:

▶ The amount of data contained in the hard disk drive. (Note: The capacity of the hard disk drive is not important, as you can have only 2 megabytes of data on a 40-megabyte drive.)

▶ The capacity of the diskette media, such as 360 or 720 kilobytes or 1.44 megabytes.

▶ The setting of the Compression option within PC Tools Backup. The amount and effect of the compression depends on the speed of your computer and the format of the data on your hard disk drive. You can select compression to minimize the number of diskettes or to minimize time.

When you start a hard disk backup, PC Tools Backup estimates the number of diskettes you need to complete the task. In my experience, the estimate is high; the program usually accomplishes the task with fewer diskettes. PC Tools Backup will provide you with its estimate before you actually start the backup process, so you can stop it if you don't have enough diskettes on hand.

On average, using 1.44- or 1.2-megabyte media (which is preferred, as it takes fewer diskettes and speeds up the process), you need about one diskette for every 1.5 megabytes of hard disk data. Accordingly, a hard disk with 15 megabytes will require approximately ten 1.44- or 1.2-megabyte diskettes.

After you make the first backups of your hard disk using the Full and Incremental methods, you can better estimate the number of diskettes you'll need to fulfill your weekly and daily backups. You'll need a single set of diskettes for the weekly backups and separate sets of diskettes for the daily backups. For instance, if your hard disk requires 20 diskettes for a weekly (Full) backup, and two diskettes for each of the daily (Incremental) backups, you'll need to have 30 diskettes on hand to fill the quota (this assumes you'll be making five daily backups per week).

Label the sets so you can readily identify them. Write WEEKLY on the weekly Full backup diskettes, and MONDAY, TUESDAY, etc., for each set of daily Incremental backup diskettes.

During the archive process, PC Tools Backup will prompt you to insert Disk Number # into the drive. Write this number on the diskette so that you can readily identify it. If and when you need to restore the hard disk with previously archived data, you'll be prompted to insert one or more of these numbered diskettes into the drive.

> ▶ **Tip:** Use the PCBDIR program, included with PC Tools, if you've forgotten to number the diskettes. PCBDIR reads the contents of the diskette and lists its number, as provided by PC Tools Backup (refer to the example in Figure 7-1). Alternately, you can use PC Backup to generate a directory of files on your backup disks. A sample printout provided by PC Backup is shown in Figure 7-2.

A Note on Diskette Quality

For obvious reasons, you don't want to skimp on the quality of diskettes used for hard disk backup. Though you'll be using

```
C:\PCTOOLS6>pcbdir B:
PCBackup Directory Report
Copyright (c) 1990 by Central Point Software. All Rights Reserved.

What drive:path contains the backup disk (default A:)B:
Disk is number 1 of a PCBACKUP set.
Disk was created with release 6.0 of PCBACKUP
Backup device was a 1.44MB drive. Media selected was 1.44MB.
Disk is formatted with 80 tracks of 18 sectors per side.
The directory starts on track 70 (46h) of this disk.
This disk is recorded in DOS standard format.
Advanced Error Correction was ON for this backup.
The compression setting for this backup is (null).
This disk was formatted by PCBACKUP.  The backup speed used was High.

C:\PCTOOLS6>_
```

166

Figure 7-1. Disk information provided by the PC Backup program.

plenty of diskettes to maintain a weekly and daily backup schedule, you reuse these diskettes so the expenditure is one-time only.

If your computer is equipped with high-density 3 1/2- or 5 1/4-inch floppy disk drives (1.44- and 1.2-megabyte capacity, respectively), purchase only high-density media for them. Standard double-density diskettes are not rated for high-density applications, and you run the risk of corrupting the data that you've spent so much time protecting. High-density media costs only a little more than double-density, but it's well worth it.

A Preview of PC Tools Backup

The PC Tools Backup program looks and "feels" much the same as the PC Tools Shell application. As shown in Figure 7-3, PC Tools Backup consists of a menu bar at the top (with four menus: Backup, Restore, Options, and Configure), two windows for displaying the directory tree and files, and a message bar at the bottom. You select commands, files, and other items in PC Tools Backup the same as you do in Shell.

```
PC Backup Directory Report 6.0
(c) Copyright 1989,1990 Central Point Software, Inc. All Rights Reserved.
Backup Performed on 06/05/1990   01:40p

Total Directories:    7
Total Files:        267

    Name            Size        Date      Time    Atrib Vol              Page 1

Directory: D:\

Directory: D:\

Directory: D:\ADLIB\
ANITRA.ROL          8103  03/14/1988    04:02p    A---    1 Compressed
ARIA.ROL            4167  09/04/1987    03:10p    A---    1 Compressed
BALLAD.ROL          1575  06/09/1987    07:14p    A---    1 Compressed
BANKMNG.EXE        12229  12/22/1988    05:11p    A---    1 Compressed
BANKMNG.TXT         3262  02/02/1989    05:49p    A---    1 Compressed
BAROQUE.ROL         9735  11/26/1987    03:35p    A---    1 Compressed
BLUES.ROL           1899  06/09/1987    12:45p    A---    1 Compressed
BOOGIE.ROL          3243  06/17/1987    12:33p    A---    1 Compressed
BOSSA.ROL           2615  09/21/1989    03:30p    A---    1 Compressed
BOSSANO.ROL         3805  09/20/1989    10:52p    A---    1 Compressed
BOSSAP.ROL          8943  05/08/1987    03:45p    A---    1 Compressed
CHOPIN7.ROL         2439  09/28/1989    10:54p    A---    1 Compressed
CLASSIC.ROL         1503  05/23/1987    04:28p    A---    1 Compressed
CLASSY.ROL          7231  09/25/1987    12:23p    A---    1 Compressed
CLOCK.ROL           8431  11/26/1987    03:30p    A---    1 Compressed
COMPOS1.EXE       196368  04/28/1989    01:47p    A---    1 Compressed
COMPOS1.RSR        22364  04/27/1989    02:34p    A---    1 Compressed
COMPOSER.BAK          35  09/20/1989    10:59p    A---    1
COMPOSER.BAT         128  09/28/1989    11:00p    A---    1
CRYSTAL.ROL         7509  09/25/1987    12:51p    A---    1 Compressed
DRIVE.ROL           9605  11/26/1987    03:04p    A---    1 Compressed
ELECROCK.ROL       13331  01/05/1989    10:15a    A---    1 Compressed
FOLKSONG.ROL        7763  11/26/1987    03:50p    A---    1 Compressed
HIGHWAYS.ROL       10543  03/03/1989    01:08p    A---    1 Compressed
INSMAK1.EXE       105785  12/22/1988    06:18p    A---    1 Compressed
INSMAK1.RSR        17370  12/22/1988    05:51p    A---    1 Compressed
INSMAKER.BAT          25  12/21/1988    11:48a    A---    1
JAZZ.ROL            1779  06/09/1987    11:56a    A---    1 Compressed
JESU.ROL           13241  05/08/1987    05:34p    A---    1 Compressed
JUKE1.EXE         104577  01/31/1989    02:46p    A---    1 Compressed
JUKE1.RSR          45925  04/20/1989    11:50a    A---    1 Compressed
JUKEBOX.BAK          593  09/20/1989    10:54p    A---    1 Compressed
JUKEBOX.BAT          256  09/28/1989    11:01p    A---    1 Compressed
JUKEBOX.DAT         1152  09/29/1989    10:47a    A---    1 Compressed
LARGO1.ROL          5467  03/30/1988    05:03p    A---    1 Compressed
LULLABY.ROL         7841  11/26/1987    03:39p    A---    1 Compressed
MINUET.ROL          5513  04/07/1988    02:50p    A---    1 Compressed
MOMENTS.ROL        12487  11/26/1987    03:29p    A---    1 Compressed
MOONLITE.ROL        9187  09/28/1989    10:58p    A---    1 Compressed
MPU401.COM          2149  05/07/1987    10:35a    A---    1 Compressed
PARADE.ROL         11559  01/14/1989    01:31p    A---    1 Compressed
PIZPOLKA.ROL        5667  04/07/1988    05:09p    A---    1 Compressed
POPTMAIN.EXE       44962  08/01/1988    04:24p    A---    1 Compressed
POPTUNES.BAT          41  07/29/1988    04:19p    A---    1
POPTUNES.DAT         614  08/05/1988    04:02p    A---    1 Compressed
RAGTIME.ROL         1579  05/25/1987    07:55p    A---    1 Compressed
```

167

Figure 7-2. Partial printed directory listing from PC Backup.

If, at any time, you need help on a particular topic, press the F1 function key, and a help screen appears.

Before you can use PC Tools Backup, you must install it on your hard disk drive. The Backup files are automatically trans-

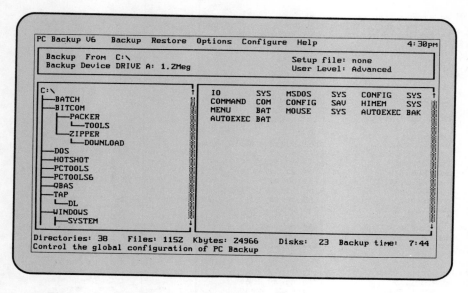

```
PC Backup V6   Backup  Restore  Options  Configure  Help                4:30PM

  Backup   From  C:\                          Setup file:  none
  Backup Device DRIVE A: 1.2Meg               User Level:  Advanced

 C:\                            ↑    IO         SYS   MSDOS     SYS   CONFIG     SYS  ↑
   ├─BATCH                            COMMAND    COM   CONFIG    SAV   HIMEM      SYS
   ├─BITCOM                           MENU       BAT   MOUSE     SYS   AUTOEXEC   BAK
   │   ├─PACKER                       AUTOEXEC   BAT
   │   │  └─TOOLS
   │   └─ZIPPER
   │      └─DOWNLOAD
   ├─DOS
   ├─HOTSHOT
   ├─PCTOOLS
   ├─PCTOOLS6
   ├─QBAS
   ├─TAP
   │  └─DL
   └─WINDOWS
       ├─SYSTEM                  ↓                                                    ↓

 Directories: 38    Files: 1152  Kbytes: 24966    Disks:  23  Backup time:   7:44
 Control the global configuration of PC Backup
```

Figure 7-3. The basic PC Tools Backup opening screen.

ferred to your hard disk with the rest of PC Tools. PC Tools Backup must be used on a hard disk. If your hard disk "crashes" (fails for whatever reason and takes some or all of its files with it), you must reinstall the PC Tools Backup files onto it. Don't worry about hurting the remaining files on the hard disk—you have a complete backup of it, right?!

Selecting Backup Options

If you haven't used PC Tools Backup before, you need to tell it a few things about your computer and the way you want to perform the backups. This configuration is automatic the first time you use PC Tools Backup, but you can change it at any time using the commands under the Configure menu.

Q Autoconfiguration of PC Tools Backup

1. Type PCBACKUP at the DOS prompt. (Of course, be sure you are logged onto the proper drive and directory.)	Starts PC Backup.
2. Read the welcome notice, and press the Continue button to go on.	
3. Define your equipment, as illustrated in Figure 7-4.	Verifies the equipment in your computer.
4. Press the OK button to continue.	
5. In the next dialog box that appears, select the drive and media capacity you want to use for your backup. You'll probably want to use the highest capacity possible, as that saves time and diskettes.	Sets drive and media type (capacity) in dialog box in Figure 7-5.
6. Press OK when done.	☐

169

Depending on the hardware configuration of your computer, there are a number of optional selections you can make in the Choose Drive & Media dialog box, shown in Figure 7-5. If you have a tape drive supported by PC Tools Backup, additional backup choices will appear:

Tape drive (40M)
Tape drive (60M)

or

Tape drive (80M)
Tape drive (120M)

Select the tape drive capacity you wish to use.

If you have two floppy disk drives that are the same capacity, PC Backup displays:

One Drive Backup
Two Drive Backup

Select the option you desire. The Two Drive Backup option can save time, as it allows you to load a diskette into one drive as PC Backup archives data to the other.

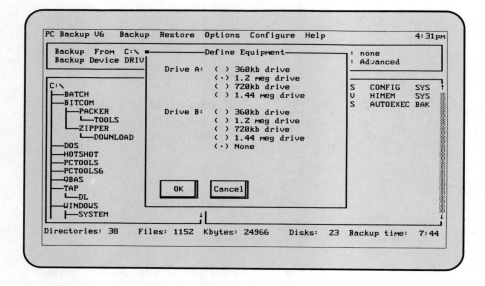

Figure 7-4. *The Define Equipment dialog box.*

Backup Speed

Before you start your first archive you should select the backup *speed*. The backup speed determines how PC Backup routes the data through the computer and what kind of shortcuts it takes. You have three choices for backup speed:

▶ The *High Speed* option (default) uses the special controller circuitry (called DMA, for Direct Memory Access) in your computer to read data from your hard disk drive while writing it to the floppy disk drive. Of course, your computer must be equipped with a compatible DMA controller. Although most PC compatibles have the required circuitry, some do not.

170

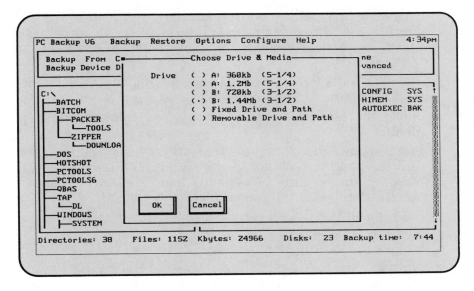

Figure 7-5. The Choose Drive & Media dialog box.

▶ The *Medium Speed* bypasses the DMA circuitry of the computer. PC Backup reads the hard disk drive and writes the data to the floppy disk drive in two distinct steps. This setting is equivalent to the /NO parameter, which you can use when you first start PC Backup (see the inside back cover of this book for additional command-line parameters you can use with PC Backup).

▶ The *Low Speed* setting should be used when backing up to a device other than a floppy disk drive and when backing up within a network.

Which option do you use? If you have the choice, pick the High Speed option. Your backups take about half the time. If you know your computer lacks the required DMA controller, opt for Medium Speed instead. Selecting High Speed DMA on a computer that lacks the DMA controller may corrupt the backup data. You won't know it until you attempt to restore the data following a hard disk mishap.

If you're not sure about the capabilities of your computer, try this simple test:

171

1. Create a new subdirectory on your hard disk (call it TEMP), and fill it with two or three small files. You can copy these files from another directory, but make a note of the contents of the files.

2. Start PC Tools Backup, and choose the Backup Speed command from the Configure menu. Select High Speed.

3. Select the cHoose directories command from the Backup menu.

4. From within the directory Tree window, select the root directory, and press Enter (or click on it with the left mouse button). All the directories in the hard disk drive should now be deselected (no longer highlighted).

5. Find the TEMP subdirectory, and select it. It should be the only one highlighted.

6. Choose the Start backup command from the Backup menu.

172

7. PC Tools Backup will now make an archival copy of just the TEMP directory and its contents. Follow the on-screen prompts until the backup is complete.

8. Select the cHoose directories command from the Restore menu.

9. Select the TEMP subdirectory in the Tree window.

10. PC Tools Backup will warn you that the restored files will overwrite existing ones on your hard disk. Choose the Overwrite option, and press OK for each of the files.

11. When the restoration is complete, leave PC Tools Backup, and examine the files in the TEMP directory. If they are intact, then the High Speed transfer option was successful. If they are not, then you should select the Medium Speed option.

> **Note:** While this test will help you determine if High Speed is appropriate for your computer, it is not entirely foolproof. You may wish to prepare additional "dummy" subdirectories and fill them with at least 1 megabyte of data. With additional files to backup and restore, there's more chance of an error occurring during the DMA data transfer process.

Additional Backup Options

Even though you can use PC Tools Backup after telling it what kind of media you plan to use for the archive, you'll probably want to set additional options before you begin. These are:

▶ Backup method.
▶ Compress.
▶ Verify.
▶ Format.
▶ Error correction.
▶ Standard format.
▶ Reporting.
▶ Overwrite warning.
▶ Time display.
▶ Save history.

173

All options are located under the Options menu.

Backup Method

The Backup method command lets you set the type of backup process you desire, either Full, Full Copy, Incremental, Separate Incremental, or Differential. These options are described earlier in the section entitled "Backup Types."

Q Setting the Backup Method

1. Choose the Backup method command from the Options menu.

2. Select the backup method. As shown in the dialog box in Figure 7-6, select the method desired.

3. Press the OK button or press Cancel.

OK returns you to PC Tools Backup; Cancel cancels any changes. ☐

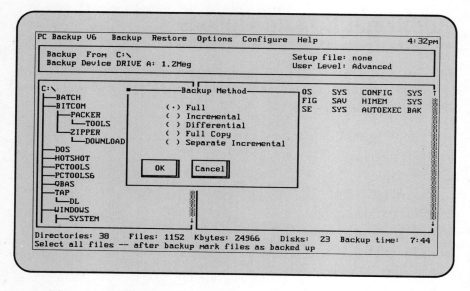

174

Figure 7-6. The Backup Method dialog box provides four types of backups.

Compress

The Compress command lets you select optional compression when backing up data. You have a choice of compression to minimize the number of diskettes, compression to minimize time, or no compression.

▶ *Minimize Space.* Reduces the number of diskettes required to make the backup (generally 10 to 60 percent, depending on the type of data stored in your computer).

▶ *Minimize Time.* Reduces the time required to make the backup. Time compression depends almost entirely on the speed of the processor in your computer. You'll enjoy little time compression if your PC or compatible is equipped with a slower 8088 or 8086 microprocessor; time compression is improved with faster 80286 and 80386 computers. This option works only with the High Speed option.

▶ *None.* Turns off all compression.

To set the Compression option:

1. Choose the Compression command from the Options menu.
2. Select Minimize Space, Minimize Time, or None, as desired.
3. Press the OK button to return to PC Tools Backup; press the Cancel button to cancel any changes.

Verify

The Verify command checks the integrity of the data recorded on the backup diskettes. You have three choices: When Formatting, Always, or None. Verification lengthens the backup process.

▶ *When Formatting.* Checks the trustworthiness of the diskette when first formatted immediately prior to backing up the hard disk. Works with the High Speed option.

▶ *Always.* Checks the backup data after it has been recorded on the diskette.

▶ *None.* Turns off all verification.

175

Here's how to set the Verify option:

1. Choose the Verify command from the Options menu.
2. Select When Formatting, Always, or None, as desired.
3. Press the OK button to return to PC Tools Backup; press the Cancel button to cancel any changes.

Format

The Format command controls when diskettes are formatted. Backups take considerably longer when the Always option is set, but better data integrity is ensured. This option applies only to backups made with the High Speed option. Your computer will automatically reformat diskettes when using the other two backup options.

To set the Format option (turn it on and off), choose the Always command from the Options menu. A checkmark appears next to the command when the option is turned on.

Error Correction

When the Error Correction option is set, PC Tools Backup uses a special error correction protocol to recover from numerous types of errors that can occur on a disk. Error correction makes disk backup a little longer, but it can be well worth it. To turn on error correction, choose the Error Correction command from the Options menu. A checkmark appears by the command when the option is turned on.

Standard Format

176

PC Tools Backup uses two types of diskette formatting procedures: nonstandard and standard. The standard format uses regular DOS disk formatting. Conversely, the nonstandard format uses a unique format employed only by PC Tools Backup. The nonstandard format uses less disk space, but requires PC Tools Backup to read the diskettes. To select the standard format, choose the Standard command from the Options menu. A checkmark appears when you select Standard. PC Tools Backup uses the nonstandard format scheme when the checkmark is absent.

Reporting

The Reporting option lets you create a report of the progress of the backup process. If you choose to make a report, you can send it to a printer or to a disk file.

- ▶ *None.* Cancels reporting.
- ▶ *Report to Printer.* Sends the report to the printer. PC Tools Backup requires that the printer be connected to the LPT1 parallel printer port.
- ▶ *Report to File.* Sends the report to a disk file.

To set the Report option:

1. Choose the Report command from the Options menu.
2. In the dialog box, as shown in Figure 7-7, select None, Report to Printer, or Report to File, as desired.

3. Press the OK button to return to PC Tools Backup; press the Cancel button to cancel any changes.

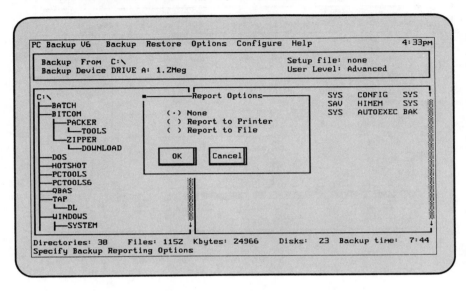

Figure 7-7. The Report Options dialog box.

Overwrite Warning

The Overwrite warning option lets you control the alert messages provided by PC Tools Backup. The Overwrite warning option is turned off or on; when on, the Overwrite warning command in the Options menu is shown with a checkmark. The Overwrite warning serves two purposes:

▶ Alerts you that PC Tools Backup is about to overwrite a previously used backup diskette (see Figure 7-8).

▶ Alerts you that existing files will be overwritten during a restoration.

Time Display

The Time display option toggles the time display during backup. The Time display option is turned off or on; when on, the Time

177

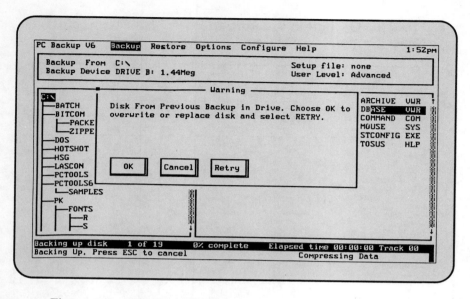

Figure 7-8. Warning dialog box displayed when using a diskette used in an earlier backup.

display command in the Options menu is shown with a checkmark.

Save History

A history file is created for each backup you make. That file is appended to the end of the last diskette in the backup set (or at the end of the tape if you are using a tape drive). When the History Files option is turned on (default), PC Tools Backup writes the history file into the PC Tools directory, as set by you or the network administrator (if you are in a network), or whatever directory contains the PC Tools Backup program.

If the Save History option is off, PC Tools Backup reads the history file recorded with the archive. PC Tools Backup works a little slower when Save History is turned off.

PC Tools Options Defaults

Table 7-2 lists the backup options and their defaults. Unless you require otherwise, you should consider the defaults as the recommended setting.

Table 7-2. PC Tools Backup Default Options.

Option	Default
Backup method	Full
Compress	Minimize Time
Verify	Verify When Formatting
Format always	Off
Error correction	On
Standard format	On
Reporting	None
Overwrite warning	On
Time display	On
Save history	On

179

Backing Up a Hard Disk Drive

With the PC Tools Backup program configured and the desired options selected, you can now back up your hard disk drive. If this is the first time you've archived the drive, you should use the Full backup method and back up everything on the drive. In the following section, you'll learn how to perform a selective backup.

Full Backup of a Hard Disk Drive

1. Choose backup From entry command from the Backup menu. If the hard disk you want to archive is not listed, as shown in Figure 7-9, enter the drive letter and press the OK button.

Starts backup operation.

2. Choose the Start Backup command from the Backup menu.

3. Provide a name for the backup, set an optional password, and press Enter.

4. As requested by PC Tools Backup, insert the first diskette.

Your hard disk drive is backed up.

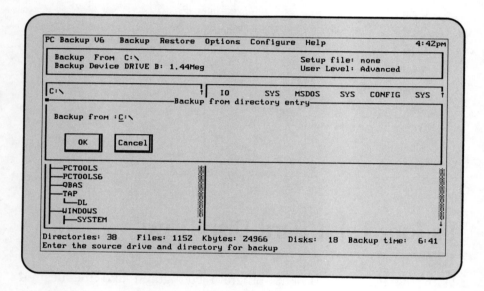

Figure 7-9. The Backup from Directory Entry dialog box.

Insert additional diskettes as the program requests. Be sure to write down the numbers of the diskettes as the program stores data on them.

When the backup is complete, store the archival diskettes in a safe place. If possible, store the diskettes in a fireproof safe or file cabinet. Do not remove the diskettes from the premises because you need ready access to them: for an emergency restoration and for the next backup at the end of the day or week.

Selective Backup

There are two types of selective backups: manual and automatic. With manual selection, you choose the subdirectories and files you want to include in the backup, in the same manner as you did when testing the High Speed option, earlier in this chapter. Manual selection employs the cHoose directory command from the Backup menu.

Automatic selection relies on PC Tools Backup to make the desired choices. You indicate the types of subdirectories or files you want to include, and the program automatically selects them. You can also tell PC Tools Backup which subdirectories or files to exclude from the backup. Automatic Selection uses the following commands from the Options menu:

181

▶ Subdirectory Inclusion.
▶ Include/exclude files.
▶ Attribute exclusions.
▶ Date range selection.

Choose Directory

The cHoose directory command from the Backup menu lets you select those subdirectories and files you want to include in the backup. Selected subdirectories and files are shown highlighted in the Tree and File List windows.

To select a subdirectory:

1. Choose the backup From entry command from the Backup menu. If the hard disk you want to archive is not listed, enter the drive letter, and press the OK button.
2. Select the cHoose directory command from the Backup menu. The Tree window is activated.
3. With the current selection on the root directory, press Enter or click the left mouse button. This deselects all subdirectories and files.

4. With the cursor keys or right mouse button, scroll through the tree until you reach the subdirectory you want to include.

5. Press Enter or click the left mouse button to select the subdirectory.

6. Repeat steps 4 and 5 until you have selected all subdirectories to archive.

If you make a mistake and select a subdirectory you didn't mean to include, highlight the subdirectory and press Enter again or click the left mouse button.

If you're using a mouse, you can select several subdirectories at once by dragging over them. Position the mouse cursor on the first directory you want, press and hold the right mouse button, press and hold the left mouse button, and drag the mouse to the last directory in the series. Release both mouse buttons.

182

> ▶ **Tip:** You can use the cHoose directory command to exclude subdirectories you don't want to back up. After selecting the cHoose directory command, don't start by deselecting the entire tree. Instead, scroll through the tree and select those subdirectories you don't want. Press Enter or the left mouse button to deselect them.

To select a file:

1. Select the cHoose directory command from the Backup menu. The Tree window is activated.

2. With the current selection on the root directory, press Enter or click the left mouse button. This deselects all subdirectories and files.

3. With the cursor keys or right mouse button, scroll through the tree until you reach the subdirectory that contains the files you want.

4. Press the Tab key to activate the File List window.

5. With the cursor keys or right mouse button, scroll through the list until you reach what you want to include.

6. Press the Enter key or click the left mouse button to select the file.

7. Reselect another file or press the Tab key to reactivate the Tree window and select another subdirectory. Repeat steps 3 through 6 as needed.

If you make a mistake and select a file you didn't mean to include, highlight the file again and press Enter again or click the left mouse button.

If you're using a mouse, you can select several files at once by dragging over them. Position the mouse cursor on the first file you want, press and hold the right mouse button, press and hold the left mouse button, and drag the mouse to the last file in the series. Release both mouse buttons.

See the Tip under the section entitled "Choose Directory" above, for details on using the cHoose directory command to exclude files.

183

Subdirectory Inclusion

The Subdirectory Inclusion option is a toggle that you turn off and on (it's normally on). When on, selecting a subdirectory also selects any subdirectories contained within it, as illustrated in Figure 7-10. When off, selecting a subdirectory affects only the current choice.

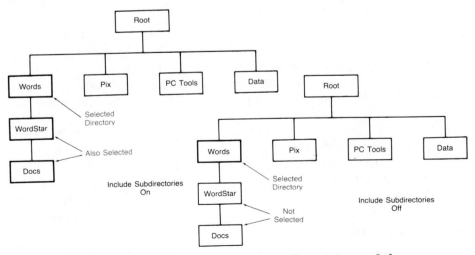

Figure 7-10. The differences between the settings of the Include Subdirectories commands.

Include/Exclude Files

The Include/exclude files command lets you indicate subdirectories and file types you want to either include or exclude in the backup. Choose the Include/exclude files command from the Option menu and enter up to 16 directories and file types, as shown in Figure 7-11.

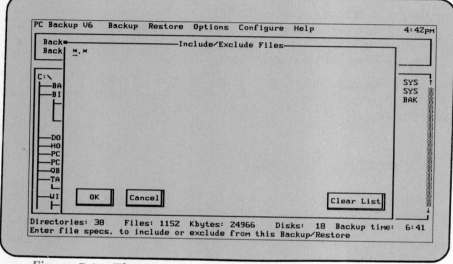

184

Figure 7-11. The Include/exclude files dialog box with the default *.* entry.

To enter a directory, type the path name. To enter a file, type the file name (you may use the * and ? wildcards, as necessary). The minus (−) character tells the program that you want to *exclude* the directory or file type. Here are some examples.

▶ *.* includes the whole disk. (This is the default PC Tools Backup starts with.)

▶ *.* includes all files under the root directory.

▶ \PCTOOLS*.* includes all files under the PCTOOLS subdirectory.

▶ − \PCTOOLS*.* excludes all files under the PCTOOLS subdirectory.

▶ *.COM includes files with the .COM extension (in all directories).

▶ *.COM includes files with the .COM extension (in the root directory only).

▶ − \WP50*.DOC excludes files with a .DOC extension in the WP50 subdirectory.

> ▶ **Note:** The setting of the Include Subdirectory option can influence the effect of included/excluded subdirectories. With the Include Subdirectory option on, including or excluding a particular subdirectory will also affect any subdirectories contained within it. If the Include Subdirectory option is off, only the indicated subdirectory is affected. You should set the Include Subdirectory option before using the Include/exclude files command. If you change the Include Subdirectory option, rechoose the Include/exclude files command, and press the OK button. This resets the selection and readies the program for the backup.

185

Attribute Exclusions

The Attribute exclusions command lets you exclude those files on the entire hard disk that conform to any or all of the following attributes:

▶ Hidden.

▶ System.

▶ Read only.

Here's how to set the Attribute exclusions option.

1. Choose the Attribute exclusions command from the Options menu. The dialog box shown in Figure 7-12 will appear.

2. Select the attribute type for the files you want to exclude in the backup. You can indicate any or all of the attribute options.

3. Press OK when you're done.

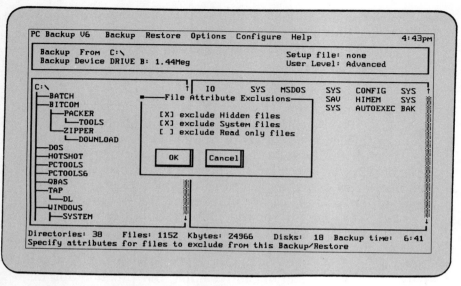

Figure 7-12. The File Attribute Exclusions dialog box.

186

Date Range Selection

The Date range selection command, in conjunction with the Include/exclude files command, lets you set a time frame for files to include in the backup. Set a starting and stopping date, and PC Tools Backup archives only those files created or edited within that date.

To set the Date range selection:

1. Choose the Date range selection command from the Options menu.
2. Turn the Date range selection function on by choosing the ON option.
3. Enter a starting date into the From data field.
4. Enter an ending date into the To data field.
5. Press the OK button to activate your date selection.

Be sure to activate the Include/exclude files command, or the settings you make in the Date range selection box will have no effect.

Other suggestions:

▶ You can archive all files made after a certain date by entering the desired date in the From data field and by using the
current date in the To field.

▶ You can archive all files made before a certain date by
entering 01/01/80 in the From date field (the start of the PC
clock time-keeping period) to the desired date.

▶ **Tip:** The Date range selection command is best used
when your computer is equipped with a clock/calen-
dar (with battery backup) function. Without the clock/cal-
endar, you may forget to reset the date each time your
computer is turned on. If the files you create always say
they were made on January 1, 1980, then your computer
does not have a battery-supplied clock/calendar, and you
should not use the Date range selection command.

187

Saving Setup Selections

You won't want to reset all your special options each time you
make a backup of your hard disk drive. Instead, save the settings
in a special .SET setup file.

Note that the changes you make with the cHoose directory
command are not saved in the setup file. The drive type, disk
media, and all option commands are saved in the setup file.

Q Saving the Current Setup

1. Make the desired changes in the options.	Changes the setup to your specifications.
2. Choose the Save setup command from the Options menu.	
3. Enter a name for the setup file. (Don't use an extension.)	Names the setup file.
4. Press the OK button.	Stores the setup file. ☐

Recalling a Saved Setup

1. Be sure that you don't need to save any options you've changed during the current session with PC Tools Backup.

   Prevents you from losing any important setting you've made in the current session.

2. Choose the Load setup command from the Options menu.

3. Select the setup file you want to use.

   Identifies the setup you want to use.

4. Press the OK button.

   Retrieves the stored setup.

▶ **Tip:** The Save Setup feature can be used to memorize the two types of backup processes you'll probably be using: Full (for weekly backups) and Incremental (for daily backups). Make the desired changes and save the setup file. Call one WEEKLY and the other DAILY. When it comes time to do the actual archive, you can start PC Tools Backup, select the setup you want, and proceed immediately to backing up your hard disk. As a shortcut, you can type

PCBACKUP WEEKLY

to start PC Tools Backup and automatically load the WEEKLY setup file, or you can type

PCBACKUP DAILY

to start the program and load the DAILY setup file.

Saving Default Settings

If you don't care for the defaults PC Tools Backup initially presents you, and you don't want to bother with creating a special setup file just for your personal preferences, use the Save as default command from the Configure menu to record your own selections. The options stored when using the Save as default command are the same as those saved in the setup file, with the addition of alterations you make to the Color Selection command.

The settings are recorded in the PCBACKUP.CFG file. If this file is ever damaged or erased, your new defaults will be lost.

Restoring a Hard Disk Drive

Should anything ever happen to the data on your hard disk drive, you can resurrect it with the archive diskettes you've made with PC Tools Backup. You can restore the entire contents of the hard disk drive, or just specific subdirectories and files.

Should you experience a complete loss of data on your hard disk, you'll need to reformat it (using the formatting programs that came with your computer or hard disk) and replace DOS before you can use PC Tools Backup. The PC Tools Backup files must reside on the hard disk before you can restore the lost data.

189

Full Restore

A full restore completely rebuilds the files and subdirectories on your hard disk.

1. Choose the restore To entry command from the Restore menu. If your hard disk drive isn't listed in the dialog box, as shown in Figure 7-13, enter its letter, and press the OK button.
2. Select the cHoose directory command from the Restore menu. Pick a backup, set to use, and press OK.
3. Choose the Start restore command from the Restore menu. PC Tools Backup may prompt you to insert the last disk of the backup series. This allows the program to sample the master backup directory.
4. If you have selected the Overwrite warning option and some or all of the original files still exist on your hard disk, you'll see the Warning dialog box shown in Figure 7-14. You have three choices: overwrite file, overwrite file only if the backup contains a new version of it, or skip this file. You can also choose to repeat your choice for the remaining files in the backup (use with the Overwrite and Overwrite with Newer file only options). This prevents the warning

box from appearing every time PC Tools Backup encounters an existing file. Press the OK button to go on.

5. Replace the backup diskettes in the drive as instructed by PC Tools Backup, until the entire hard disk has been restored.

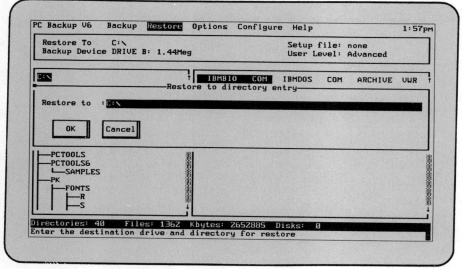

Figure 7-13. The Restore to Directory Entry dialog box.

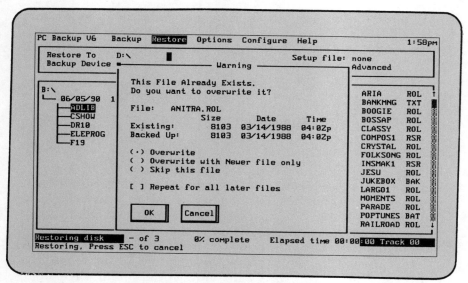

Figure 7-14. PC Tools Backup warns you if your hard disk already contains a file with the same name as the one you're restoring to the drive.

As soon as possible, you should check the integrity of the program and data files to make sure the restoration was a success. If you make another backup of the hard disk, use a new set of diskettes and keep the original archive until you are sure that all files on your hard disk are intact.

> ▶ **Tip:** You can use the restore To entry command to replace the backup data onto a hard disk drive other than the original. You can select a different drive letter (like D: instead of C:) if your computer has more than one hard disk drive on it. You can also use restored data from your hard disk on another computer. (Its hard disk drive should be empty, however, and should use the same version of MS-DOS/PC DOS as yours.)

191

Partial Restore

A partial restore lets you recondition only selected files or subdirectories. Use this procedure if only some of the files on your hard disk have become corrupted or erased. (Before using Restore, try to unerase files using the PC Tools Unerase command, found in the Shell program.)

For a partial restore of hard disk data:

1. Choose the restore To entry command from the Restore menu. If your hard disk drive isn't listed in the dialog box, enter its letter and press the OK button.
2. Select the cHoose directory command from the Restore menu. PC Tools Backup prompts you to insert the last diskette of the backup series. This allows the program to sample the master backup directory.
3. Select subdirectories and/or files you want to restore, following the same basic procedures outlined earlier in this chapter. Or, use the Subdirectory inclusion, Include/exclude files, Attribute exclusions, and Date range selection commands, as previously discussed, to select subdirectories and file types you want to restore.
4. If you have selected the Overwrite warning option, and some or all of the original files still exist on your hard disk,

PC Tools Backup will alert you that proceeding with the restoring will overwrite some files. Make your selection from the available options, and press the OK button to go on.

5. Replace the backup diskettes in the drive as instructed by PC Tools Backup, until the entire hard disk has been restored.

As soon as possible, you should check the integrity of the program and data files to make sure the restoration was a success. If you make another backup of the hard disk, use a new set of diskettes and keep the original archive until you are sure that all files on your hard disk are intact.

Refer to the PC Tools Hard Disk Backup manual for additional information if you are attempting to restore hard disk data with damaged or lost disks.

192

Comparing Data on Disks

Making backups helps to preserve your data. But things can go afoul. There's always a danger that you will lose perfectly good files by restoring them with earlier versions. For example, you create a file on Monday, then back it up on Tuesday. On Wednesday, you edit the file making significant changes. Then, something happens to the hard drive on Thursday. Do you use Tuesday's backup to restore the data? If you do, you forfeit the alterations you made to the file.

You may not always be aware of the number and extent of changes between the data on your hard drive (if any of it is still good) and the data on your backup disks. Too, you may want to be sure that the information on your backup disks are an exact duplicate of the data on your hard drive. PC Tools Backup offers a Compare feature where you can compare the data on a hard drive against that on your backup diskettes (or tape). Differences are noted.

We'll assume you are checking the data on new set of backup diskettes with the original on your hard drive.

1. Select the cHoose directory command from the Restore menu.

2. If you have the Save History option turned on (default), select a backup set to use. Otherwise, insert the last diskette of the backup set you want to verify. Press the OK button to proceed.

3. Choose the start Compare command from the Restore menu. PC Tools now compares the backup with the original. You are prompted to insert the diskettes from the backup set as the program continues its comparison.

4. As PC Tools Backup compares the files, it marks each one in the file window with a special marker character, as described in Table 7-3. No symbol means that the file has not been compared yet.

5. At the end of the comparison, PC Tools Backup summarizes its findings, indicating the number of files that were equal, and those that were missing, older, newer, mismatches, and/ or had different times/dates. Click OK when you are done.

193

Table 7-3.   Symbols Used During Backup Comparison.

Symbol	Meaning
=	Backup file is identical to original.
<	Backup file is older than original, but otherwise files compare.
<<	Backup file is older than original, and files do not compare.
>	Backup file is newer than original, but otherwise files compare.
>>	Backup file is newer than original, and files do not compare.
s	Size of backup file does not match size of original, but dates/times are the same.
–	Backup file missing from hard disk.
x	Backup file does not compare with original, but date/time matches.

▶ Note: "Original" means backed-up file on hard drive.

Notice that file comparisons are not always accurate if:

▶ A terminate-and-stay-resident program is currently running.

▶ You have changed backup speeds.

Changing User Levels

As with PC Shell, PC Tools Backup lets you adjust the user level. The default user level is Advanced, meaning that all the commands are available to you and listed in the menus. If you desire, you can change the user level to Beginning or Intermediate. Doing so will remove some of the more advanced commands from the menus, making the program less intimidating.

To change the user level:

1. Choose the User Level command from the Configure menu.
2. Select one of the user level options, either Beginner, Intermediate, or Advanced.
3. Click OK to accept the change.

194

Review

In this chapter you learned the procedures for backing up and restoring hard disk drives using PC Tools Backup. You also learned:

▶ Backups are only as good as the last archive you made. An old archive means you have old data.

▶ PC Tools Backup recognizes the archive bit and can use it to decide which files on your hard disk need to be backed up.

▶ There are five types of backups: Full, Full Copy, Incremental, Separate Incremental, and Differential.

▶ An ideal backup policy is one Full backup every week, plus an Incremental backup at the end of each day.

▶ Before you can use PC Tools Backup for the first time, you must tell it what drive types you have in your computer and the type of media you'll be using.

▶ Backups made with the High Speed option go faster, but your computer must be compatible.

▶ You can archive your entire hard disk drive or just selected portions of it.

▶ PC Tools Backup allows you to restore the entire hard disk or just selected subdirectories and files.

195

Recovering Lost Files and Disks

In This Chapter

▶ *DOS disks are structured*
▶ *Reclaiming accidentally erased files*
▶ *Rebuilding hard disk drive directories*
▶ *Running PC Tools Mirror and Rebuild*
▶ *Verifying files and disks*

Computer disks are not safe deposit boxes where you can stockpile files and always expect to retrieve them unharmed. While you can be reasonably sure files you place on the disk will remain in good health, not all fare so well. You may accidentally erase a file or reformat your hard disk drive. Or, maybe your computer experiences a glitch and accidentally records data on the disk where it's not supposed to.

PC Tools provides many features to help you restore lost files and disks. These include an Undelete command to assist you in reclaiming files you or an applications program deleted in error. PC Tools also offers the Mirror program for recording backups of the all-important file allocation table, as well as Rebuild for putting damaged disks back together again.

Limitations and Caveats

As with all tools, your success in using PC Tools to restore lost files and disks relies heavily on your personal knowledge and expertise. While PC Tools provides many automatic measures for restoring lost files and disks—and these measures will be used for the majority of file and disk recovery operations you supervise—certain situations may require manual intervention. The more you know about your computer and the way it operates, the better chance you have in bringing back lost data.

You may never need to use the file and disk recovery features of PC Tools, but it's nice to know they're there in case you need them. If a problem arises, don't panic. Often, the error can be corrected with one or two minor steps. Working in a frenzy because you're afraid you've lost valuable data will cloud your reasoning. Slow down and analyze the situation before you proceed. If you're not sure about what you're doing, seek capable help.

198

Important Terms

Whether you use PC Tools for automatic or manual file and disk recovery, you need to acquaint yourself with some basic terms. These terms relate to data files and how they are recorded on your disks.

Data on a computer disk is recorded in concentric tracks. If you could see the tracks, they would appear as rings starting at the center of the disk and spreading outward. Unlike the groove on a record, which is a continuous spiral from the outside to the inside, computer disk tracks are self-contained rings, as shown in Figure 8-1.

The number of tracks varies between media type and capacity. Standard double-sided, double-density (360-kilobyte) diskettes contain a total of 80 tracks—40 on each side. A moderate size hard disk, say about 40 megabytes, may contain 600 or more tracks, divided among three or four separate disks.

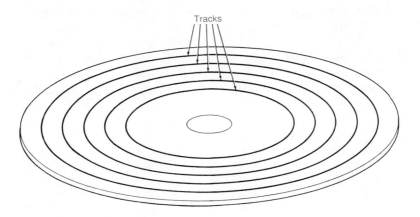

Tracks

Figure 8-1. The tracks on a computer disk.

The data on the disk is further divided into sectors. A sector
is a particular segment of the track. By dividing each track into
individual sectors, the computer can more readily store and later
retrieve data. As with tracks, the number of sectors differs from
disk to disk. Regular IBM 360-kilobyte floppy diskettes contain
nine sectors per track; many hard disk drives use 25 or 30 sectors per track. Some hard disk drives exceed 31 sectors per track,
but these are considered "nonstandard" to many PC utility programs. Fortunately, PC Tools is not one of them.

Just as tracks are composed of many sectors, sectors are sub-
divided into clusters. A cluster is the smallest unit the computer
can manipulate. Cluster size is expressed in kilobytes and determines the smallest amount of space that a given file will take up.
Even if a file is only 2 bytes long, it will still consume an entire
cluster.

The cluster size in double-sided, double-density media is 1
kilobyte. That means that file size is always in 1-kilobyte increments. If a file is 500 bytes, it still takes up 1 kilobyte of actual
disk space (although its size is still listed as 500 bytes). If a file
is 1,025 bytes, it will consume two clusters, or 2 kilobytes of
space (recall that 1 kilobyte is really 1,024 bytes, not 1,000
bytes). Generally speaking, cluster size increases with larger
media. Hard disk drives generally have cluster sizes of 2 to 4
kilobytes. With a 4-kilobyte cluster size (as found on 20- and 30-
megabyte hard disks for the XT), minimum file size is 4,096
bytes.

199

Each disk you format on your computer—whether it's a hard or floppy disk—is composed of four parts: the boot record (or boot block), the file allocation table, the root directory, and the data area. These parts are located on the disk in a specific sequence, as shown in Figure 8-2. Depending on the type of media and its capacity, the physical size of the file allocation table, root directory, and data area may vary from disk to disk.

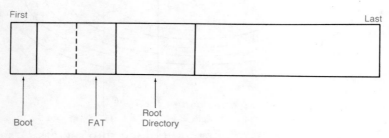

Figure 8-2. Arrangement of vital data on your hard disk drive, starting with the boot record.

Boot Record

Every disk has a boot record, even if the disk isn't bootable, that is, even if you can't use it to start your computer. The boot record contains vital information that your computer uses to begin operation when it's first turned on. If the disk also contains the necessary system files (IBMBIO.COM, IBMDOS.COM, and COMMAND.COM), the computer will start up, and you can begin work. If the disk lacks system files, and you try to use it to boot your computer, you'll get a "non system disk" error.

The data in the boot record is necessary if you want to start your computer with that disk. If something happens to the boot record data, it's likely that the disk will no longer start your computer.

File Allocation Table

The file allocation table, or FAT, can be likened to an attendance sheet in a school room. On the sheet is a check box for each student in the room. When a student is present, the corresponding check box is marked. When the student is absent, the check box is empty.

The FAT records all the clusters on the disk that contain valid data. Valid data is considered a file that you (or your applications program) record on the disk, but have not yet erased. Once you erase a file (and the term "erase" is used with specific emphasis, as we'll soon see), the space on the disk that contained the deleted file is now considered free and can be used to store a new file.

It's important to note that the FAT is not really a directory of files on the disk, but rather a scorecard of clusters that are either occupied (also called allocated) or empty, along with which clusters belong to which files.

Damage to the FAT can be disastrous; your computer won't be able to tell a full disk from an empty one, and it won't know what portion of the disk holds a particular file. Files are often stored in many clusters, and the clusters aren't always together on the disk. An error in the FAT can corrupt data retrieval because the computer may fetch only a portion of the file, and not all of it. Or worse, the computer may retrieve part of one file, and part of another, thinking both parts belong to just one file.

201

Root Directory

Every disk has a root directory, even if you don't use subdirectories. The root directory contains a list of all the files and subdirectories contained within the disk. (From the root directory, subdirectories are treated like files.) Damage to the root directory generally means that one or more of the files or subdirectories on your disk may be inaccessible.

The root directory plays an important role when formatting a hard disk using the DOS FORMAT command. Because reformatting the entire disk can consume a lot of time, DOS takes a shortcut and simply erases the file and subdirectory names in the root directory. The actual files and subdirectories remain. PC Tools uses this method to its advantage when reclaiming a hard disk you've accidentally reformatted.

Data Area

The actual files—whether they are contained in subdirectories or not—are placed in the data area of the disk. Each file consumes a specific amount of the data area, as dictated by the size of the file and the cluster size of the disk.

Files larger than the cluster size are distributed among two or more clusters. As illustrated in Figure 8-3, these clusters may not always be together (contiguous) on the disk. In fact, depending on how often you erase and add data, files may be strewn all over the disk. PC Tools, with its Compress program, allows you to rejoin all the files, thus making your computer and hard disk more efficient.

202

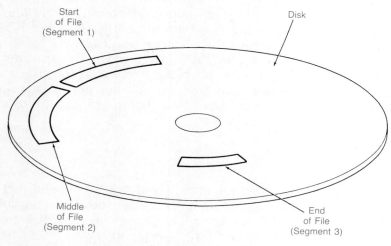

Figure 8-3. A fragmented file is one that contains many noncontiguous segments distributed over the disk.

Reclaiming Erased Files

The Undelete command, found under the Special and File menus in the PC Tools Shell program, lets you restore files that you accidentally erase from your disks.

Suppose, for example, that you're using WordStar and you've just finished a report on departmental acquisitions. You name the file REPORT.DOC. As you write, WordStar keeps an earlier version of the file as a backup, in case something happens to the original. The program automatically names this file REPORT.BAK.

After the report is finished and spell-checked, you decide to delete the backup file to clean up your work disk. But instead of entering REPORT.BAK you mistakenly type REPORT.DOC (you've been writing that file name all day long). Normally, a mistake like this means you'll have to retype or reedit at least some of the document, requiring a great deal of extra effort on your part. With Undelete, you can use PC Tools quickly to select the erased file and restore it to its original form.

Another example: You've decided to do some house cleaning on your computer hard disk drive. Several subdirectories are no longer needed, and you clear them out by typing

ERASE *.*

All goes well—until you accidentally move to the wrong directory and erase all the files in it. Again, PC Tools comes to the rescue. With PC Tools, you quickly select all the deleted files. Then, with the Undelete command you bring them all back.

How Undelete Works

Many PC users are surprised to learn that erasing a file from a hard or floppy disk doesn't actually obliterate the data. Rather, it deletes the file entry in the disk directory and tells DOS that the space previously occupied by the file is now available for use again. This information is stored in the directory and FAT of the disk.

When DOS deletes a file entry, it marks it as erased (actually, unallocated) and removes the first letter of the file name. For example, if the file name was REPORT.DOC, when erased the file becomes EPORT.DOC.

During the Undelete process, PC Tools selects those files that have been recently deleted. You select the file you want to recover, and add the missing letter at the beginning of the file name; PC Tools takes care of the rest.

For best results, you should recover accidentally lost files immediately after erasing them. That way, there's no chance that DOS will refill the space on the disk with new data. If you delete a file, then go on and store several others, there's a good chance that DOS will fill at least some of the empty space provided by the erased file with other data. You cannot retrieve a lost file if other data has been written over it.

After pressing the file button, a message appears giving you the option of using the Delete Tracking method or the DOS directory. The following example uses the DOS Directory.

To recover an erased file:

204

1. If you haven't done so already, start Shell in the normal manner. You can recover files using Shell in stand-alone or memory-resident mode.
2. Choose the Undelete files command from the Special menu.
3. Select the drive and/or directory that contains the lost file, and press Continue to go on.
4. Shell asks if you want to recover a lost file or subdirectory. (It also asks if you want to attempt to create a file using whatever remaining data is on the disk; more about this option later.) In most instances, you'll press the File button to reclaim a lost file.
5. As illustrated in Figure 8-4, Shell presents a list of files within the disk or directory that have been recently erased. The first letter of each file will be missing, but enough of the file name should remain to make your choice. You can also find the file you want by noting when the file was created or deleted.
6. Select the file you want.
7. Press the F5 function key for Go.
8. Type the first letter of the file name (such as R for EPORT.DOC). Press Enter twice.
9. Press either the Automatic button or the Manual button.
10. Shell will inform you if the file was recovered successfully. If it was, press the Continue button to return to Shell. If the file was not successfully undeleted, you'll have to try the manual method of recovery. See the section entitled "Manual File Recovery" below for more details.

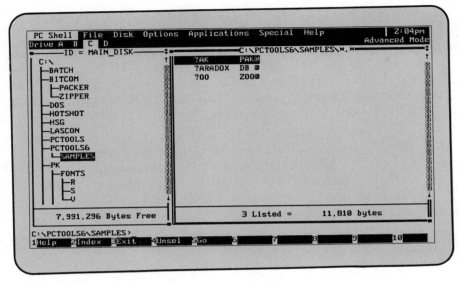

Figure 8-4. Files that can be recovered using the Undelete command (DOS Directory method).

Shell may display an asterisk (*) or at-symbol (@) after some or all of the files. These symbols tell you that some or all of the file can be recovered.

▶ The @ character after a file name means PC Tools can successfully recover the entire file automatically, requiring no further intervention on your part. If the file you want has an @ after it, press the Automatic button to recover the file.

▶ The * character means that at least some of the original file has been overwritten by new data. You will need to manually piece some or all of the file back together again. If the file you want has an * after it, press the Manual button to start recovery.

▶ No symbol means that while the old file name is still listed in the disk directory, none of its data remains. Press the Exit button to return to Shell.

Using the Delete Tracking Option

As an option, PC Tools can supplement the data stored in the disk directory. The Delete Tracking file (named PCTRACKR.DEL and stored in the root directory of the disk) stores the names of files you erase. Unlike the disk's own directory, the Delete Tracking file contains the entire file name, including the first character.

The Delete Tracking file is updated every time you erase a file, but it can hold only a certain number of entries, depending on the capacity of the disk. The number of delete file names that can be stored varies between 25 entries for a 360-kilobyte floppy diskette to up to 999 entries for a large hard disk drive.

The Delete Tracking option is activated with the Mirror program, detailed in full later in this chapter. To use the Delete Tracking option, type

MIRROR /T

at the DOS prompt. (Or better yet, include the command in your AUTOEXEC.BAT file so your computer starts Mirror for you automatically each time it is started.) You can set Delete Tracking for a particular drive and include the maximum number of erase file entries, as explained in the section entitled "Running Mirror" later in the chapter.

The Delete Tracking option allows for greater latitude when reclaiming lost files, although it won't improve your chances of recovery if the file has been overwritten with new data.

To recover an erased file with Delete Tracking:

1. If you haven't done so already, start Shell in the normal manner. You can recover files using Shell in stand-alone or memory-resident mode.
2. Choose the Undelete Files command from the Special menu.
3. Select the drive and/or directory that contains the lost file, and press Continue to go on.
4. Shell asks if you want to recover a lost file or subdirectory. To undelete a file, press the File button.
5. Indicate that you want to use the entries stored in the Delete Tracking file by pressing the Del Track button, as depicted in Figure 8-5.

6. Shell presents a list of files within the disk or directory that have been erased recently. Select the file you want.

7. Press G for Go.

8. Shell will inform you if the file was recovered successfully. If it was, press the Continue button to go to the next file or return to Shell. If the file was not successfully undeleted, you'll have to try the manual method of recovery. See the section entitled "Manual File Recovery" below for more details.

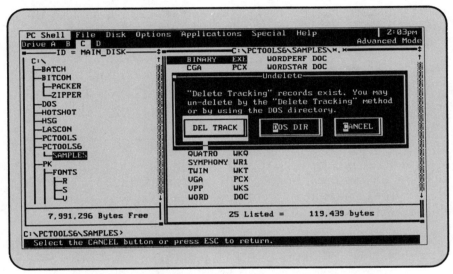

207

Figure 8-5. The Undelete dialog box lets you select between the Delete Tracking (optional) method or the DOS Directory (standard) method.

As with file recovery using the DOS directory, Shell may display an * or @ character after some or all of the files.

▶ The @ character after a file name means PC Tools can successfully recover the entire file using the Delete Tracking option. If the file lacks the @ character, you can't use the Delete Tracking option.

▶ The * character means that at least some of the original file has been overwritten by new data.

▶ No symbol means that while the old file name is still listed in the disk directory, none of its data remains. Press the Exit button to return to Shell.

Manual File Recovery

Shell provides some advanced tools for reconstructing files that can't be undeleted automatically. Manual file recovery is most often used when a file has been erased and partially overwritten by new data. But it can also be used to resuscitate a file that's been corrupted by a computer or disk error.

> ► **Tip:** If you are recovering a file from a floppy diskette, make a backup of the original diskette first. Use the DOS DISKCOPY command or the Copy Disk command in PC Tools Shell. (Don't use the DOS COPY command, as this copies only valid files and not the entire contents of the disk.) Work with the copy and not the original, in case things get messed up. If you're recovering a file from a hard disk and you're not absolutely sure what you're doing, back up the drive first.

208

Manual recovery is intended primarily for straight ASCII documents and binary text documents, and not binary-only files. Recall from Chapter 4, "Managing Files with Shell," the differences between these three:

► ASCII documents contain just text and no special control characters. A text-only file (created by a word processor or communications program) is an ASCII document.

► Binary text documents contain mostly text, but can also include special control characters. Most word processing programs, including WordStar and WordPerfect, and some electronic spreadsheet programs produce binary text files as their main document type.

► Binary-only files contain little, if any, text. All you see when looking at a binary-only file is a collection of weird control characters. Applications programs are examples of binary-only files.

Manual file recovery requires you to look for clusters on your disk and indicate the data you think goes with the file you're trying to restore. Obviously, you need to be able to identify the data to piece the file back together. You can easily recognize portions of an ASCII and binary text document because you can read along with it. Binary-only files provide no coherency.

To reclaim a file using the manual recovery method, follow the same basic steps outlined above for automatic recovery, except press the Manual button instead of the Automatic button. Choosing manual file recovery presents the editing screen shown in Figure 8-6. Shell displays, in order, the sectors and clusters that probably contain the data you need to complete the file.

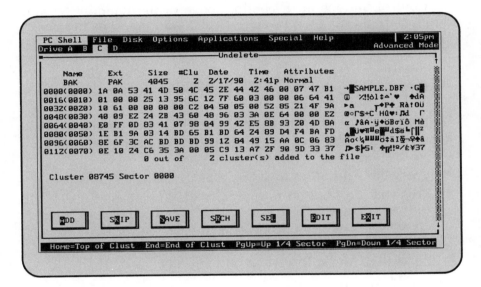

Figure 8-6. The manual file recovery editing screen.

If you've never seen hexadecimal data before, the window contents can look mighty peculiar.

▶ The name of the file, along with further information about the file (such as size, total number of clusters, and attributes) is displayed along the top of the window.

▶ The numbers on the far left of the box indicate the byte number: starting at 0000 in hex, or (0000) in decimal.

▶ The characters in the middle of the window are the hexadecimal form of the data. Hexadecimal notation is base-16; the first six letters of the alphabet provide the extra "digits" for the counting scheme.

▶ The characters on the left of the window are the decimal form of the data. Here, the data is in an ASCII form, but all 254 printable ASCII characters may be used.

▶ The currently displayed cluster and sector are provided near the bottom of the screen.

Control buttons at the bottom edge of the window let you add clusters or move on to more likely candidates, as desired.

210

▶ Press the *Add* button to add the currently selected cluster to the file.

▶ Press the *Skip* button to bypass the selected cluster, without adding it to the file.

▶ Press the *Save* button to save the file under reconstruction.

▶ Press the *Srch* button to search for additional clusters to add to the file.

▶ Press the *Sel* button to select a new cluster number.

▶ Press the *Edit* button to reorder added clusters to a deleted file (see Figure 8-7). You can Move a cluster before or after another cluster. You can also Remove a cluster if you find it doesn't fit the file.

▶ Press the *Exit* button when you're done.

After you've recovered the file, you should try it out to make sure everything fits properly. If the file contained only ASCII text, make sure there are no breaks or obvious defects in the progression of the data. If the document is a binary text file, pay particular attention to the words as well as the formatting and layout.

The total number of clusters needed to complete the file is listed under the hexadecimal display. Use this information to help determine if a file you're piecing together has all its component parts.

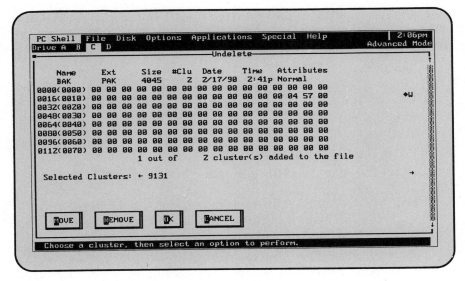

Figure 8-7. Shell allows you to move and remove clusters within a file.

211

> ▶ **Tip:** Binary text files (created with a program like WordStar or WordPerfect) often include special header and trailer sections that provide certain information about the file. Without the header and trailer, the applications program will likely reject the file, even if the remainder of data from the file is intact. When recovering files, pay special attention to the very beginning and end of the file, as these play a pivotal role in your success at reconstituting the file. Note that in some documents, the header contains a code for the length of the file. This code helps the program determine the amount of RAM it should provide to load the complete document. Further data corruption could occur if the code and actual length of the file don't match.

Recreating a Lost File

The name of the erased file must be in the directory before you can undelete it. But there are times when the directory entry for a file is replaced by a new file, but the data for the old file still remains on the disk. As a last ditch effort, you can scour the disk in search of the lost data, and use the Undelete Create command to piece the file back together.

To recreate a file:

1. Choose the Undelete command from the Special menu.
2. Select the disk and/or directory that contains the erased file, and press the Continue button.
3. Press the Create button in the dialog box that appears.
4. Provide a name for the file, and press the Create button.

Follow the steps outlined above in the section entitled "Manual File Recovery" on how to locate lost portions of the file and piece it back together again.

As with manual file recovery, the create file method is best suited for ASCII text and binary text documents only. You cannot reliably recreate a binary-only file.

212

Mapping the Disk

Two additional Shell commands—File Map and Disk Map—provide extra flexibility when recovering lost files and even the disk itself.

The File Map command in the Special menu lets you visually check the placement of a file on the surface of the diskette. As shown in Figure 8-8, clusters occupied by the selected file are indicated with a dotted square. You can readily see if the file is scattered over the disk in several noncontiguous clusters. Shell provides some important information about the file at the top of the disk display area, including the first cluster occupied by the file.

Each block on the grid contains a special symbol that tells you the status of the clusters:

▶ *Shaded square*—The cluster is unused and available for file storage.
▶ *Dotted square*—Allocated cluster; belongs to a file.
▶ *B*—Boot record.
▶ *F*—File allocation table.

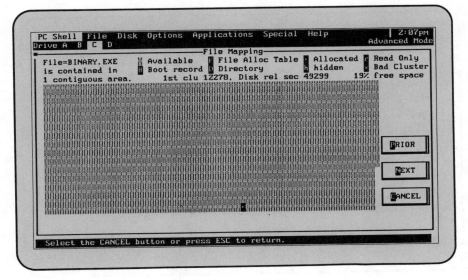

Figure 8-8. The File Mapping display shows the relative position of a file on the disk.

▶ *D*—Root directory.
▶ *h*—Hidden file.
▶ *r*—Read-only file.
▶ *x*—Cluster marked as bad.

Press the Next or Prior buttons to select different files in the disk or directory. When you are done, press the Cancel key to return to Shell.

The Disk Map command in the Special menu shows you the placement of all of the files and their clusters. The Disk Mapping display, illustrated in Figure 8-9, is best used as a "snapshot" of the contents of a floppy or hard disk. You can easily see how much empty space is left on the disk, gaps of unallocated clusters within the disk. A disk with many unallocated clusters is highly "fragmented" and can benefit from the PC Tools Compress program, detailed fully in Chapter 9, "Maintaining Your Hard Disk Drive."

Press the Exit key when you're done looking at the disk map.

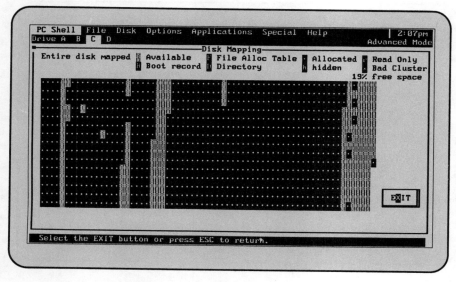

Figure 8-9. The Disk Mapping display shows the arrangement of all files on the disk.

214

Rebuilding Hard Disk Drive Directories

Catastrophe strikes! You turn on your computer one day and find that an unexplained glitch has ruined your hard disk. Files that were there yesterday seem permanently lost. Your directories, your files—everything is gone.

Regular backups are your best protection against calamities such as this. But we're humans after all, and despite the importance of hard disk backups, we occasionally forget to do it. PC Tools equips you with several life-saving devices for recovering disks that have been accidentally damaged or even purposely reformatted. PC Tools makes the process of reclaiming lost disks almost automatic. You issue the command, and PC Tools takes care of the rest.

Central to PC Tool's disk recovery are the Mirror and Rebuild programs, included in the PC Tools diskettes. Mirror is intended to make an extra copy of the all-important file allocation table, root directory, and boot record of the disk and store them safely out of the way of most of the other data on the disk. The Rebuild program literally rebuilds the file allocation table and root directory using the data stored in the Mirror file.

The main purpose of the Mirror and Rebuild duo is to undo an accidental ERASE *.*, RECOVER, or FORMAT command. Suppose you or someone else in your office intended to format a new floppy diskette, but instead wound up reformatting the hard disk. Normally, it would mean most or all of the data on the hard disk is lost. But with Rebuild, the original file allocation table and root directory (the parts erased during a hard disk format) are replaced with backup copies.

> ⊘ **Caution:** Do not use the Rebuild program until you absolutely need it. Using it when it's not required may cause data loss, depending on the last time the Mirror program was run. As Rebuild depends on the contents of the Mirror backup file to reconstruct the contents of the hard disk, an old backup means you won't regain your most recent work.

215

Running Mirror

Each time the Mirror program is run, it samples the contents of the file allocation table, root directory, and boot record of your hard disk. (You can also use Mirror on floppy disk drives; the technique is the same.) Mirror is not a memory-resident program. Once you run it, it creates the backup file of the FAT, root directory, and boot record and returns control to your computer.

Mirror optionally creates a separate Delete Tracking file, as explained earlier in this chapter. The purpose of the Delete Tracking file is to maintain a list of the files most recently deleted from the disk. When the Delete Tracking option is enabled, a small memory-resident program is installed in your computer's memory. Should you find that the Delete Tracking option is upsetting the operation of other memory-resident programs in your computer, or even your main applications, turn the option off. You should, however, continue to use Mirror.

You can run Mirror manually or automatically each time your computer starts. To run it manually, type

```
MIRROR
```

at the DOS prompt. Mirror automatically assumes you want to take a snapshot of the FAT, root directory, and boot record of the same disk that contains the Mirror program. If you want to take a snapshot of another disk, type

```
MIRROR d:
```

where d: is another drive in your computer.

As mentioned earlier in this chapter, to turn on the Delete Tracking option, enter

```
MIRROR /T
```

216

at the DOS prompt. Normally, Mirror retains the name of a set number of files, depending on the capacity of the media, as indicated in Table 8-1. You can optionally specify the maximum number of entries with the /T-nnn parameter. Replace nnn with the maximum number of entries you want to store.

Table 8-1. Delete Tracking File Size and Entries.

Disk Size	File Size	Number of Entries
Floppy Disks		
360K	5K	25
720K	9K	50
1.2M	14K	75
1.44M	14K	75
Hard Disks		
20M	18K	101
32M	36K	202
Over 32M	55K	303

You can combine parameters as required; for example:

```
MIRROR A: B: C: /TC:256
```

takes individual snapshots of drives A, B, and C and installs the Delete Tracking option for drive C using a maximum of 256 entries.

To run Mirror automatically when you start the computer, merely add the MIRROR command to your AUTOEXEC.BAT file. The PC Tools manual suggests you run Mirror after you've loaded the mouse drivers and print spooler (if any) but before you install any other memory-resident programs, including PC Tools Shell and Desktop.

At the very least, you should run Mirror once a day. If you've done a lot of work during a particular day, you may want to stop for a moment and reset your computer. That will rerun Mirror and update the backup file.

Running Rebuild

217

Remember: Use Rebuild only when you need it. Otherwise, you could loose important data.

To run rebuild, type

```
REBUILD X:
```

at the DOS prompt (where X is the drive you want to recon-struct, such as C or D). Rebuild will display the time and date Mirror was run the last time. Rebuild asks if you want to use this latest copy of the Mirror backup file. Answer Yes or No accord-ingly. If you answer No, Rebuild will look for an older copy of the Mirror backup file. (You'd want to use the older copy if you've run Mirror since a serious hard disk crash.)

> ▶ **Tip:** If your computer can't boot from the hard disk, start Rebuild from a floppy diskette using the PC Tools distribution disks. (Or better yet, use a copy of the original distribution disk.) If you're using 5 1/4-inch disks, the Rebuild program is on Disk 4. If you're using 3 1/2-inch disks, Rebuild is on Disk 2.

Verifying Files and Disks

Never assume that once you use PC Tools to recover a file or disk the data is returned to its original form. If you've undeleted an erased file, inspect it with Shell's View command or—if the file is a program document—use the application that created it.

Disks, especially hard disks, are harder to check. At a minimum, you should check the disk with the DOS CHKDSK command. This command will identify a possible problem with the file allocation table. For best results, use the /V parameter with CHKDSK as follows:

```
CHKDSK /V
```

218   Each file on your hard disk will be scanned in turn. You'll see the subdirectories and files whiz by on your screen.

The PC Tools Shell program also provides useful file and disk verification commands. The Verify File command in the File menu verifies individual files you have selected. The Verify Disk command in the Disk menu checks the integrity of the entire disk. Refer to Chapters 4 and 5, respectively, for more information on using the Verify File and Verify Disk commands.

If your hard disk crashed unexpectedly, taking one or more files with it, the formatting of the disk could be impaired. The PC Tools Compress program, detailed in Chapter 9, "Maintaining Your Hard Disk Drive," will analyze the entire surface of the disk and detect any errors that may occur.

Using DiskFix

DiskFix (new to version 6.0 of PC Tools Deluxe) automatically tests for, and optionally corrects, problems on hard and floppy disks. DiskFix can repair a number of disk failures, like lost clusters, missing data, even problems in the all-important FAT and root directories. The benefit of DiskFix is that it does not require intimate knowledge of disks, DOS, or computers. With very few exceptions, the program is completely menu-driven, with English-language instructions, prompts, and warnings.

You can start DiskFix from with Shell (choose DiskFix from the Applications menu) or directly from the DOS prompt by typing

`DISKFIX`

When you run DiskFix it first checks that the critical data on your hard drive is not corrupt. It also checks that your computer and hard drive mechanism are running properly. These initial checks are necessary so that your disks are not damaged even more by improper repair. Assuming that your hard drive is able to at least limp along, DiskFix asks if you want to repair a disk now. Answer Yes to continue. Note that you can test any disk in your computer with DiskFix without actually repairing it. DiskFix always asks if you want to repair any damage it finds.

DiskFix asks which drive you want to analyze, as shown in Figure 8-10. The drives shown are all those that DiskFix could find in your computer. If a drive is missing it means that DiskFix is unaware of it, and thus cannot repair it. Highlight a drive, and press Enter.

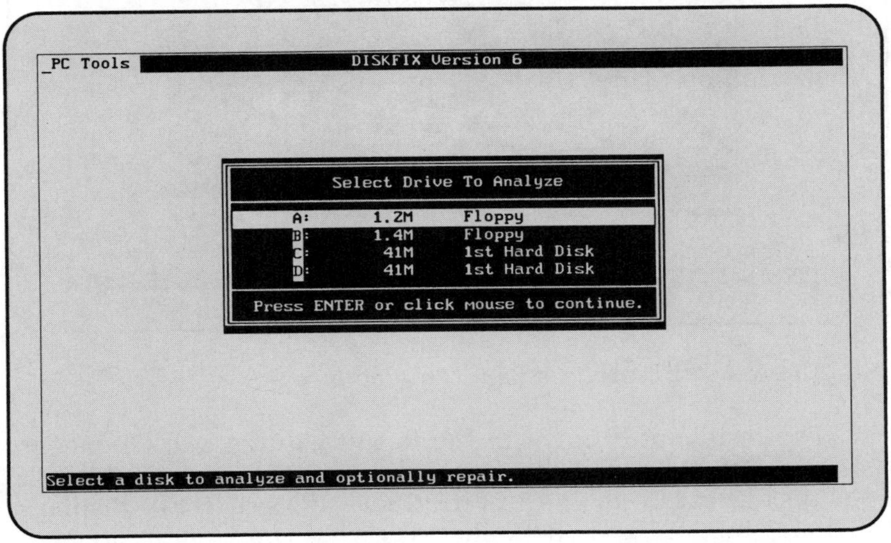

219

Figure 8-10. DiskFix Drive Analysis dialog box.

DiskFix now analyzes the drive (see Figure 8-11) and checks the:

▶ *DOS Boot Sector.*
▶ *Media Descriptors* identify the type of disk.
▶ *File Allocation Tables.*
▶ *Directory Structure.*
▶ *Cross Linked Files* (portions of data that appear to belong to more than one file).
▶ *Lost Clusters* (portions of data that don't appear to belong to a file).
▶ *Media Surface* (the general well-being of the disk).

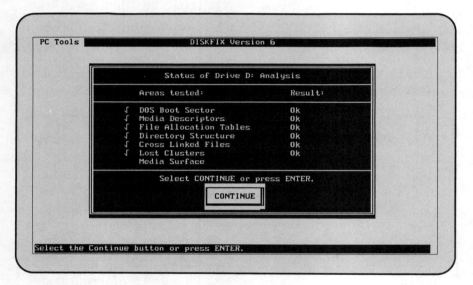

Figure 8-11. Analysis Report dialog box.

The results are shown in the Result column. An Ok means that DiskFix did not detect a problem for that examination. If your disk checks out fine in all critical areas, DiskFix displays the dialog box in Figure 8-12 and asks what you want to do next. You can:

▶ *Fix a disk* (this is really the procedure you just did).
▶ Perform a *surface scan* of the entire media surface (to look for individual media defects).

▶ *Revitalize a floppy* diskette (this reads a damaged floppy in a different manner than DOS and tries to extract data).

▶ *Exit to DOS*—or go back to Shell.

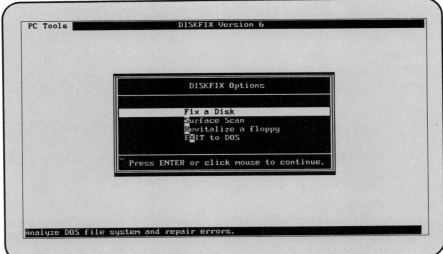

Figure 8-12.   DiskFix function menu.

221

Note that a surface scan can take a long time, depending on the size of your hard drive. All clusters of your hard drive are analyzed, not just those parts that have data. So even if your 120-megabyte hard disk drive only has 10 megabytes of data in it, DiskFix will still check all 120 megabytes of real estate.

An "ERROR" during media analysis means that DiskFix has sensed a problem, and that you'll probably want to have it corrected. DiskFix will ask if you want to correct the problem now; answer Yes or No accordingly. Important note: Answering No to certain repair questions will terminate the remainder of the analysis, as the repair tasks must be conducted in a specific sequence.

DiskFix attempts to do what it can for a damaged disk, especially for clusters that are cross-linked or lost. Occasionally, lost clusters cannot be reunited with the rest of the file, so DiskFix saves the data in a lost cluster file, in much the same way that the DOS CHKDSK program corals lost data into error files. The DiskFix lost cluster files are named PCTxxxx.FIX, where the xxxx begins at 0000 and increments by one for every separate file you have. If the data in the lost cluster file is recognizable text, you may be able to piece it back into a usable form.

Similarly, if DiskFix locates lost subdirectories, the subdirectories are placed under the root directory and given new names, using the format LOSTxxxx, such as

LOST0000

LOST0001

LOST0002

and so forth. Now that the subdirectories are reclaimed, you can look inside and retrieve important data.

If DiskFix identified a number of errors, it may be a good idea to make a special backup of your hard drive, and use the Compare feature of PC Tools Backup to make sure that the archive and hard disk data are identical. You can then reformat your hard drive, preferably using a low-level format program or a utility (such as Advanced Disk Technician or SpinRite) that rejuvenates your hard drive.

Review

This chapter detailed ways to use PC Tools to recover files and disks that have been accidentally erased or damaged. You also learned:

▶ Every disk has a boot record, even if the disk can't be used to start the computer.

▶ The file allocation table (or FAT) records the locations of files on the disk.

▶ The root directory contains a list of all the files and subdirectories contained within the disk.

▶ The PC Tools Shell Undelete command can unerase files that have been recently deleted.

▶ For best results, you should recover accidentally lost files immediately after erasing them.

▶ The Delete Tracking option stores a record of files deleted from the disk and can aid in recovering erased files.

▶ The Mirror and Rebuild programs are designed to reconstruct a hard or floppy disk.

▶ The Rebuild program should be used only when needed. Otherwise, important data could be lost.

▶ The DiskFix program can be used to reclaim damaged disks automatically.

223

Maintaining Your Hard Disk Drive

In This Chapter

225

► *Increasing hard disk efficiency*
► *Testing your disks for errors*
► *Formatting disks quickly and safely*
► *Parking your hard disk drive for safety*

Keeping your hard disk in shape is the best way to protect your valuable data. PC Tools provides numerous facilities for maintaining your hard disk drive. Most maintenance procedures take only a few moments but go a long way to extend the life of your data. This chapter provides you with a variety of techniques you can use to keep your hard disk drive in top working order. Note that many of the functions and procedures also apply to floppy diskettes. For the sake of clarity, we'll assume you're using a hard disk drive.

Hard Disk Fragmentation

Hard disk fragmentation is not dropping the drive and watching it shatter into thousands of tiny pieces. Rather, fragmentation refers to the order and continuity of the individual files on your hard disk.

Recall from Chapter 8, "Recovering Lost Files and Disks," that a disk (hard or floppy) is divided into many tracks. These tracks are further divided into sectors, which are even further divided into clusters. The smallest chunk of data that your hard disk can deal with is a cluster. Cluster size varies between drives (considering media type and capacity) but is generally 1 to 4 kilobytes in size. That is, your files are composed of many 1- to 4-kilobyte chunks, all placed strategically on the disk.

When files are fragmented, their component parts are located among two or more noncontiguous clusters on the disk. The first half of a file may occupy cluster 1000, for instance, but the second part may be located in cluster 2050. To retrieve the entire file, your hard disk must first move to cluster 1000, read the data stored there, then jump to cluster 2050.

Depending on the size of the file, it may be composed of several dozen clusters. A large database file may even be composed of several hundreds clusters. Imagine each cluster of a large file located in some distant part of the disk. Your drive must work overtime to retrieve all the parts.

226

At a minimum, file fragmentation slows down your hard disk. The actual degree of speed decrease depends on the hard disk, the data, and the amount of fragmentation, but you can expect some loss of performance. Perhaps worse is that fragmented files are harder to recover after they have been accidentally erased. Files that are contained in contiguous clusters are undeleted more reliably than those scattered over many noncontiguous clusters.

Fortunately, PC Tools provides a handy and easy-to-use program that eliminates file fragmentation. The Compress program is designed to detect and purge file fragmentation on both hard and floppy disks. You can access Compress from within Shell (as long as you've loaded Shell as a stand-alone program, and not as a memory-resident program) or directly from the DOS prompt.

Note that the PC Tools Compress program is technically considered a disk defragmentor. It is not a file compression utility that condenses data into a smaller packet. PC Tools does provide this facility with the PC Secure program, detailed in the Data Recovery DOS Shell manual that accompanies PC Tools Deluxe.

Starting Compress

Compress uses the same menu and window interface shared by all the PC Tools programs. The program includes on-line help in case you need assistance in using any of the commands. You can also start Compress using one or more command-line parameters. These parameters assist you in automating disk defragmenting, especially if you develop the habit of regularly compressing your hard disk.

You have the option of starting the Compress program from within Shell or at the DOS prompt.

To start Compress from within Shell:

1. Start Shell in the usual manner.
2. Choose Compress from the Applications menu. (The Compress program should be listed in the menu unless you've removed it.) In a few moments, Compress loads and displays the screen shown in Figure 9-1.

227

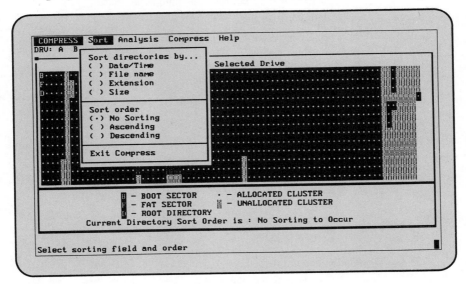

Figure 9-1. The Compress opening screen.

To start Compress from the DOS prompt:

1. If you haven't done so already, log onto your hard disk drive.

2. At the prompt, type COMPRESS and press Enter.

Table 9-1 shows the command-line parameters you can use when starting Compress. The options invoked by these parameters are detailed later in this chapter. To use one or more of these parameters, add them after the COMPRESS command at the DOS prompt. For example:

COMPRESS /SF

starts the Compress program and automatically selects the Sort by File Name option. If you want to defragment a disk other than your hard disk, add the drive letter immediately after the COMPRESS command, as in

COMPRESS A:

Table 9-1. Compress Command-Line Parameters.

Parameter	Function
Compression Technique (choose one only)	
/CU	Unfragment with minimum compression
/CF	Full compression
/CC	Full compression and clear
Ordering Options (choose one only)	
/OS	Standard ordering
/OD	DOS ordering (directories with files)
/OO	DOS ordering (subdirectory first)
/OP	Programs (.EXE and .COM) first
Sorting Options (choose one only)	
/SF	Sorts files by file name
/ST	Sorts files by time
/SE	Sorts files by extension
/SS	Sorts files by size
Sort Order Options (choose one only)	
/SA	Sorts files in ascending order
/SD	Sorts files in descending order
Additional Options	
/NM	Suppresses running Mirror after Compress is done
/BW	Suppresses color display

> 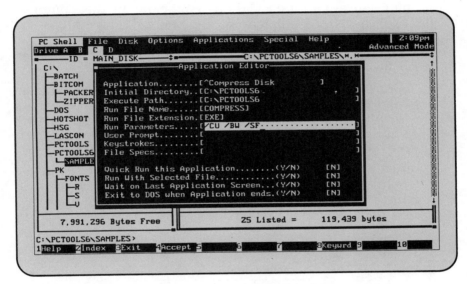 **Tip:** You can also include these command-line parameters in the Applications menu of Shell. You can edit the run-time parameters of programs listed in the Applications menu with the Application Editor window. Add those parameters you want to include, as shown in Figure 9-2. Now, whenever you run Compress, your command-line parameters are automatically included.

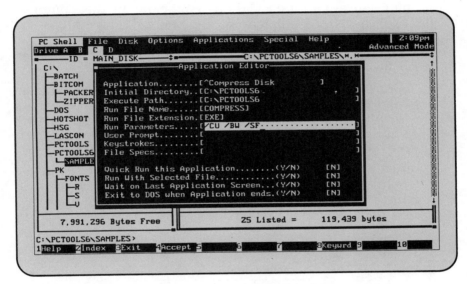

Figure 9-2. Editing the run parameters of Compress in the Shell Application Editor window.

229

Note that with the exception of the /NM and /BW parameters, you can select any option directly from within the Compress program.

Sorting and Ordering Options

For added efficiency, the PC Tools Compress program can optionally sort the files on the hard disk while it is defragmenting them. You can sort files within directories by date/time, name, extension, or size, in either ascending or descending order. To set the sort order, choose one of the options under the Sort menu. Note that you select one option in the first group of selections

(Date/Time, File name, etc.) as well as one option in the second group (either Ascending or Descending).

You can also choose no sorting, in which case Compress will replace the files on the hard disk in about the same order as it found them. Compressing with sorting off speeds up the defragmenting process a bit.

In addition to setting the File Sort option, you can select the physical ordering of the files on the disk. To set the ordering of files, choose the Ordering Options command in the Compress menu. You have three choices, as depicted in Figure 9-3.

▶ *Standard.* Places your files in no particular physical order. Compress will place the files onto the disk as it sees fit.

▶ *.COM & .EXE first.* Places executable programs at the front of the disk. If you don't add new programs to your hard disk often, this option can save some time in subsequent compresses.

▶ *DOS.* Places your files in DOS order, where all files in a directory are placed together and the subdirectory is moved toward the front of the disk. You can choose either DOS with subdirectories first or DOS with subdirectories and files held together.

230

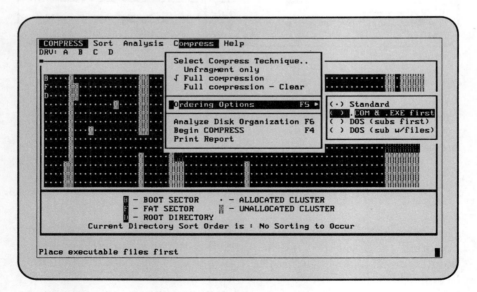

Figure 9-3. Available ordering options within Compress.

Setting the Compression Technique

The compression technique tells Compress the depth of defragmentation you wish. All three techniques defragment the files on the disk; the options differ in extra enhancements provided during the defragmentation process.

To select the compression technique, choose one of the following options in the Compress menu.

▶ *Unfragment only.* Defragments the files, but doesn't attempt to consolidate the empty clusters toward the end of the disk. Use this option when you're short on time. Note that interleaving empty and allocated clusters promotes fragmentation as you add more files; DOS fills the first unallocated clusters it finds, going toward the end of the disk only as the rest gets filled up.

▶ *Full compression.* Unfragments files, and moves the unallocated clusters toward the end of the disk, as shown in Figure 9-4.

▶ *Full compression—Clear.* Same as Full compression, but also erases all data in the unused sectors. Use this option if you work with restricted or classified data and want to prevent prying eyes from looking at what you've been up to. (Note: You can achieve an even higher degree of privacy by using the PC Secure program.)

231

Testing for Fragmentation

PC Tools Compress runs a quick test to see if defragmenting is advisable. If you think that the files in your disk are fragmented, choose the Disk analysis command from the Analysis menu. As shown in Figure 9-5, Compress will report the number of allocated and unallocated clusters, the number of bad clusters (as marked in the disk's file allocation table), and other technical data. In almost every case, Compress will detect at least some fragmentation and encourage you to complete the Compress option.

You can obtain more concrete information on which files on the disk are fragmented using the File analysis command, also found in the Analysis menu. As shown in Figure 9-6, The File analysis command displays:

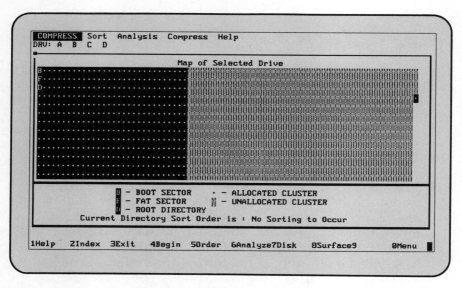

232

Figure 9-4. A disk with all unallocated clusters placed at the end of the disk (the few allocated clusters are PC Tools Mirror files).

► The files in the currently selected directory (as well as any subdirectories located within the directory).
► The number of clusters occupied by each file.
► The number of pieces each file is broken into (areas).
► The percent of fragmentation of each file.

If any file is shown as located in more than one area, it's fragmented. You can view other subdirectories by choosing one of the buttons located along the bottom of the File Analysis window.

Problems in the File Allocation Table

PC Tools Compress checks the integrity of the file allocation table while analyzing the disk. If the program detects a mismatch in the file allocation table (one or more files are allocated to the same clusters or one or more clusters previously allocated clusters are now mysteriously detached from a file, for example), it will warn you to use the DiskFix program before running Compress.

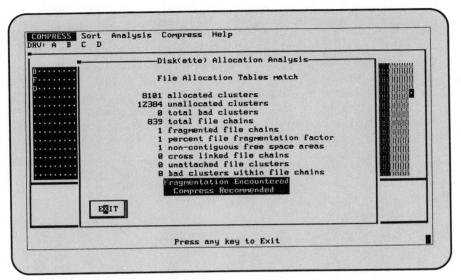

Figure 9-5. *The result of a Disk Allocation Analysis test.*

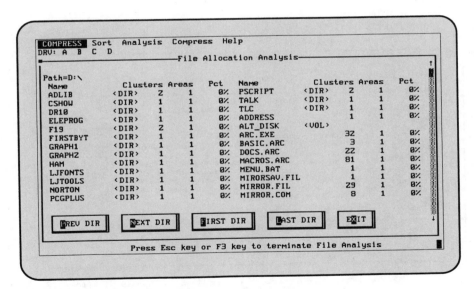

Figure 9-6. *The result of a File Allocation Analysis test.*

Running Compress

Once you've selected those options you want to use, you're ready to run Compress and defragment the files on your hard disk.

> ▶ **Tip:** Before running Compress you should disable or unload all memory-resident programs (with the exception of PC Cache). Memory-resident programs could interfere with the proper operation of Compress and actually cause considerable data corruption. To really play it safe, back up your hard disk before running Compress. If anything should happen to the data, you can restore it using the previously backed up version.

Q Running Compress

1. Choose the Begin COMPRESS command from the Compress menu.

   Invokes Compress command.

2. Read the warning that appears (as shown in Figure 9-7), and press Continue or Exit, as desired.

   Continue starts Compress; Exit takes you back to Shell.

234

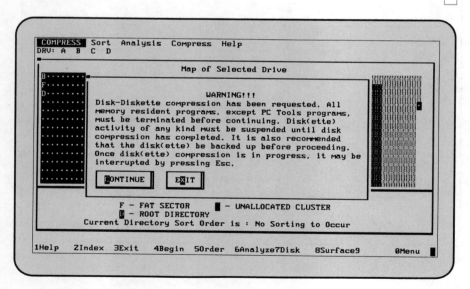

Figure 9-7. This warning dialog box appears each time you compress a disk.

Compress now proceeds to examine your hard disk and defragment its files. You can safely interrupt the Compress option at any time by pressing the Escape key. PC Tools Compress will finish shuffling the cluster it's currently working on, then ask if you want to cancel. Answer accordingly.

When the defragmenting process is complete, Compress asks if you want to exit or run the Mirror program. Since you've moved the files on the disk, your old Mirror backup file is no longer valid, and it should not be used. You are advised to run Mirror at this time, then restart your computer.

Printing a Compression Report

If you feel like you need a printed report of the defragmenting process and what it did to your files, choose the Print Report command from the Compress menu before starting Compress. Select the destination of the report: printer (connected to LPT1:) or a disk file. When choosing a disk file, Compress automatically names it COMPRESS.PRT.

235

Analyzing and Verifying Your Disks

Even if you're not from Missouri, you'll want to periodically prove to yourself that your hard disk and its files are in good operating condition. PC Tools offers some rudimentary disk-checking capabilities that can spot clusters that have gone bad. (Unlike other programs, such as Disk Technician or Spinrite, PC Tools does not perform a "crystal ball" check to find weak clusters that may fail in the near future.)

Disk analysis is best used to pinpoint clusters on a hard disk drive that have gone bad since you originally formatted the disk. If a bad cluster belongs to a file, PC Tools will attempt to retrieve the entire file and move it to a safer place on the disk, then mark the cluster as bad in the file allocation table. If the cluster is unallocated, PC Tools will lock it out against future use.

The main PC Tools facilities for checking the disk are the DiskFix program and the Surface analysis command in the Compress program.

Here's how to use the Surface analysis command.

1. If you haven't done so already, start the Compress program. There's no need to select any of the optional parameters unless you plan on defragmenting the files after you analyze the disk.

2. Choose the Surface analysis command from the Analysis menu.

3. Indicate the number of disk passes you want (one is the default), and press the OK button. Or press the Continuous button for an endless surface analysis. (The analysis will stop when you press the Escape key.)

4. Indicate where you want the exception report sent. (The exception report includes any errors found by the Compress program.) Choose Printer, Disk, or No Report, as desired. The No Report option is sufficient if you plan on staying at your computer during the analysis.

236

PC Tools Compress will now check each cluster on the disk several times to determine if it's good or bad.

> ▶ **Tip:** A surface analysis of an average 32-megabyte hard disk drive attached to an AT-class computer can take up to several hours (faster drives on faster computers take less time). You'll probably not want to sit at your computer during the whole test, but if you're away, you may miss some of the error messages that occur. When you can't stay to watch the surface analysis in person, ask Compress to provide a report. The Disk option saves a report on a drive other than the one being checked. (If you're checking drive C, indicate drive A or B for the report; be sure to load a diskette in the drive to store the report.) After the surface analysis is complete, view the report using PC Tools Shell, the Notepads word processor in the PC Tools Desktop desk accessory program, or your favorite stand-alone word processing program.

During the surface analysis, Compress uses the following codes to indicate the status of the clusters on the disk:

▶ *B*—Boot sector.

▶ *F*—FAT sector.

▶ *D*—Root directory.

▶ *X*—Bad cluster.

▶ *Dotted square*—Allocated cluster.

▶ *Shaded square*—Unallocated cluster.

▶ ***—Unreadable cluster.

Every disk has a boot record, file allocation table, and root directory. Blank portions of the disk are indicated by a shaded square; occupied portions, by a dotted square. Clusters that have already been marked as bad in the file allocation directory are marked X. When PC Tools Compress finds a cluster it can't read, the program displays it with an asterisk. Compress then marks the cluster as bad (and indicates it with an X), so it can't be used by DOS again.

Disks that reveal a number of bad clusters, as shown in Figure 9-8, indicate a catastrophic hard disk crash or partial erasure. If you're testing a hard disk, you should make a backup of the files that remain and reformat it completely. If you're testing a floppy diskette, copy those files that are still intact and throw the disk out.

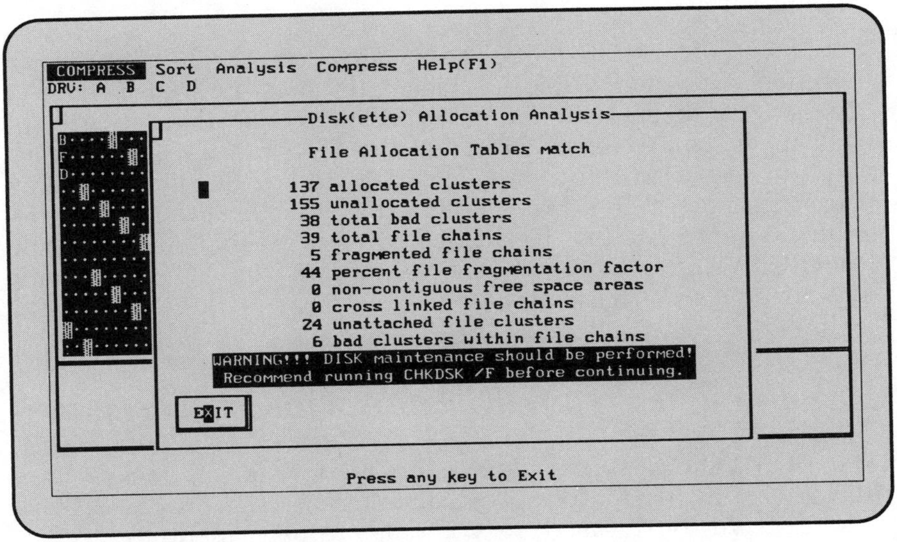

237

Figure 9-8. Analysis report of a severely damaged disk.

The DiskFix Program

PC Tools also comes with a handy disk diagnosis and repair program called DiskFix (DISKFIX.EXE). Start this program from within Shell, by using the Applications menu, or from the DOS prompt directly. Refer to Chapter 8, "Recovering Lost Files and Disks," for more information on using DiskFix. Note that DiskFix is a new utility starting with version 6.0 of PC Tools Deluxe.

Using PC Format

238

PC Tools comes with a replacement program for the DOS FORMAT command. The PC Tools Format program, called PC Format (and named PCFORMAT.COM on the PC Tools diskettes), does the same basic function as its DOS counterpart, but it also helps guard against accidental formatting of hard disks. PC Format also prevents complete data loss when reformatting a previously used floppy diskette.

If you've installed PC Tools using the PCSETUP program included with the PC Tools package, the existing DOS FORMAT program has been renamed FORMAT!.COM so that it won't be used when you enter FORMAT at the DOS prompt (conversely, you can still use it by entering FORMAT!). PCSETUP adds a batch file named FORMAT.BAT that starts the PC Format program. When installed by PCSETUP, both the batch file and PCFORMAT.COM program are located in the PCTOOLS subdirectory on your hard disk.

Formatting a Floppy Diskette with PC Format

The DOS FORMAT command completely fills all tracks of the diskette with a string of special blank characters. If the diskette has been previously used, its contents are permanently erased.

Conversely, the PC Format program is intelligent enough to know when a floppy diskette has already been used. If the diskette has never been used (it's unformatted), PC Format initializes it in the same manner as the DOS FORMAT program. But if the diskette has been used before and is already initialized, PC Format will leave the actual data intact but will clear the entries in the file allocation table, as well as delete the first character of all files in the root directory.

Note that this is the same operation performed by the DOS FORMAT command when formatting a hard disk. As you know by now, since the actual data of the diskette is still intact, it's possible to recover it in case you actually format the disk.

You can access PC Format from within the PC Tools Shell program (as long as Shell has been loaded in stand-alone mode and not in memory-resident mode) or directly from the DOS prompt.

Ⓠ Running PC Format from Shell

1. If you haven't done so already, load Shell in the usual manner. (Don't load it as memory-resident.)

2. Choose PC Format from the Applications menu. PC Format now loads, assuming you want to format a diskette in drive A. If you are formatting a diskette other than in drive A, you'll need to run PC Format manually using Shell's Run command or run it from the DOS prompt.

Starts PC Format, and formats the disk in the drive you've specified.

239

Ⓠ Running PC Format from the DOS Prompt

1. If you haven't done so already, log onto the directory that contains the PCFORMAT.COM program.

2. At the DOS prompt, type FORMAT or PCFORMAT, and indicate the drive you wish to format, such as FORMAT B:.

Runs PC Format, and formats the diskette in the drive you've specified.

PC Format asks you to insert the diskette you want to format in the drive and press any key to continue. If you decide you don't want to format a disk at this time, press the Escape key or Ctrl-C to exit.

PC Format supports a number of optional command-line parameters. Most of these don't need to be used but are handy to have if you want to control the formatting process. The most common are:

240

▶ *x*—Indicates the drive you want to format. Substitute x with a valid drive letter, such as A, B, or C.

▶ */1*—Formats the disk single-sided.

▶ */4*—Formats a 360- or 180-kilobyte diskette in a 1.2-megabyte floppy disk drive.

▶ */8*—Formats the disk with 8 sectors per track, instead of the usual 9 (for 360-kilobyte diskettes) or 15 (for 1.2-megabyte diskettes).

▶ */F*—Specifies a "null" format. PC Format reads the data on each track, formats each track, then rewrites the data. This provides a "renewal" of formatting when using previously used diskettes.

▶ */F:nnn*—Formats the disk with a specific capacity. Valid numbers are 160, 180, 320, 360, 720, 1200, and 1440.

▶ */N:nn*—Formats the diskette with a specified number of secors per track. It is always used with the /T parameter.

▶ */P*—Prints format information to LPT1 printer port.

▶ */Q*—Quickly reformats an already formatted disk. This erases the directory and FAT from the diskette, but doesn't check its integrity.

▶ */R*—Reformats and rewrites every track, but leaves the file allocation table, root directory, and data intact. This option also requires the /4, /8, or /F:nnn parameters.

▶ */S*—Formats the diskette and copies the system files to it. This step is necessary if you want to make a bootable disk. (To make the diskette bootable, copy the COMMAND.COM file to it.)

▶ */T:nn*—Specifies the number of tracks to format. It is always used with the /N parameter.

▶ */V*—Indicates you want to provide a label to the diskette when formatting is complete. Provide the name when requested. Note: You can also add disk (or volume) names to diskettes using Shell.

▶ */DESTROY*—Formats the disk and erases it (same as a DOS format).

▶ */TEST*—Simulates a format without actually formatting the diskette.

▶ **Tip:** Use the /R command-line parameter to rejuvenate a previously formatted diskette that contains data you want to keep. The /R parameter reformats and rewrites every sector on the disk, including the boot record, file allocation table, and root directory. If any sectors on the disk are found bad or marginal, data is moved (if possible) to another area of the disk.

241

Formatting a Hard Disk with PC Format

PC Format is not strictly required when formatting a hard disk drive, but you can use it for the task just the same. Command-line parameters you can use are:

▶ *x*—Indicates the drive you want to format. Substitute x with a valid drive letter, such as C or D.

▶ */S*—Formats the disk and copies the system files. This step is necessary if you want to be able to start the computer from the hard disk. In addition to the system files, you'll also need to copy the COMMAND.COM file to the hard disk drive as well.

▶ */V*—Indicates you want to provide a label to the hard disk when formatting is complete. It provides the name when requested.

Disk Caching

The dictionary defines the word "cache" as "a hiding place for storing provisions and other necessities." In computer terms, a cache is a portion of random access memory (RAM) set aside for storing bits of data.

The most common form of cache is disk caching, where commonly used data from the disk is temporarily stored in memory. By keeping the information in fast RAM instead of fetching it from the disk every time it's needed, many operations go much faster. Depending on the amount of memory set aside for the cache, you can practically store entire programs in memory. Your work will go faster because your computer won't have to access the disk so much.

242

If you have a late model AT-, 386, or 486 class PC or clone, it probably already has a caching program. The caching program included with PC Tools is compatible with almost every PC compatible, and it is designed to be safely used with the rest of the PC Tools cadre, including Compress, PC Format, Shell, and Desktop. The PC Tools caching program, called PC Cache, also provides additional features that you may not find in similar caching utilities, including the ability to use regular, expanded, or extended memory.

⊘ **Caution:** If you're already using a caching program with your computer, you must disable it before installing PC Cache. Under no circumstances should you run two caching programs at the same time. It may cause serious data loss.

Using PC Cache

PC Cache is straightforward. Because it's a memory-resident program, you'll probably want to load it when your computer is first started, so you should include the PC Cache command in your AUTOEXEC.BAT file. Simply add the following line in the AUTO-EXEC.BAT file, and PC Cache will be activated the next time you start or reset your computer:

```
PC-CACHE
```

> ▶ **Tip:** If you installed PC Tools using the PCSETUP auto-
> mated installer program, PC Cache may already be
> included in your AUTOEXEC.BAT file. Check first using
> Shell's View command.

Entering the name of the PC Cache program alone installs PC Cache with its defaults. This enables caching on all available drives and assigns 64 kilobytes of base RAM to caching.

If this arrangement is not satisfactory to you, you can include command-line parameters. The most common are shown in Table 9-2.

Table 9-2. PC Cache Optional Command-Line Parameters.

Parameter	Function
/ Ix	Ignores (does not enable) the indicated drive. Substitute the x for a valid drive letter, such as / IA or / IB. You can use the / I parameter as many times as you need to ignore multiple drives.
/ SIZE = nnnK	Sets the amount of base memory for use by PC Cache. The default is 64 kilobytes; the maximum is 512 kilobytes.
/ SIZEXP = nnnK	Sets the amount of expanded memory for use by PC Cache.
/ SIZEXT = nnnK	Sets the amount of extended memory for use by PC Cache.
/ EXTSTART = nnnnK	Specifies the starting address of the cache in extended memory. The EXTSTART number must be greater than 1024. Use this option with care.
/ FLUSH	Empties the cache.
/ INFO	Displays a table of available drives and their sizes, and the type and size of the cache. Use this parameter before you install PC Cache.

continued

Table 9-2. *(continued)*

Parameter	Function
/ MAX = nn	Specifies the maximum number of sectors that can be saved in the cache during a single read request. Select a low number to optimize PC Cache for use with large applications. The default is 4.
/ MEASURES	Displays the relative performance and speed improvements provided by PC Cache.
/ PARAM	Displays the parameters of PC Cache currently in effect.
/ PARAM*	Displays memory disk use. Extended parameter display showing available expanded memory, number of disk drives and their sizes, and how extended memory is allocated (see Figure 9-9).
/ QUIET	Disables the sign-on display when PC Cache first starts.
/ UNLOAD	Clears the cache, and unloads PC Cache from memory.
/ WRITE = nn	Controls the time delay before write operations are sent to the disk. Enter a number from 1 to 14; the higher the number, the longer the delay. Use this option with care.
/ ?	Displays help on PC Cache parameters.

244

Here are some examples of using PC Cache with some of the more common command-line parameters:

▶ PC-CACHE / IA / IB—Starts PC Cache and ignores (disables from cache) both drives A and B.

▶ PC-CACHE / SIZE = 128K—Starts PC Cache and allocates 128 kilobytes of base memory for caching.

▶ PC-CACHE / IA / IB / SIZEXP = 512K—Starts PC Cache, ignores (disables from cache) both drives A and B, and allocates 512 kilobytes of expanded memory for caching.

```
C:\PCTOOLS6>pc-cache
  PC-CACHE, Version 6
  Unauthorized duplication prohibited
  PC-CACHE has been set up as follows:
        Perform batch copies to/from cache
        Read a maximum of   4 sectors ahead
        Write optimize set to   1 second(s).
        256 K Extended memory cache at   1024K has been set up as follows:

                        Conventional        Extended
        Dos/Resident        198K              832K
        PC-CACHE             10K              256K
        Available           432K              192K
        Total               640K             1280K

  PC-CACHE program successfully installed.
  Specify /? for information on parameters

C:\PCTOOLS6>_
```

Figure 9-9. A sample report provided with the /PARAM*
PC Cache parameter.

Testing the Performance of PC Cache

PC Cache provides a handy indicator for testing its performance. For a cache utility, performance is rated in the number of "transfers" saved between disk and computer. By reducing the number of transfers, overall performance of the computer is increased.

After you've loaded PC Cache, you can view the transfer savings by entering

PC-CACHE /MEASURES

at the DOS prompt. PC Cache displays the following tidbits of information, as shown in Figure 9-10.

▶ *Logical transfers.* The total number of data transfers that have occurred between the cache and the current application since loading PC Cache.

▶ *Physical transfers.* The total number of data transfers that have occurred between the disk and the current application since loading PC Cache.

▶ *Transfers saved.* The number of physical transfers saved by PC Cache.

▶ *Percent saved.* The percentage of transfers saved by PC Cache.

```
C:\PCTOOLS6>pc-cache /measures
 PC-CACHE, Version 6
 Unauthorized duplication prohibited
 Measurements are as follows:
        713    logical transfers.
        542    physical transfers.
        171    transfers saved.
        23%    percent saved.

C:\PCTOOLS6>_
```

Figure 9-10. A sample efficiency report provided with the /MEASURES PC Cache parameter.

Use the /MEASURES parameter to test various installations of PC Cache. Try loading PC Cache with just 32 kilobytes of memory and perform a strict set of commands on your computer. (For example, start PC Tools Shell, access a couple of commands, and quit.) Note the performance as displayed with the /MEASURES parameter and reset the cache using an extra 32 kilobytes of RAM. (Note: Use the /UNLOAD parameter to unload PC Cache, then manually reload it using more memory.)

Repeat these steps several times until PC Cache displays no extra performance even when adding more RAM. At a certain point—and it differs among computers—the performance of PC Cache will top out, no matter how much memory you give it.

If you're unsure how much memory is being used by PC Cache or how your computer is set up, use the /PARAM or /PARAM* command-line parameters. The /PARAM switch displays the parameters of PC Cache currently in effect. The

/PARAM* switch shows available expanded memory, the number of disk drives and their sizes, and how extended memory is allocated.

Differences in Memory Types

PC Cache can allocate memory for caching in regular, extended, or expanded RAM. If your computer is equipped with just 512 or 640 kilobytes of RAM (the minimum suggested for running PC Tools), you'll be using a portion of regular RAM as a cache reservoir. But if your computer is equipped with additional RAM—either extended or expanded—you should use it instead. This frees the regular (also called base) 512 or 640 kilobytes of memory to your applications programs.

The terms "extended" and "expanded" can be confusing, and they are often used interchangeably. However, they indicate two different forms of memory installed in your computer. Expanded memory is the term applied to bank-switched memory using the Lotus/Intel/Microsoft specification (such as the Intel Above Board). The amount of memory varies—from as little as 64 kilobytes to as much as 8 megabytes; most computers nowadays come with 1 or 2 megabytes of expanded memory.

247

Extended memory is a special memory scheme used in the AT that adds RAM above the 1-megabyte mark reserved by DOS. ATs (as well as most computers that use the 80386 and 80486 microprocessors) can have both extended and expanded memory.

Note what kind of extra memory, if any, your computer has. Once again, PC Tools comes to the rescue. To determine the type and amount of memory in your computer:

1. Start the PC Tools Shell program.
2. Choose the System Info command from the Special menu.
3. Inspect the memory entries near the bottom of the window for base, expanded, and extended memory, as shown in Figure 9-11.

If there are no entries for expanded or extended memory, it means your computer doesn't have any. You may want to consider adding some. You can add expanded memory by installing an expanded memory board inside your computer. Along with

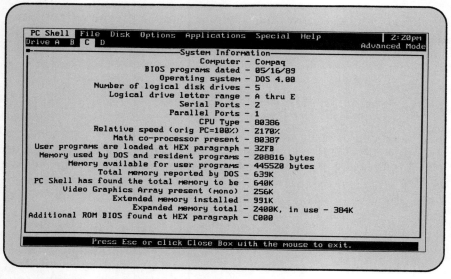

```
 PC Shell  File  Disk  Options  Applications  Special  Help        │ 2:20pm
 Drive A  B  C  D                                                Advanced Mode
 ┌─────────────────────────System Information─────────────────────────┐
                            Computer - Compaq
                  BIOS programs dated - 05/16/89
                     Operating system - DOS 4.00
          Number of logical disk drives - 5
             Logical drive letter range - A thru E
                           Serial Ports - 2
                         Parallel Ports - 1
                               CPU Type - 80386
            Relative speed (orig PC=100%) - 2170%
                Math co-processor present - 80387
    User programs are loaded at HEX paragraph - 32FB
  Memory used by DOS and resident programs - 208816 bytes
       Memory available for user programs - 445520 bytes
             Total memory reported by DOS - 639K
  PC Shell has found the total memory to be - 640K
         Video Graphics Array present (mono) - 256K
                 Extended memory installed - 991K
                   Expanded memory total - 2400K, in use - 384K
    Additional ROM BIOS found at HEX paragraph - C000
 │        Press Esc or click Close Box with the mouse to exit.        │
```

Figure 9-11. A System Information window, showing such items as number of serial and parallel ports, total and available memory, operating system, and relative performance (speed of CPU) as compared to the original IBM PC.

248

the board you'll receive a diskette containing driver software that enables the memory.

Parking Your Hard Disk Drive

One of the most dangerous moments for your hard disk drive is when you turn your computer off at the end of the day. When the power is switched off, the spinning metal platters inside the drive coast to a stop. The air pressure that has been built up inside the drive subsides as the platters slow. This air has been keeping the delicate magnetic heads floating a safe distance from the disk media, but now that it's beginning to diminish, the heads begin to float toward the metal.

If the heads happen to strike against the metal disks while they are still turning, damage to the hard disk could result. While the heads themselves probably won't be hurt, whatever data was recorded at the point of impact could be gone.

You can eliminate almost all hard disk crashes caused by the heads striking the disk when the computer is turned off by using the Park Disk command in the PC Tools Shell program. The Park Disk command, found under the Disk menu, moves the heads in the hard disk to a safe area. While the Park Disk command won't prevent the heads from striking the disk surface accidentally, if it does happen, at least no valuable data will be lost.

You'll especially want to park the heads of your hard disk if you plan on moving the computer. Even with the computer off and the hard disk drive inactive, moving the mechanism could cause the heads to impact against the disk surface.

Note that many late-model hard disks include their own automatic head-parking mechanism. This mechanism retracts the heads after a short period of inactivity, or the moment the computer's power is turned off (enough power remains in the circuitry of the hard disk drive to move the heads to the "safe zone").

249

Although it's rare, double-parking could damage your hard disk drive. That is, damage could result if the heads are parked first with PC Tools Shell, then by the drive's own internal auto-parking mechanism. Check the instructions that came with your computer or hard disk drive to be sure.

Follow these simple steps to park the heads in your hard disk.

Q **Parking the Hard Disk Drive**

1. If you haven't done so already, load the PC Tools Shell program.
2. Choose the Park Disk command from the Disk menu.

   Parks the hard disk drive.

3. Turn off the computer.   ☐

Unlike some disk-parking programs, Shell doesn't disable the computer when the hard disk is parked. If you choose another command or click the Cancel button, as shown in Figure 9-12, the heads will "unpark." You'll have to repeat the steps outlined above to repark the heads before you turn the computer off.

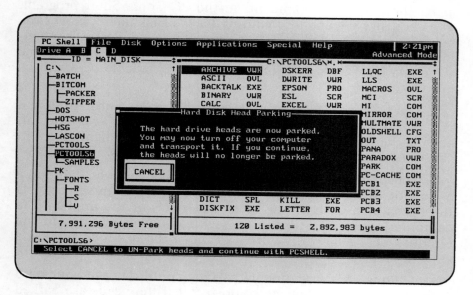

Figure 9-12. The Hard Disk Head Parking dialog box.

Review

In this chapter you learned how to maintain your hard disk drive and keep it in good working order. You also learned:

► Hard disk fragmentation is when one or more files are located among two or more noncontiguous clusters on the disk.

► The main task of the PC Tools Compress program is to eliminate fragmentation.

► Compress can optionally provide a printed report of the defragmentation operation.

► The Surface analysis command in Compress can be used to test for formatting and data errors.

► When Compress finds a cluster it can't read, the program marks it as bad so it can't be used by DOS again.

▶ Disk caching, as provided by the PC Cache program, improves hard disk performance by storing commonly used data in memory.

▶ When you're finished using your computer for the day, you should park the heads in the hard disk drive using the Park Drive command.

251

Using PC Tools Desktop

In This Chapter

- ▶ *Loading PC Tools Desktop*
- ▶ *Using the Desktop word processor*
- ▶ *Checking the spelling in your documents*
- ▶ *Maintaining data using the data manager*
- ▶ *Calling and conversing with other computers*

PC Tools offers a collection of handy miniapplications that you can use by themselves or within one of your applications programs. You can use these desk accessories, which are all contained within the PC Tools Desktop program, to augment your regular applications or in place of a more complex stand-alone program.

Included with the PC Tools Desktop collection are:

- ▶ A word processor.
- ▶ A data manager.
- ▶ A communications terminal.
- ▶ A appointment scheduler.
- ▶ A selection of multifunction calculators.

This chapter covers only the basics of the PC Tools Desktop applications, providing quick start introductions to get you going. You should refer to the Desktop Manager manual that accompanies the PC Tools Deluxe package for in-depth coverage of the desk accessories.

In Review: Running Desktop

In Chapter 2, "Getting Started with PC Tools," you learned how to start Desktop as either a stand-alone or memory-resident program. For your convenience, we'll quickly review the methods of starting Desktop here.

254

Recall there are three ways to run Desktop: as a stand-alone program at the DOS prompt, as a memory-resident program (loaded manually by you), and as a memory-resident program (loaded automatically by the AUTOEXEC.BAT batch file when the computer is first turned on).

The following steps assume you are using a hard disk drive, and you are currently logged onto the drive that contains the PC Tools programs—usually drive C. Note that there is no need to move to the PC Tools subdirectory unless you have deleted or edited the PCTOOLS directory in the PATH statement in your AUTOEXEC.BAT file.

To run Desktop:

At the DOS prompt	Type DESKTOP and press Enter
As memory-resident/ manual load	Type DESKTOP /R and press Enter, then press Ctrl-Spacebar to activate
As memory-resident/ AUTOEXEC.BAT load	Press Ctrl-Spacebar to activate

The Control and Spacebar keys are hot-keys that activate Desktop from memory. Under most circumstances, you can activate Desktop from within DOS or any application. Some PC programs may require all the memory in your computer, however, and Desktop may not load.

You press these same keys to deactivate Desktop and return to the DOS prompt or your application. Remember that even though Desktop is deactivated, it still resides in your computer's memory, so you can call it back up any time. It also continues to consume a portion of your computer's RAM, so if you need to reclaim that memory for use by another application, type

KILL

at the DOS prompt. This removes Desktop (as well as Shell, if it has also been loaded as memory-resident) from the computer's RAM. Note that KILL.COM is a PC Tools program and must be on the currently selected drive, or DOS won't be able to find it.

After Desktop is loaded (and activated if you're using it in memory-resident mode), your computer screen should look like that in Figure 10-1. The illustration includes a description of the various components of the Desktop display.

255

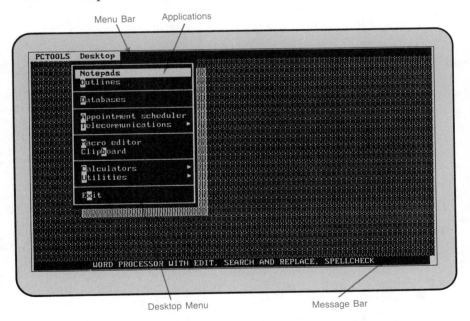

Figure 10-1. The opening Desktop display, with component parts.

Special Desktop Parameters

Parameters are "switches" or options you select when you load a program into your computer. Desktop supports about ten parameters that control the way the program works and interacts with your computer. To use a parameter, enter it after typing PCSHELL at the DOS prompt. You've already learned about one of Desktop's parameters, the /R switch that loads Desktop as a memory-resident instead of a stand-alone program. In most cases, you can combine switches to activate many options.

/BW

256

Starts Desktop in black-and-white mode.

/CS

Clears the screen and displays a background pattern when Desktop is running in memory-resident mode. The background is automatically included when Desktop runs in stand-alone mode.

/C3 or /C4 = IRQ/xxx

Assigns a serial port to the Desktop autodialer.

/DQ

Disables quick-load feature when activating Desktop from the DOS prompt. (Quick-load helps load Desktop faster when you activate it; it's used only when Desktop is loaded as a TSR.) Use the /DQ switch if you are experiencing problems running Desktop as memory-resident when activating the program from the DOS prompt.

/IM

Disables the mouse. It is helpful if you are using an older mouse driver that is not supported by PC Tools.

/IN

Runs Desktop in color with a Hercules InColor graphics card (memory-resident mode only).

/LE

Exchanges right and left mouse buttons to accommodate left-handed persons.

257

/LCD

For use with laptop computers equipped with liquid crystal displays.

/MM

Allows you to start Desktop without invoking a Desktop application that may have been running during the last session.

/Od

Selects a different drive to contain the Desktop overlay files (these include DESKTOP.OVL, DESKTOP.IMG, and DESKTOP.THM). Ordinarily, Desktop places these overlay files in the drive and directory containing the PC Tools files; you can change it if your drive (or RAM disk) gets too full. Replace the d with a drive letter, such as /Oa.

/350

Displays Desktop in 350 line resolution; used only with VGA monitors.

/R

Loads Desktop memory-resident.

/RA

Loads Desktop memory-resident and automatically starts the Appointment Scheduler.

258

Table 10-1 offers a quick reference guide to using the parameter switches with Desktop running as a stand-alone program from the DOS prompt, or as a TSR.

Table 10-1. Parameter Switches for Desktop Operating Modes.

Parameter	From DOS Prompt	As a TSR
/ BW	X	X
/CS		X
/C3 & /C4	X	X
/ DQ		X
/ IM	X	X
/ IN		X
/ LE	X	X
/ LCD	X	X
/ MM		X
/Od	X	X
/350	X	X
/ R		X

In the remainder of this chapter, we'll assume you've already loaded Desktop.

Processing Words

PC Tools calls its Desktop word processor Notepads. With a name like that you'd think the word processor would be a simple note keeper, offering just rudimentary text writing and editing capabilities. Surprisingly, Notepads is a full-function word processor that boasts many "power" features, including a built-in spelling checker, search and replace, and headers and footers. If you're a WordStar user, you'll be pleased to learn that Notepads is compatible with WordStar files. Notepads can read and write documents in WordStar format.

Q Starting Notepads

1. Choose the Notepads command from the Desktop menu.

   Starts Notepads. The dialog box in Figure 10-2 appears.

   259

2. Press the New button if you want to create a new document, or select a file from the list and press the Load button.

   Creates a new document (named WORK.TXT), or opens an existing document.

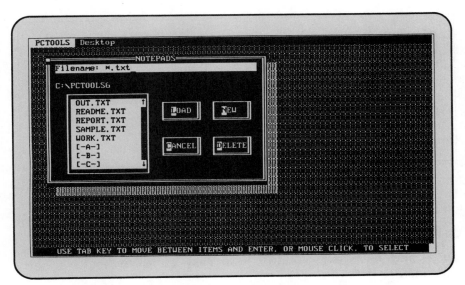

Figure 10-2. The Notepads open/new document dialog box.

When started, Notepads displays its own editing window and menu bar, as shown in Figure 10-3. As illustrated in the figure, the Notepads display contains the following basic parts:

▶ *Menu bar.* Located at the top of the screen.

▶ *Window border.* Shows the currently active window (double border). You can have as many as 15 windows open at one time in Desktop, depending on available memory.

▶ *Status line.* Shows where the cursor is located in the document, as well as the name of the file and the current edit mode (INS means insert mode).

▶ *Selection bar.* The blank space at the far left of the window between the window border and text. It allows you to select entire rows at a time with the mouse.

▶ *Ruler line.* Indicates current tabs or margins for document.

▶ *Vertical scroll bar.* Scrolls through the length of the text.

▶ *Horizontal scroll bar.* Scrolls from side to side when you have set margins wider than will fit in the window.

▶ *Message bar.* Located at the bottom of the screen, displays shortcut keys for common tasks, such as Load, Save, and Find/Replace.

▶ *Resize box.* Used for resizing the window.

▶ **Tip:** A shortcut to using the resize box to change the size of the Notepads window is the Zoom command in the Window menu. Choose the command once, and the window balloons to full size. Choose it again and the window returns to its smaller state. If all your new files open at partial size, open a new document (it will automatically be called WORK.TXT), zoom the window to full size, and choose the Save setup command from the Controls menu.

Writing and Editing Text

The most common task you'll do with any word processor is write and edit text. Follow these easy steps to begin a new document:

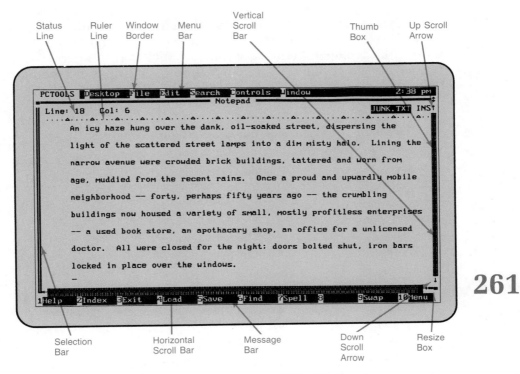

Status Line — Ruler Line — Window Border — Menu Bar — Vertical Scroll Bar — Thumb Box — Up Scroll Arrow

Selection Bar — Horizontal Scroll Bar — Message Bar — Down Scroll Arrow — Resize Box

Figure 10-3. The component parts of the Notepads display.

261

1. Choose the Notepads command from the Desktop menu.
2. Press the New button to start a blank document. All new documents use the blank template document WORK.TXT. Notepads will warn you that a file with that name already exists (unless you've erased it). At the dialog box that appears, press the OK button to continue.
3. Start writing when the empty window appears.

If you're familiar with computer word processors, you'll find Notepads intuitive and easy to learn. Words that are too long to fit the current line are automatically wrapped to the next line. When you want to start a new paragraph or line, press Enter. If you make a mistake, press the Backspace key to erase characters to the left of the cursor. You can also use the Delete key to erase characters to the right of the cursor.

Press the cursor keys to move the cursor without editing or writing text. Table 10-2 shows the functions of the cursor keys within the Notepads editing window. Note that the cursor cannot be moved to an area in the window that does not contain text.

Table 10-2. Cursor Key Functions Within Notepads Editing Window.

Key	Function
Right	Moves the cursor one character to the right
Left	Moves the cursor one character to the left
Up	Moves the cursor up one line
Down	Moves the cursor down one line
Ctrl-Right	Moves the cursor right one word
Ctrl-Left	Moves the cursor left one word
Home	Moves the cursor to the beginning of the current line
End	Moves the cursor to the end of the current line
Ctrl-Home	Moves the cursor to the top of the document
Ctrl-End	Moves the cursor to the end of the document
Home, Home	Moves the cursor to the top line of the window
End, End	Moves the cursor to the bottom line of the window
Page Up	Scrolls up one window
Page Down	Scrolls down one window
Ctrl-Page Up	Scrolls up one line (cursor remains stationary)
Ctrl-Page Down	Scrolls down one line (cursor remains stationary)

Selecting Text

Sometimes, you may wish to work on a group of text together, rather than deal with each individual character. Let's say, for example, that you don't want the middle paragraph shown in Figure 10-4. Instead of deleting each character one at a time, you can select the whole paragraph and delete all the text in one step.

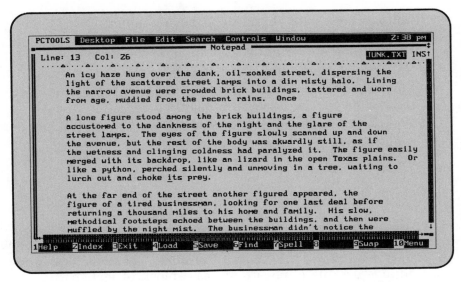

Figure 10-4. Notepads window with three paragraphs.

The task of selecting, or marking, text is made easier if you have a mouse. Simply position the mouse pointer over the start of the paragraph, press and hold the left button, then drag the mouse button to the end of the paragraph. As shown in Figure 10-5, the entire paragraph is selected. Press the Delete key and the paragraph vanishes.

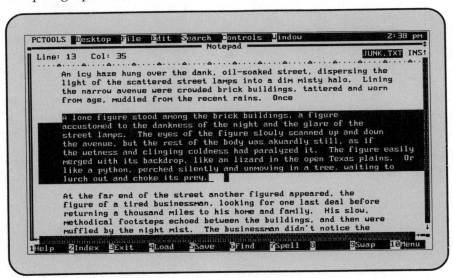

Figure 10-5. Notepads window with center paragraph selected, ready for deletion.

Follow these steps if you don't have a mouse:

1. Position the cursor at the beginning of the paragraph.
2. Choose the Mark block command from the Edit menu.
3. Move the cursor to the end of the paragraph. As you move the cursor, text in between is highlighted.
4. Choose the Delete all text command from the Edit menu.
5. Confirm that you want to delete the paragraph by pressing the OK button.

Cutting, Copying, and Pasting

264

A powerful feature of the Notepads word processor is its temporary clipboard. This clipboard stores a block of text that you've previously selected and cut or copied using the appropriate commands in the Edit menu. You can then paste this text anywhere within the document, or even in another Notepads document.

To cut or copy a block of text to the clipboard, select it following the steps outlined above. Then choose the Cut to Clipboard or Copy to clipboard command from the Edit menu.

▶ Cut to clipboard removes the selected text from the document and stores it in the clipboard.

▶ Copy to clipboard takes a snapshot of the selected text and stores the copy in the clipboard. The original selection remains intact.

To paste the contents of the clipboard, move the cursor to where you want the text moved, then choose the Paste from clipboard command from the Edit menu.

▶ **Tip:** The text stored in the clipboard remains until you quit Desktop or cut or copy other text. You can use this feature to paste the same block of text within one or more documents repeatedly. You can use this technique, for instance, as a quick means to fill in your return name and address in a series of letters you're writing.

Spell-Checking

You should get into the habit of checking the spelling of your documents before printing and distributing them. Spell-checking not only keeps a watchful eye over your spelling—"seperate" instead of the proper "separate", for instance—but also helps nab the occasional typographical error.

To spell-check a document:

1. With the cursor anywhere within the document, choose the Spellcheck File command from the Edit menu.

2. When Notepads catches a word it thinks is misspelled, it highlights the word and displays the dialog box shown in Figure 10-6. Press the appropriate key according to the action you want to take: Ignore (skip the word), Correct (provide a new spelling), Add (add the word as is to the spelling dictionary), or Quit (finished with spell-checking).

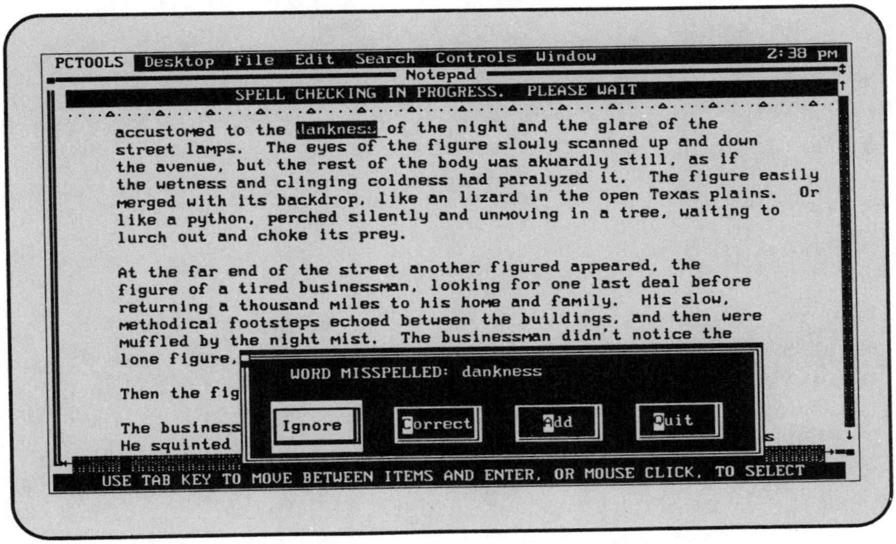

265

Figure 10-6. The Spellcheck dialog box, asking you to ignore, correct, or add the highlighted word.

If you press the Correct key, Notepads quickly scans its dictionary and displays a list of words close to the one that's misspelled. Scroll through the list (illustrated in Figure 10-7) with the mouse or keyboard, and press Enter or the Accept button to confirm the new spelling.

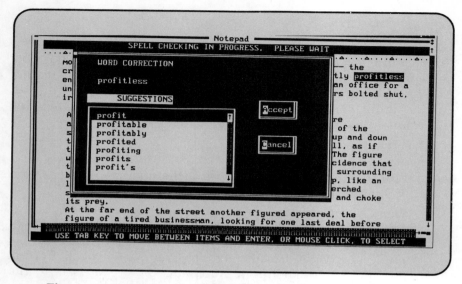

Figure 10-7. Alternative spellings suggested by Notepads for the word "profitless," which is spelled correctly but is not contained in the Notepads spelling dictionary file.

You can also spell-check just the current word or the text in the current window. Choose the Spellcheck Word or Spellcheck Screen commands, as desired.

Saving a File

Notepads automatically saves your documents for you when you exit Desktop, but you'll want to save the document periodically while you work. To do so manually, at say 10 to 15 minute intervals, choose the Save command from the File menu. If you'd like to change the name of the file, edit the entry in the file name field. The File Format selectors let you save the file in PC Tools Desktop (WordStar) format or straight ASCII text.

If you select the Make Backup File option, Notepads will keep the previously saved version of the document and name it FILENAME.BAK, where FILENAME is the unique name of your document.

You can also tell Notepads to save the document for you automatically. Chose the Autosave command from the File menu. Turn Autosave on, and indicate a time delay between savings (a 5 to 10 minute delay should be satisfactory). Press OK.

Loading a File

Documents that you or someone else have previously written and saved can be called up from the disk at any time, even when another document is open (depending on the size of the documents and available memory).

Q Loading a File

1. Choose the Notepads command from the Desktop menu.

2. Highlight the file you want from the list.   Selects the file to open.

3. Press the Load button.   Loads the file into Notepads.

☐ **267**

> ▶ **Tip:** If the file is on another disk, highlight one of the drive letters (A, B, C, etc.) in the Open File dialog box, and press Enter or the Load button. Then highlight the file of your choice. If the file is in another subdirectory, highlight the subdirectory, and press Enter. You may need to navigate around the directory tree to find the file you want. To move up a subdirectory level, highlight the ".." entry, and press Enter.

Changing the Format

Notepads lets you specify the unique formatting of your document. You can add a header or footer to every page, control the margins, indicate line spacing, and more.

▶ To set a header or footer (text that appears on the top or bottom of every page), choose the Header/Footer command from the Controls menu. As shown in Figure 10-8, enter one line of text in the Header or Footer fields.

▶ To set the margins, choose the Page layout command from the Controls menu. Indicate the left, right, top, and/or bottom margins. The left and right margin settings are in characters, assuming 10 characters per inch. Both numbers are relative to the left side of the page. The top and bottom margin settings are in lines, assuming six lines per inch.

► To set a new paper size, choose the Page layout command from the Control menu. Type a new number in the Paper size field. Sixty-six lines is the default for 11-inch paper.

► To set line spacing, choose the Page layout command from the Control menu. Type a new number in the Line spacing field.

► To set a new starting point for page numbering, choose the Page layout command from the Control menu. Type a new number in the Starting page # field.

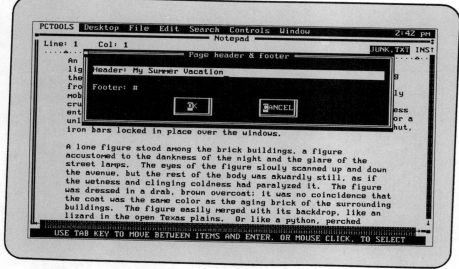

Figure 10-8. Sample header entry.

Printing a File

After you've written, edited, spell-checked, and formatted the document to your liking, you're now ready to print it out. To print the file, choose the Print command from the File menu. Select the port your printer is connected to (LPT1, COM1, etc.), and press the Print command. If you wish to print more than one copy of your document at a time, enter a new number in the Number of copies field.

Writing Outlines

Desktop contains an outline generator (sometimes referred to as a thought organizer) that lets you easily write and format outlines. You start and use the Outlines feature much the same way as Notepads. In fact, Outlines uses the basic text writing, editing, and formatting functions as Notepads, but adds special commands for controlling the appearance of the outline headings and formatting. When using Outlines, an additional menu—called Headlines—appears in the menu bar, as shown in Figure 10-9.

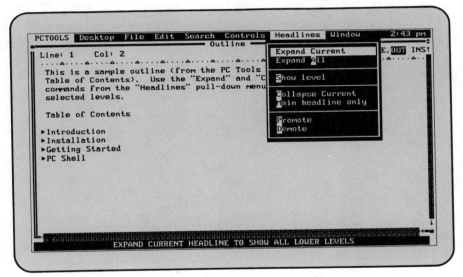

269

Figure 10-9. The Headlines menu.

To best understand the commands in the Headlines menu, you need to know a little about the way Outlines works with text. Outlines have headlines, such as

    A. Introduction
    B. Chapter 1
    C. Chapter 2

and so forth. Each headline occupies a certain level. The levels start at Level 1 for a headline that starts at or near the left margin. Subsequent levels (Level 2, Level 3, etc.) are indented from the main headline. Each level is indented five spaces over from the one preceding it, to create an outline format as depicted in Figure 10-9.

Outlines gives you the ability to manipulate the display of levels and headlines, so that you can work with only certain parts of the outline at one time. For example, you may wish to view only the most important topics of an outline, so you display just the Level 1 headlines. Figure 10-10 shows the previous outline with all levels under Level 1 "collapsed." At any time, you can "expand" the collapsed headlines to reveal additional levels.

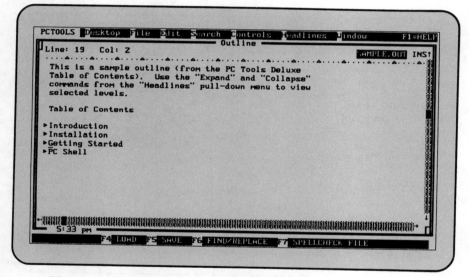

Figure 10-10. An outline with all headlines but Level 1 collapsed. (The paragraph at the beginning of the outline is straight text and is not formatted as a level.)

Here's what the commands in the Headlines menu do:

▶ *Expand Current.* Expands all the headlines below the current headline. Works only when headlines under the current one have been collapsed.

▶ *Expand All.* Expands all collapsed headings in the outline. Works only when headlines have been collapsed.

▶ *Show level.* Displays the headlines to the level you indicate. For example, if you select to Level 3, you'll see Levels 1, 2, and 3.

- ▶ *Collapse Current*. Collapses all levels following the one that's current.
- ▶ *Main headline only*. Collapses all levels except for the main headline.
- ▶ *Promote*. Moves a headline to the next higher level.
- ▶ *Demote*. Moves a headline to the next lower level.

Keeping Track of Data

The PC Tools Desktop database manager lets you organize, store, and manage information. For example, you can create a form that lets you enter the names and addresses of everyone on your season's greetings list. The Databases database manager will organize automatically the list according to options you select. You can display only those people who live in a certain city, for example, or list only those people who sent you a card last year.

271

Of Fields and Records

A database is a complete document or file that is divided into individual records, as shown in Figure 10-11. Each record is further divided into fields. The field is the smallest chunk of data that the database can manipulate. One field may be the last name of a client; another field may be the ZIP Code where the client resides. Each record contains the fields of a separate person or thing. One record may list the name and address of Uncle Joe, and another the name and address of Grandpa Fred.

Like most data managers, Databases has certain limitations regarding the number of fields and records it can contain.

- ▶ You can store up to 3,500 records per database file.
- ▶ Each record can contain up to 4,000 characters.
- ▶ Each record can be divided into as many as 128 fields.
- ▶ Each field can contain up to 70 characters.

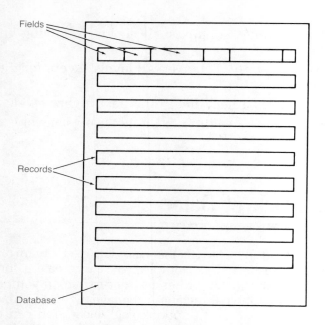

Fields

Records

272

Database

Figure 10-11. The component parts of a database file.

Creating a New Database

The best way to learn how to use Databases is to create a new database. The process involves three discrete steps: defining the structure of the new database, customizing a new form file, and entering record data.

To define the structure of a new database, you must create a special .DBF document file. This document file (compatible with dBASE III and IV) specifies how the database fields are named and classified. Follow these steps to make and define the structure of a new database:

1. Choose the Databases command from the Desktop menu.
2. Press the New button in the dialog box that appears. Another dialog box pops onto the screen, as shown in Figure 10-12.
3. Fill out the dialog box for each field you want to create. Specifically, give the field a unique name, indicate its type (whether character, numeric, logical or date), and its length

(in number of characters), then save the field structure by pressing the Add button.

4. At any time, you can examine the fields you've created by pressing the Next and Prev buttons.

5. Delete a field you don't want by pressing the Delete button.

6. When you're done defining the structure, press the Save button.

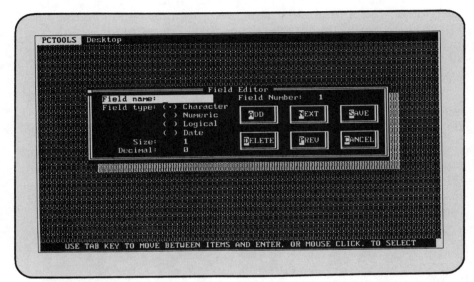

Figure 10-12. The Field Editor dialog box, used to create a new database.

The four field types indicate the type of information that will be stored in each field.

▶ A *Character* field contains letters, numbers, and special characters that you want treated as text. Examples: name, address, telephone number.

▶ A *Numeric* field contains numbers you might want to use in a math calculation. (PC Tools Desktop lacks a math calculation feature in Databases; the Numeric field is intended for use when sharing Databases files with dBase.) Examples: Balance due, age.

▶ A *Logical* field contains a single character that represents true or false. Enter Y or N, T or F, as desired. Use the Logical field to provide additional field entries if a certain con-

273

dition is met. Example: If customer has not paid, enter N or n.

▶ A *Date* field contains eight characters for storing numeric data codes. The format follows the MM/DD/YY standard.

For each field you create you need to indicate its length. The maximum is 70 characters. Plan ahead to give each field enough space to contain the required information. You should provide a minimum of 30 characters for names, 40 characters for street addresses, 20 characters for cities. If you plan on entering only local phone numbers, leave room for just 7 characters. Long distance numbers must have at least 10 characters to store the area code.

When dealing with dollars and cents (in numeric fields), you may want to indicate the number of digits to the right of the decimal point. Select the Decimal field and enter a number.

274

When you press the Save button, Databases automatically stores the new structure and displays the fields in a database window, as shown in Figure 10-13. Each field name you create is shown in the window, followed by one or more dots. The dots represent the length of the field.

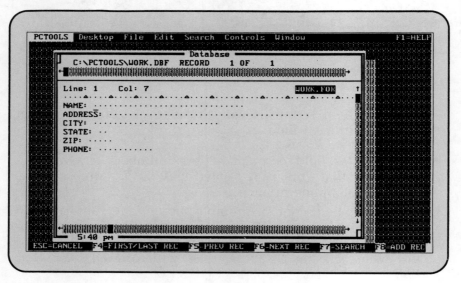

Figure 10-13. Completed database, showing entry fields (the dots represent the length of each field, as indicated by you in the Field Editor dialog box).

Fill out the form by moving the cursor to the desired field and typing.

▶ Press the Tab key to move to the next field quickly.
▶ Press the Shift and Tab keys together to move to the preceding field quickly.

When you're done entering all the data for the first record, press the F8 function key to add the record to the database. Enter the data for the next record, press F8, and so forth, until your database is complete. Bear in mind that at any time you can reopen this database file and add new records. You don't need to provide all the records for the database in one sitting. When you're done entering all the records for the current session, close the window.

You can display previously entered records at any time. Press the F5 function key to move to the previous record; press the F6 function key to move to the next record. Press the F4 function key to toggle between the first record in the database and the last. Record number 1 is always blank and is the one you use when you want to add a new record, even though newly added records are always placed at the end of the database.

Databases lets you display the fields in just about any way you want. When you create a new .DBF database file, the program also creates a special .FOR document that you can edit with the Notepads word processor. As shown in Figures 10-14 and 10-15, use the word processor to manipulate the file names and placeholders (where the actual data from the .DBF file will be placed) within the window.

275

▶ **Tip:** If you're preparing a form letter, for use with a name and address database file, for example, write the standard text that will appear in the letter and indicate where the data is to be placed by entering the placeholders at the appropriate spot. Figure 10-16 shows the form letter that prints the name, address, city, state, and ZIP Code of the entries in a correspondence database.

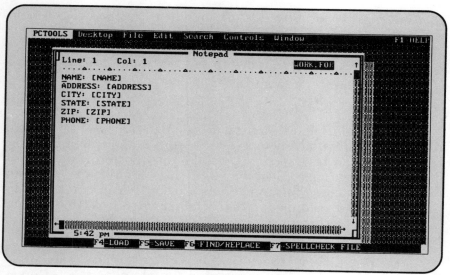

276

Figure 10-14. A sample unformatted database form.

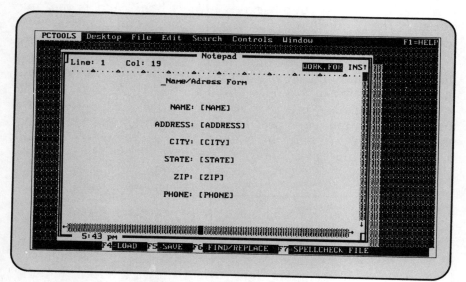

Figure 10-15. A sample database form, formatted with all fields centered in the window.

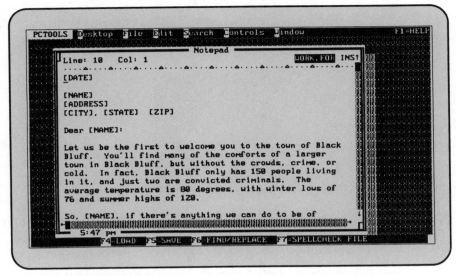

PCTOOLS **D**esktop **F**ile **E**dit **S**earch **C**ontrols **W**indow   F1=HELP

Notepad

Line: 10   Col: 1   WORK.FOR INS↑

[DATE]

[NAME]
[ADDRESS]
[CITY], [STATE] [ZIP]

Dear [NAME]:

Let us be the first to welcome you to the town of Black
Bluff. You'll find many of the comforts of a larger
town in Black Bluff, but without the crowds, crime, or
cold. In fact, Black Bluff only has 150 people living
in it, and just two are convicted criminals. The
average temperature is 80 degrees, with winter lows of
76 and summer highs of 120.

So, [NAME], if there's anything we can do to be of

5:47 PM

F4=LOAD F5=SAVE F6=FIND/REPLACE F7=SPELLCHECK FILE

277

*Figure 10-16. A database form combined with a "mail
merge" document.*

After the form has been edited, save it, and return to
Databases. If you haven't done so already, open the .DBF file
you've been working with. You can now view the data merged
into the rest of the form by choosing the Load Form command
from the File menu. To print the filled-in form, choose the Print
command, also located in the File menu.

Sorting Records

To make Databases more efficient and to help you find records
you've previously added, you'll want to sort the records within
the database file.

 Sorting the Database

1. Choose the Sort database command from the Edit menu.	Activates the Sort database command.
2. Highlight the field you want to sort on, such as by Name or by City.	Selects a field to sort on.

3. Press the Next and
   Previous buttons as
   required to highlight
   different fields in the
   database.

4. When the field you want to   Sorts the database.
   sort on is displayed, press
   the Sort button.

Searching and Selecting Records

While you could hunt through hundreds or even thousands of
records to find the one you want, an easier way is to use
Databases' built-in record searching and selecting tools.

278   To search for a particular record, choose the Find text in all
fields command from the Search menu. In the dialog box that
appears, as illustrated in Figure 10-17, select the Search Selected
Records option, and press the Search button.

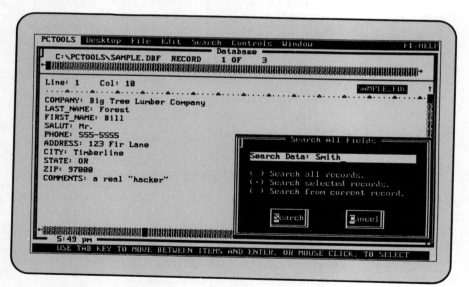

Figure 10-17. The Search All Fields dialog box.

Let's review an example of how the search feature might
work; suppose you want to find a client named Smith. Choose
the Find text in all fields command, type Smith in the dialog box,

select the Search selected records option, and press the Search button. Databases finds the first entry with Smith and displays its records. If you have more than one Smith in the database, you can use the search command again.

Selecting records provides a means to display only those that meet certain criteria, like City or State. Normally, Databases selects all records in a database; changes you make in the selection criteria narrows the number of records that are displayed.

To select records that meet a certain criteria:

1. Choose the select Records command from the Edit menu.
2. In the dialog box that appears (as illustrated in Figure 10-18), enter the field names you want to select from and the criteria you want to use for the selection.
3. Press the Select button when you're done.

279

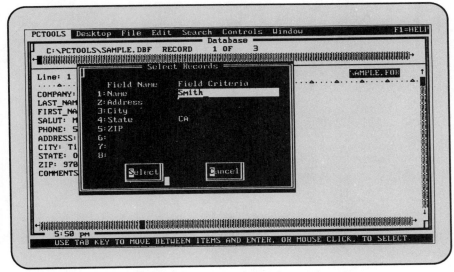

Figure 10-18. Sample Select Records dialog box, with field names and criteria entered.

> ► **Tip:** The selection criteria can be explicit—a certain
> name or state, for example—or it can be a range of
> entries. To display all records where the AGE field is
> between 18 and 24, for instance, enter 18..24 beside the
> AGE field, as shown in Figure 10-19. The range can be open
> ended, for either the start or finish: 18.. starts the AGE crite-
> ria at 18, with no stop range; ..24 starts the AGE criteria at
> the lowest number contained in the database and stops it at
> 24. You can also use letters to display a range of text
> entries: A..C entered in the Name field displays those
> records where the Name begins with A, B, or C.

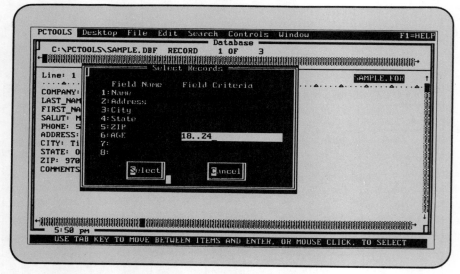

*Figure 10-19. This entry in the Select Records dialog box
will select fields that contain an age of between 18 and
24 in the AGE field.*

Communicating with Other Computers

If you have a modem connected to your computer, you can use it
and PC Tools Desktop to converse with another computer anywhere
on the globe. All you need to complete the link is a phone line
between yourself and the remote computer.

The communications function built into Desktop, called Telecommunications, is a "smart terminal." Not only can you use it to dial a remote computer automatically, but you can also use it to send and receive files, even when you're busy working in another application.

To start the terminal, choose the Telecommunications command from the Desktop menu . The Telecommunications window appears as shown in Figure 10-20. The entries in the window are preprogrammed communications settings. PC Tools comes with a collection of setting files, including MCI Mail, EasyLink, and CompuServe. You can edit these settings files or create your own. The settings files allow you to select the number you want to dial quickly and to initiate the call. There's no need to reset communications parameters manually for each call you make.

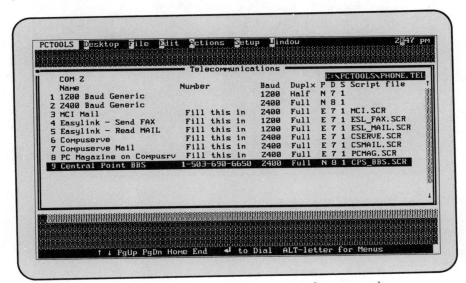

Figure 10-20. The Telecommunications phone number window.

Entering a New Setting

Before you can use Telecommunications, you need to enter a phone number and other settings options in the Telecommunications window. Follow these simple steps:

1. Choose the Create new entry command from the Edit menu.
2. In the dialog box that appears (shown in Figure 10-21), provide details about the modem connection you desire. Enter the phone number, the terminal type, port, parity, and so forth.
3. Press the Accept button when you're done.
4. Store your changes in the PHONE.TEL settings file by choosing the Save command from the File menu.

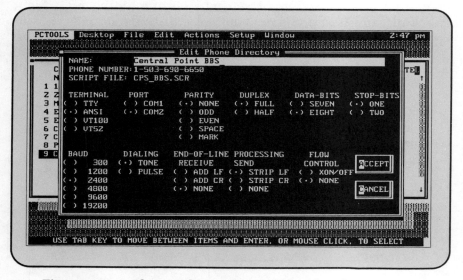

Figure 10-21. Change the options in the Edit Phone Directory window for each remote computer you want to contact.

The most common communications settings are:

▶ *Terminal*: TTY.
▶ *Port*: COM1 or COM2 (depending on where the modem is connected to).
▶ *Parity*: None.
▶ *Duplex*: Full.
▶ *Data-bits*: Eight.
▶ *Stop-bits*: One.
▶ *Baud*: 1200 or 2400 (depending on the capabilities of your modem and the modem you're connecting to).

▶ *Dialing*: Tone.
▶ *End-of-Line Receive*: None.
▶ *Processing Send*: None.
▶ *Flow Control*: XON/XOFF.

Placing the Call

After you've established the number to call and the parameters to use, you can establish the modem link. Select the setting file you created and press Enter. PC Tools Desktop will provide a running commentary.

▶ **Tip:** You don't absolutely need to enter a phone number in the settings directory. If the modem and computer you're talking to accepts 1200 Baud Generic or 2400 Baud Generic settings, you can use one of these to place the call. Dial the phone by choosing the Dial command from the Actions menu, and enter the phone number in the dialog box that appears.

283

Using Screen Autodial

If you are using Notepads, Outlines, Databases, or a stand-alone application (such as WordStar or WordPerfect), and you've loaded Desktop in memory-resident mode, you can use the screen auto-dialing feature of Telecommunications to read automatically a number you've entered on the screen. Telecom "captures" the number and dials it. For example, write the number 555-1212, then press Ctrl-O (Ctrl and the letter O). It dials the number 555-1212. This feature is particularly handy when working with Databases. You can dial automatically a number displayed in the Telephone field.

> $\bigcirc$ **Caution:** Many programs, including WordStar, use the
> Ctrl-O for a specific function. If you've loaded Desktop
> in memory-resident mode, pressing Ctrl-O when you meant
> to activate some command in your applications program
> will instead provoke Telecom's autodial feature.

You can readily change the hot-key used by PC Tools Desktop to activate the autodial feature. Within Desktop, choose the Utilities command from the Desktop menu. Choose the HotKey Selection option, and enter a new hot-key for Screen Autodial.

Hanging Up the Phone

284 When you're done with the computer conversation, choose the Hangup phone command from the Actions menu. In a few moments, the phone will hang up.

Sending and Receiving Files

The PC Tools Telecommunications terminal can send and receive files using ASCII or XMODEM transfers.

- ▶ ASCII transfers send or receive plain text, one character at a time. ASCII transfers are susceptible to errors caused by noise on the phone line.

- ▶ XMODEM transfers send data in discrete blocks. XMODEM includes a built-in error detection/correction scheme to ensure that transfers are error-free, even on relatively noisy phone lines.

ASCII transfers are appropriate for ASCII-only text documents. You need to use XMODEM when transferring binary text or binary-only files. Although the XMODEM protocol is the most common error-free file transfer method, it's not always supported. Both you and the remote computer must use the XMODEM protocol.

To send a file:

1. Initiate the connection with the remote modem.
2. For an ASCII transfer, choose the ASCII command from the Send menu. For an XMODEM transfer, choose the XMODEM command from the Send menu.
3. Select the file you want to send from the list that appears, and press the Load button.

   To receive a file:

1. Initiate the connection with the remote modem.
2. For an ASCII transfer, choose the ASCII command from the Receive menu. For an XMODEM transfer, choose the XMODEM command from the Receive menu.
3. Type a name for the file you will be receiving.
4. When receiving an ASCII file, choose the End Transfer command from the Actions menu when the transmission is complete.

285

Fax Communications

PC Tools Desktop supports background fax communications. If you have a fax board in your computer, you can use Desktop to send and receive facsimile transmissions. You can use the Notepads word processor to create the fax document and/or a cover sheet. Desktop works with only a select number of PC fax boards, specifically the Connection CoProcessor (Intel) and the SpectraFax (SpectraFax Corp.). The fax board can be installed in a Novell network (but should not be installed in the network server PC).

The fax communications control panel allows you to enter the phone number of the recipient and optionally a time and date to place the call. That way you can use your computer to place fax transmissions after hours, when the long distance rates are lowest. Conversely, you can keep your computer on and receive faxes at any time. It keeps a log of faxes sent and received.

Advanced Topics

The PC Tools Desktop Telecommunications module includes an enhanced "script" feature that lets you automate many common communications procedures. For instance, you can place a call to Dow Jones News/Retrieval, and a script previously written by you automatically navigates through the Dow Jones service and obtains the latest stock quotes on the stocks in your portfolio.

Telecom also provides for background communications using the BACKTALK memory-resident program included with PC Tools. With Backtalk installed, you can use your computer for another task while it is sending or receiving files with the communications terminal.

For more information on these advanced topics, refer to the Desktop Manager manual included with the PC Tools package.

286

Desktop Companions

PC Tools Desktop contains several additional miniapplications, including an appointment scheduler, several desktop calculators, keyboard macros, and a data clipboard for sharing text. Here's a rundown of each.

Appointment Scheduler

The appointment scheduler is shown in Figure 10-22. The appointment scheduler is an electronic cross between an appointment book and a to-do list. For each day of the month (for any month of the year), you can enter a list of tasks you need to get done. Desktop automatically numbers the tasks you must do in the to-do list. If you have more than about six tasks for any particular time frame, you can scroll the to-do list display to see the rest.

The appointment scheduler helps you set the pace for your day. You can set appointments every half hour or every 15 minutes, using the Appointment Settings options shown in Figure 10-23. You'll note that you can turn on or off certain days of the

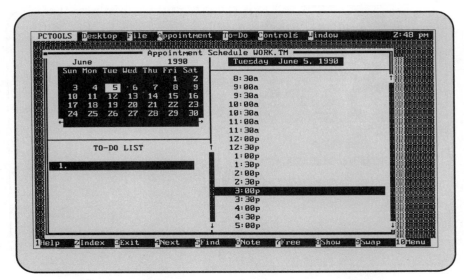

Figure 10-22. Basic Appointment Scheduler window.

week. For each appointment time, you can enter a short note to remind you that you're busy that part of the day, as illustrated in Figure 10-24.

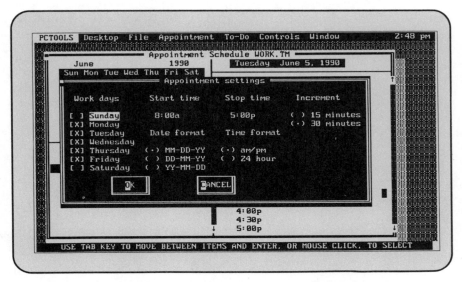

Figure 10-23. The Appointment Settings dialog box.

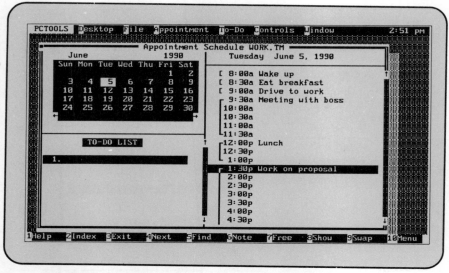

288   *Figure 10-24. An appointment schedule filled in for
one day.*

By highlighting the calendar and moving the current day
selection, you can prepare your appointments days or weeks in
advance. Appointments can be made without an automatic
alarm. With the alarm option turned on, you can program Desktop to chime at the scheduled appointment, or 5 or 10 minutes
in advance.

The appointment scheduler desk accessory provides several
time-saving features. For example, you can have it search
through your schedule to find a block of free time. Or it can tally
the use of your time according to how your appointments are
scheduled.

Desktop Calculators

PC Tools Desktop comes with four different types of electronic
calculators:

▶ *Algebraic calculator* for routine arithmetic.
▶ *Financial calculator* for figuring out financial matters, such
   as computing present value, future value, and bonds.
▶ *Programmer's calculator* for converting between hexadecimal, octal, binary, and decimal notation.

▶ *Scientific calculator* for solving trigonometric and other "scientific" equations.

The calculators are shown in Figures 10-25 through 10-28. To call up any calculator, choose the Calculators command in the Desktop menu, then select the calculator type you want to use.

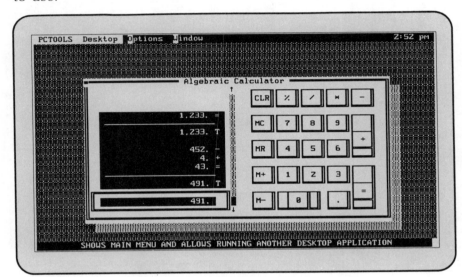

Figure 10-25. The algebraic calculator.

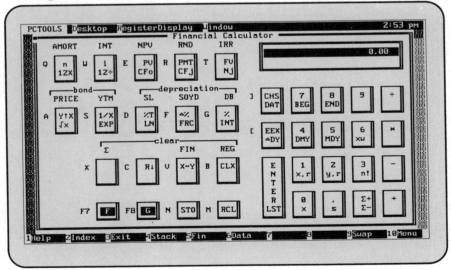

Figure 10-26. The financial calculator.

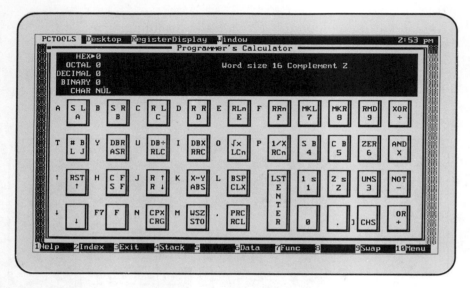

Figure 10-27. The programmer's calculator.

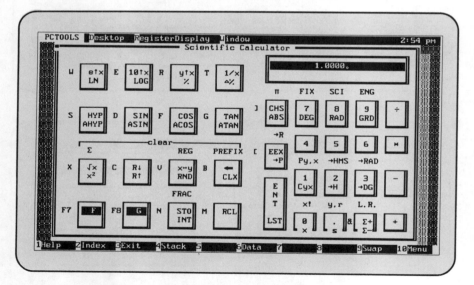

Figure 10-28. The scientific calculator.

The algebraic calculator includes a "paper tape" that scrolls like a regular PC Tools window. As you complete your computations, the results print out on the tape. You can easily go back and view a previous result by scrolling the tape window in the usual manner.

Keyboard Macros

Keyboard macros are preprogrammed shortcuts. A macro is akin to a tape recording. What you record on the tape can be instantly played back. With PC Tools macros, you enter a series of keystrokes into the PC Tools Desktop Macro Editor. To play back the keystrokes you recorded, press just one or two special hot-keys.

The Macro Editor, shown in Figure 10-29, operates like the Notepads Desktop accessory. You can create macros by entering the keystrokes explicitly into the Macro Editor window, or by turning on the Learn mode and recording those keys you press on the keyboard. For instance, you can start the Telecommunications terminal, select a phone number to call, and initiate the call just by pressing the Alt-C keys.

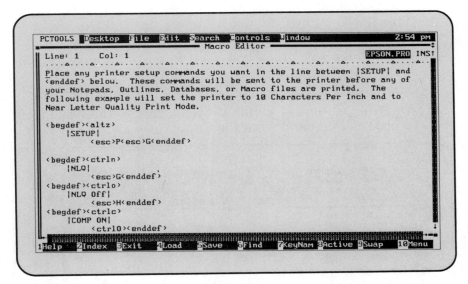

Figure 10-29. Sample Macro Editor document.

You can use the macros you create with the Macro Editor for a variety of functions. For example, you can use macros to embed special printing codes in your Notepads documents (to turn on bold print or to change the font size, for example).

You can use the macros you define with the Macro Editor within Desktop or another application (such as PC Tools Shell, WordPerfect, and Lotus 1-2-3). When used in another application, you must load Desktop in memory-resident mode.

Data Clipboard

The clipboard is a unique PC Tools feature that lets you temporarily store snippets of text you've cut or copied from another application. As long as Desktop is loaded in memory-resident mode, you can use the clipboard to transfer text between two different word processors—WordStar and Microsoft Word for example—even though these two applications aren't data file compatible.

To use the clipboard:

1. Choose the Clipboard command from the Desktop menu.
2. When the Clipboard window opens (shown in Figure 10-30), choose the Copy to Clipboard command from the Copy/Paste menu.
3. With the keyboard or mouse, select the text you want to copy.
4. Move the cursor where you want to paste the text (or start another application).
5. Choose the Clipboard command from the Desktop menu.
6. When the Clipboard window opens, choose the Paste from Clipboard command from the Copy/Paste menu.

292

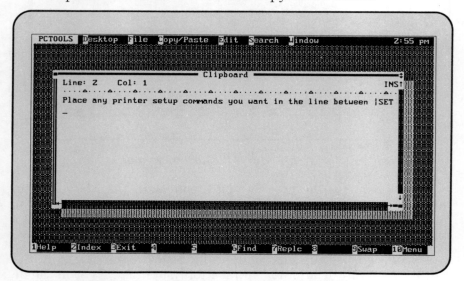

Figure 10-30. A clipping of text temporarily stored in the Desktop clipboard.

Review

This chapter introduced you to the desk accessories included in the PC Tools Desktop program. You also learned:

▶ You can load Desktop as a stand-alone program at the DOS prompt or as a memory-resident program.

▶ Notepads, the Desktop word processor, can read and write documents in WordStar format.

▶ You can easily cut and copy text by selecting the text and using the Copy and Cut to Clipboard commands in the Edit menu.

▶ The built-in spell-checker checks for spelling and typographical errors.

▶ Outlines is a thought organizer that lets you easily create and format outlines using headlines and multiple levels.

▶ Creating a database with the Databases module of Desktop involves three steps: defining the structure of the new database, customizing a new form file, and entering record data.

▶ You can readily sort records and display records using selection criteria you enter.

▶ The Telecommunications module lets you communicate with other computers via a modem or fax board.

293

Appendix A
PC Tools Program Files

The PC Tools program is composed of several dozen files. Only some of the files are absolutely necessary to run the program, while others can be safely discarded (but keep a backup copy of all files in case you ever need to replace missing ones). You can readily determine the function of a file by noting its extension:

▶ *COM*—Program; can be run directly from DOS or within Shell.

▶ *EXE*—Program; can be run directly from DOS or within Shell.

▶ *OVL*—Overlay; contains messages, screen prompts, and other data for use with an associated program (COM or EXE) file.

▶ *CFG*—Configure; configuration file that stores user-selectable settings.

▶ *HLP*—Help; help text file.

▶ *SYS*—System driver; loaded into the computer upon startup, usually in the CONFIG.SYS file.

General Files

These files are used for the general operation of PC Tools. The PCSETUP.COM program is needed only when installing PC Tools on a hard disk, so it can be safely deleted from the hard disk after installation. (However, you may want to keep it handy in case you want to use it again.) The KILL.EXE program is used only when Shell and Desktop are loaded as memory-resident programs.

PCSETUP.COM	PC Setup program.
KILL.EXE	Removes Shell and Desktop programs when installed in TSR mode.

Shell Files

These files manage the Shell program. All files are required when using the Shell application.

PCRUN.COM	Shell run-time program; runs other application when Shell is in TSR mode.
PCSHELL.EXE	Main Shell program.
PCSHELL.HLP	Shell on-line help text.
PCSHELL.OVL	Shell program overlay.
PCSHELL.CFG	Shell saved configuration.

Desktop Files

These files manage the Desktop program. All files are required when running the Desktop application. Text in parentheses indicate the miniapplication in Desktop that accesses the file.

DESKTOP.EXE	Main Desktop program.
DESKTOP.HLP	Desktop on-line help text.
ASCII.OVL	ASCII table utility overlay (Utilities).
CALC.OVL	Algebraic calculator overlay (Calculators).
DBMS.OVL	Database manager overlay (Databases).
FINCALC.OVL	Financial calculator overlay (Calculators).
SCICALC.OVL	Scientific calculator overlay (Calculators).
HEXCALC.OVL	Programmer's calculator overlay (Calculators).
HOTKEY.OVL	Hot-key utility overlay (Utilities).
INKILL.OVL	Desktop program removal utility overlay (Utilities).
RECOLOR.OVL	Screen colors utility overlay (Utilities).
SPELL.OVL	Spelling-check overlay (Notepads).
TALK.OVL	Telecommunications overlay (Communications).
TIME.OVL	Appointments overlay (Appointment Scheduler).
BACKTALK.EXE	Background communications program (Communications).
DICT.SPL	Spelling-check word dictionary (Notepads).
PHONE.TEL	Phone numbers directory (Communications).

297

Utility Files

The PC Tools stand-alone utilities comprise these files. The files are needed only when running the associated utility.

COMPRESS.EXE	Compress program.
COMPRESS.HLP	Compress program help.
COMPRESS.CFG	Compress configuration; created first time Compress is run.
MIRROR.COM	Mirror program.
MIRROR.FIL	Mirror system area image; created by Mirror each time the program is run. Do not delete.
MIRROR.BAK	Mirror system area image backup. Do not delete.
MIRORSAV.FIL	Mirror pointer file; created by Mirror. Do not delete.
PCTRACKR.DEL	Delete file tracker file (optional feature of Mirror). Do not delete.
PARTNSAV.FIL	Mirror partition save file (optional feature of Mirror). Create once, and store file on a floppy disk. After copying, OK to delete.
REBUILD.COM	Rebuild program.
PC-CACHE.COM	PC Cache program.
PCFORMAT.COM	PC Format program.
PCSECURE.EXE	PC Secure program.
PCSECURE.HLP	PC Secure help text.
PCSECURE.CFG	PC Secure configuration; created first time PC Secure is run.

298

Backup Files

These files are required for the PC Backup utility.

PCBACKUP.EXE	Main PC Backup program.
PCBACKUP.HLP	PC Backup on-line help text.
PCBACKUP.CFG	PC Backup saved configuration.

PCB1.EXE	PC Backup program file.
PCB2.EXE	PC Backup program file.
PCB3.EXE	PC Backup program file.
PCB4.EXE	PC Backup program file.
PCB5.EXE	PC Backup program file.
PCB6.EXE	PC Backup program file.
PCBDIR.COM	Disk identification program.

In addition, PC Backup creates two user-created files that should not be tampered with or erased.

PCBACKUP.RPT	Backup report (optional).
<name>.SET	User-defined backup set.

299

Support Files

PC Tools comes with an assortment of support files not required for the basic operation of Shell, Desktop, or the various utilities. You don't need to save these files if you have no personal use for them.

CSERVE.SCR	CompuServe log-on script (use with Telecommunications).
CSMAIL.SCR	CompuServe mail log-on script (use with Telecommunications).
ESL_FAX.SCR	Easylink FAX log-on script (use with Telecommunications).
ESL_MAIL.SCR	Easylink mail log-on script (use with Telecommunications).
EPSON.PRO	Epson printer macros.
HPLJF.PRO	HP Laserjet printer macros.
LETTER.FOR	Sample form letter form (use with Databases).
MCI.SCR	MCI mail log-on script.
MEMCHK.COM	Memory check program; checks available memory. Generally used as a troubleshooting tool.

MI.COM	Memory mapping program; maps memory used by DOS. Generally used as a troubleshooting tool.
PANA.PRO	Panasonic printer macros.
PC-CACHE.SYS	PC Cache system driver for use with the Bernoulli box.
PCMAP.SCR	PC Magazine MagNet (on CompuServe) log-on script (use with Telecommunications).
PROPTR.PRO	IBM Proprinter macros.
README.TXT	Additions and updates to the documentation (delete only after reading or printing).
SAMPLE.DBF	Sample database document (use with Databases).
SAMPLE.FOR	Sample database form document (use with Databases).
SAMPLE.OUT	Sample outline (use with Outlines).
SAMPLE.PRO	Sample macros used in examples (used with Macro Editor).
SAMPLE.TXT	Sample text (use with Notepads).

300

In addition, PC Tools creates a number of temporary files during execution. These include files with an IMG, IMX, THM, TRE, and FIL file extension. These should not be deleted while using PC Tools, or the program could fail. The files are recreated each time the program is run or when PC Tools can't locate an older copy.

Index

301

304

305

307

S

Sample Select Records dialog box, 279
SAMPLE.DBF file, 300
SAMPLE.FOR file, 300
SAMPLE.OUT file, 300
SAMPLE.PRO file, 300
SAMPLE.TXT file, 300
Save as command, 188
Save command, 266
Save Configuration command, 80-81
Save Configuration File command, 72
Save History option, 178
Save Setup command, 187-188
SCANEXCP.RPT file, 129
SCICALC.OVL file, 297
scientific calculator, 289-290
screen autodial, Telecommunications, 283-284
Screen Colors option, 71
screens
    components, 27-28
    Desktop, 10
    Shell, 53
scroll
    arrows, 44
    bars, 30
Search All Fields dialog box, 278
Search Disk command, 69
sectors, disk, 199
Select command, 109
select Records command, 279
selection criteria, Databases record, 280
separate incremental backup, 162
SET file, 187
Setup Configuration command, 71
Shell (F8) key, 40
Shell Application Editor window, 229
Shell
    adding to AUTOEXEC.BAT file, 148
    Applications menu
        adding programs to, 153-157
        supported programs, 152-153
    as way station for applications, 147-148
    attaching documents to applications, 157-158
    changing current drive, 64
    directory maintenance, 135-140
    directory, printing contents, 143-144
    disks
        bootable, 133-134
        comparing, 126-128
        copying, 121-125
        formatting, 130-134
        formatting errors, 133
        formatting while copying, 122
        mapping, 212-214
        printing contents, 143-144
        re-reading the tree, 120-121
        renaming, 134-135
        verifying, 125-126
        viewing contents, 118-120
    DOS Command Line, using, 78-79
    exiting, 24
    File Edit editing keys, 108
    file management, 83-116
    files, 296
        attributes, 111-112
        comparing, 100-102
        copying, 87-93

deleting, 97-99
displaying, 61-63
editing, 107-109
getting information, 112-114
locating, 114-115
manual recovery, 208-211
moving, 93-95
moving with mouse, 94-95
printing, 109-111
renaming, 95-97
selecting, 59-61
sorting, 142-143
verifying, 99-100
view filters, 105-107
viewing, 102-107
viewing two lists, 64-65
wildcard searches, 115
hot keys, 52
load parameters, 53-57
loading, 51-57
managing disks, 117-146
menus, 65-75
network, running on, 80
running, 21-24
running applications, 147-158
saving configuration, 80-81
screen, 53
setting file display options, 85
subdirectory
    adding, 136-137
    attributes, 140
    deleting, 138
    modifying attributes, 140
    prune and graft, 139
    renaming, 137
    selecting, 59
user-definable function keys, 79
variable user levels, 75-78
viewing directories/files, 57-65
Short Cut Keys option, 71
shortcut keys
    File List window, 61
    Tree window, 59
Show level command, 270
Single rename option, 97
size box, 30
Size command, 39
Size/Move Window command, 39, 72
Sort database command, 277
Special menu, 74-75
spell-checking, Notepads text, 265-266
SPELL.OVL file, 297
Spellcheck dialog box, 265
Spellcheck File command, 265
stand-alone programs, 16
    Desktop, 25
    Shell, 21-22
Standard Format command, 176
start Compare command, 193
Sub Directory Rename dialog box, 138
subdirectories
    adding, 136-137
    deleting, 138
    modifying attributes, 140
    prune and graft, 139
    renaming, 136-137
    selecting for backup, 181-183

309

Reader Feedback Card

Thank you for purchasing this book from Howard W. Sams & Company's FIRST
BOOK series. Our intent with this series is to bring you timely, authoritative
information that you can reference quickly and easily. You can help us by taking a
minute to complete and return this card. We appreciate your comments and will use
the information to better serve your needs.

1. Where did you purchase this book?

☐ Chain bookstore (Walden, B. Dalton)   ☐ Direct mail
☐ Independent bookstore   ☐ Book club
☐ Computer/Software store   ☐ School bookstore
☐ Other _____

2. Why did you choose this book? (Check as many as apply.)

☐ Price   ☐ Appearance of book
☐ Author's reputation   ☐ Howard W. Sam's reputation
☐ Quick and easy treatment of subject   ☐ Only book available on subject

3. How do you use this book? (Check as many as apply.)

☐ As a supplement to the product manual ☐ As a reference
☐ In place of the product manual   ☐ At home
☐ For self-instruction   ☐ At work

4. Please rate this book in the categories below. G = Good; N = Needs improvement;
   U = Category is unimportant.

☐ Price   ☐ Appearance
☐ Amount of information   ☐ Accuracy
☐ Examples   ☐ Quick Steps
☐ Inside cover reference   ☐ Second color
☐ Table of contents   ☐ Index
☐ Tips and cautions   ☐ Illustrations
☐ Length of book
☐ How can we improve this book? _____
  _____

5. How many computer books do you normally buy in a year?

☐ 1—5   ☐ 5—10   ☐ More than 10
☐ I rarely purchase more than one book on a subject.
☐ I may purchase a beginning and an advanced book on the same subject.
☐ I may purchase several books on particular subjects.
  (such as _____)

6. Have you purchased other Howard W. Sams or Hayden books in the past year? ___
   If yes, how many? _____

7. Would you purchase another book in the FIRST BOOK series? _____

8. What are your primary areas of interest in business software?
   - ☐ Word processing (particularly _____)
   - ☐ Spreadsheet (particularly _____)
   - ☐ Database (particularly _____)
   - ☐ Graphics (particularly _____)
   - ☐ Personal finance/accounting (particularly _____)
   - ☐ Other (please specify _____)

Other comments on this book or the Howard W. Sams book line: _____
_____

Name _____
Company _____
Address _____
City _____ State _____ Zip _____
Daytime telephone number _____
Title of this book _____

Fold here

- -

‖‖‖

NO POSTAGE
NECESSARY
IF MAILED
IN THE
UNITED STATES

BUSINESS REPLY MAIL
FIRST CLASS   PERMIT NO. 336   CARMEL, IN

POSTAGE WILL BE PAID BY ADDRESSEE

Sams

11711 N. College Ave.
Suite 140
Carmel, IN 46032–9839